Digital Political Cultures in the Middle East since the Arab Uprisings

Digital Political Cultures in the Middle East since the Arab Uprisings

Online Activism in Egypt, Tunisia and Lebanon

Dounia Mahlouly

I.B. TAURIS

LONDON • NEW YORK • OXFORD • NEW DELHI • SYDNEY

I.B. TAURIS
Bloomsbury Publishing Plc
50 Bedford Square, London, WC1B 3DP, UK
1385 Broadway, New York, NY 10018, USA
29 Earlsfort Terrace, Dublin 2, Ireland

BLOOMSBURY, I.B. TAURIS and the I.B. Tauris logo are trademarks
of Bloomsbury Publishing Plc

First published in Great Britain 2023
This paperback edition published 2025

Copyright © Dounia Mahlouly 2023

Dounia Mahlouly has asserted her right under the Copyright,
Designs and Patents Act, 1988, to be identified as Author of this work.

For legal purposes the Acknowledgements on p. vii constitute an
extension of this copyright page.

Series design by Catherine Wood & Adriana Brioso
Cover image: Beirut, Lebanon, 20th Oct, 2019.
(© Marwan Naamani/dpa/Alamy Stock Photo)

A catalogue record for this book is available from the British Library.

A catalog record for this book is available from the Library of Congress.

ISBN: HB: 978-0-7556-4517-6
           PB: 978-0-7556-4521-3
           ePDF: 978-0-7556-4518-3
           eBook: 978-0-7556-4519-0

Typeset by Integra Software Services Pvt. Ltd.

To find out more about our authors and books visit www.bloomsbury.com
and sign up for our newsletters.

Contents

Figures

Acknowledgements

I am forever grateful to all the young revolutionary spirits who motivated me and inspired me to conduct this research. Thank you to Mohammed, Nasreen, Ralph, Amar, Magd, Fadil, Omar, Dalia, Habib, Nino, Mahdi, Zine and all those who could not be named.

ألف شكر لنساء القويات حياتي :خديجة، أمينة وبنتي نورة

I would not have published my work without the support of Dina Matar, Andrew Hoskins and Marie Gillespie who encouraged me at various stages of this project. I am thankful to Nicolas and my dear friends Inna, Inga, Zaina and Mahmoud

1

Introduction

The field of political communication traditionally understands the media as a power structure and a system of control. It is primarily concerned with the question of political influence and seeks to understand the relationship between the sphere of power and the media. This top-down perspective is as central to the idea of an elitist public sphere as it is to the Marxist critique of the media. Indeed, the latter traditionally advocates for structural change. In this regard, the study of political communication stands out from other disciplines like Cultural Studies, which rely on a bottom-up approach. Whereas political communication tends to focus on the discourse of the elite, Cultural Studies is interested in the popular culture of the masses and the informal power of the audience. Media theorists in fact rarely endeavour to reconcile these two seemingly opposing perspectives. I certainly did not have this ambition when I first started working on this research ten years prior to writing this book. And yet although this enquiry began within the field of political communication, it did not end there. With ten years of hindsight, I realized that my findings supported a theory of agency that challenges our understanding of the popular and the masses.

When I undertook this research in 2012, my objective was to study the evolution of the social media sphere in post-revolutionary Tunisia and Egypt. I examined the online campaigning strategy of those leading political actors, who intended to restore their legitimacy in the aftermath of the 2011 uprisings. This drew my attention to the rapid politization of the social media sphere that became visible over the course of the post-revolutionary transition. I relied on both online and fieldwork ethnographic research to show how digital platforms had benefitted these well-established political groups in the context of presidential and constitutional debates. This approach eventually led me to formulate a structural critique of digital media and demystify the idea that it was instrumental to the civil movements of the revolution. When I completed my initial research in 2014, I concluded that these new communication technologies were just as likely to serve the actors of the counterrevolution. In the following years, this argument was corroborated by a larger body of research that presented a structural critique of digital technologies. Many of these theories in fact recently gained traction by outlining the downside of online political engagement (Fuchs, 2012a; Tufekci, 2016). They indicated that networked activism was not the best way to achieve long-term political change, arguing that opposition voices needed to resort back to well-organized political structures. This idea certainly resonated with many young people, who witnessed how the practice of web activism transitioned from the emergent to the mainstream. It reflected a growing scepticism and a general sense of disenchantment about decentralized channels as well as the informal communication practices of the grassroots.

Prior to the global pandemic, the world witnessed a wave of civil protests in countries like Chile and India, as well as in Sudan and the city of Hong Kong. However, with the exception of the Black Lives Matter movement, this recent wave of mobilizations generated little interest in grassroots communication networks. That is surprising considering the fact that this topic has been extensively researched in the past. Back in the late 1990s, a number of transnational anti-globalization movements triggered the curiosity of communication scholars, who began to study early forms of web activism. Ten years later, a new wave of protests sparked around the time of the Occupy Wall Street movement. This later case of civil mobilizations raised questions about the role of social media as a logistical tool and a platform for political dissent. In comparison, it appears that the worldwide protests of 2019 did not generate as much interest for the communication tools used by activists and their reach amongst the grassroots. This may be due to the shock of the 2020 pandemic, which created a sense of disconnect with the rest of the world. Or perhaps another possible explanation is that we became more cautious about assuming that grassroots networks can effectively apply these tools to bring progressive change.

Our experience of communication technologies is indeed not the same today as it was ten years ago. Digital media rapidly expanded into the mainstream, eventually reaching a mass audience. In the last ten years, it has proved to be conducive to populist rhetoric and instrumental to political leaders whose message is designed to appeal to 'the masses'. In Europe and the United States, the increasing popularity of the far right became visible across both mainstream and encrypted social platforms. This ultimately generated more scepticism with regard to grassroots communication networks. Popular online channels are now viewed as likely to circulate disinformation and conspiracy theories as was the case during the 'info-demic' of the Covid-19 crisis. Grassroots audiences are accordingly assumed to be receptive to these types of online messages, which are tailored for the masses. Yet this perspective remains very much centred on the experience of Western neoliberal societies. It specifically pertains to growing concerns over the decline of public trust, which has been described as the crisis of liberal democracy. In the West, this point of view supposes that liberal elites need to restore their legitimacy, in order to save the grassroots in distress from the pernicious influence of evil populists. This argument does not, in other words, attribute much agency and critical thinking to the audience. Instead, it tends to focus on what the progressive wing of the liberal establishment can do to inform the public debate and restore our faith in democracy. Because in the context of the Global North, populism often belongs to a more conservative wing of the political leadership, which deceitfully portrays itself as an alternative to the establishment in claiming to represent the voices of the grassroots.

Yet in many other parts of the world, ruling conservative elites indulged in a more outward and perhaps less insidious form of populism. Many authoritarian leaders have capitalized on the postcolonial identity crisis to construct a narrative of national (or sectarian) identity. They historically relied on symbolism and populist rhetoric to create a facade of religious or national unity, by imposing themselves as charismatic father figures. In such contexts, the voices of the progressive opposition were often marginalized and limited to the peripheries of the public sphere. The obstacles they face when trying to challenge this form of reactionary populism are therefore significantly different from the concerns of Western liberal elites. In these other political environments, the progressive opposition has no choice but to rely on decentralized communication channels and find creative ways to engage with the grassroots. This approach alternatively starts from the assumption that grassroots audiences are able to exercise agency and informal power. As such, it offers an original angle to rethink the potential of bottom-up communication practices. Most importantly, it allows us to question Eurocentric assumptions about those communication tools that become popular amongst the grassroots.

One would thus expect that public concerns over the recent rise of populism in the West would raise more awareness about the challenges faced by the progressive youths, who have tried to overthrow their own populist leaders elsewhere in the world. However, the resurgence of Western populism often encourages the liberal establishment to advocate for the recentralization of the public debate. As I will argue, this discourse has been exported elsewhere in the world and weaponized by other governments to justify the ongoing securitization of the online space. Such argument has significant implications for other parts of the world and may indirectly restrict avenues for peripheral communication in the Global South.

This book precisely addresses this conundrum, by considering how the Arab Spring and the coincidental media revolution of the digital came to inspire conflicting feelings of hope, fear and disillusionment to a Western public. It reflects on the antagonism between the elite and the masses, as well as the process through which a media from the emergent to the mainstream. In doing so, it also asks the questions of who is expected to formulate the message of a revolution and examines how this message can be expressed in the popular language of the grassroots.

This reflection expands way beyond the scope of my initial study, drawing on ten years of research and interviews with activists and civil society actors. It further investigates the challenges related to the securitization of digital media and re-examines the latest evolution of the online debate in post-revolutionary Tunisia and Egypt. This book specifically reports on the emergence of a new market for media development, which is internationally funded and supported under the banner of 'countering violent extremism'. It shows how this new market is conditioned by the Eurocentric argument of recentralization and argues that this approach to media development disempowers civil society actors involved in the local independent media sphere. Besides the cases of Tunisia and Egypt, the book also discusses the impact of this security lens on the 2019 wave of protests that became known as the 'second wave of the Arab Spring'. In order to introduce this discussion, it lays out the findings of a new research, which explores the most recent case of the Lebanese revolution. This part of my updated research features additional fieldwork interviews with members of the Lebanese pro-revolutionary opposition, which I conducted between the civil mobilizations of 2019 and the parliamentary election of 2022.

Overall, this research will also bring me to reflect on what distinguishes the first from the second wave of the 'Arab Spring', from the perspective of media and communication. The first wave of the 'Arab Spring' refers to the events of 2011, which included the Tunisian revolution and the Egyptian uprisings of 25 January. These mobilizations toppled the regimes of Ben Ali and Mubarak, leading to a chain of events that reshaped the politics of the region. In countries like Syria, Libya and Yemen, similar uprisings were met with violent repression, which resulted in civil conflicts involving foreign interventions. Indeed, this first wave of protests marked a defining moment in the contemporary history of the Middle East. Despite the fact that these civil movements have been coined under the same term, they had very different outcomes in each country depending on the geopolitical stakes and particularities of the national context. Yet many international observers initially focused on the similarities between these events, with a particular focus on the role of digital media. Indeed, the first wave of the Arab Spring arose around the time of the Occupy Wall Street movement. It was concomitant with other civil mobilizations such as the Spanish 'Indignados' protests, the London riots and the anti-austerity movement in Greece, which all seemed to involve some form of digital activism. International commentators drew analogies between these events, suggesting that digital technologies had significantly changed the way young people engaged in political action (Fuch, 2012a; Mason, 2011; Tefekci, 2016). Within that context, the 2011 Arab Spring was briefly yet memorably framed as a 'Twitter revolution' (Lotan et al., 2011).

The first wave of the Arab Spring was carefully studied with the aim of investigating the effects of online activism (Gerbaudo, 2012; Howard and Hussein, 2013; Iskander, 2011; Lim, 2012; Papacharissi, 2015; Tufekci, 2016). Some communication scholars suggested that new media had considerably facilitated the logistics of the protests (Breuer, 2012). Others argued that digital technologies had introduced a more causal form of political engagement, which contrasted with partisan politics (Bennett and Segerberg, 2013; Tufekci, 2016). Alternatively, those who approached the topic from a postcolonial perspective challenged the myth of a 'Twitter revolution' (Beinin, 2012; Lynch, 2011). They demonstrated that, from a communication perspective, the revolution was not so much about technological innovation as much as it was about social creativity and resilience (Allagui and Kuebler, 2011; Aouragh and Alexander, 2011).

Today, it is indeed admitted that the narrative of 'Twitter revolution' misrepresented the full scope of the 2011 uprisings. In countries like Tunisia and Egypt, online activism was initially limited to a highly educated youth from the urban middle class (Breuer, 2012). As an emergent media, new communication technologies were viewed as playful, experimental and empowering. Yet the practice of web activism was not accessible to anyone (Gerbaudo, 2012; Tufekci, 2013), for it required some degree of technical skills and political literacy. Those who approached the Arab Spring from the perspective of online activism initially focused on the role of a young intelligentsia. In reality, this approach may have initially comforted international observers in the belief that the revolutionary movements should be led by a progressive intellectual elite.

In 2019, another series of civil movements sparked across the region, which was referred to as the 'second wave of the Arab Spring' (Fahmi, 2019a; Young, 2019). Sudanese revolutionaries mobilized against the regime of president Omar al-Bashir, demanding a fair transition towards a civil democratic government. During the same period of time, the nationwide demonstrations of the Algerian Hirak led to the resignation of President Abdelaziz Bouteflika. In Iraq, young people took the streets, joining a series of brutally repressed protests to express their discontent and demonstrate against corruption and political sectarianism. Meanwhile, in Lebanon, the pro-revolutionary opposition was challenging the legitimacy of the entire political establishment, contesting the legacy of the 1975–90 civil war. In comparison, this second wave of protests was not extensively researched in the field of media and political communication.

Yet, beyond the scope of digital activism, these two generations of civil movements both involved interesting art forms and informal communication practices. As was the case in 2011, the second wave of the Arab Spring brought together different social actors who relied on a range of decentralized channels and creative forms of expression in the early days of the mobilizations. In both cases, a broad range of grassroots emergent media were applied collaboratively to ensure that the language of the revolution would resonate with the political praxis of the street. Communities of football supporters played a significant role in the 2019 Algerian Hirak, as they did in the context of the 2011 Tunisian revolution. In 2019, the process through which protesters reclaimed ownership of the street was reminiscent of Egyptian street art and its symbolic value for the 2011 Arab Spring. Besides, the martyrs of the 2019 Lebanese revolution became as iconic as the ones who were remembered as the faces of the 2011 Egyptian uprising. Like in 2011, the second wave of the Arab Spring engaged different voices from civil society, relying on informal communication channels that intended to engage women, the youths and the diaspora. Digital activism therefore needs to be studied in relation to these broader range of creative social practices that are used to communicate the revolution in the popular language of the grassroots.

In light of this, the research outlined in this book will show how the pro-revolutionary youth struggled to maintain the spirit of the revolution as soon as counterrevolutionary forces regained ownership of the public space. It will quote from fieldwork interviews and a sample extracted from the blogosphere to explain how this young progressive opposition came to formulate an introspective critique of digital activism.

The book will highlight the particularities of these different media environments and political contexts. I will comment on how the pro-revolutionary youths experienced contentious politics in the years following the uprisings and will show how these tensions played out in the distinct cases of Tunisia, Egypt and Lebanon.

The book focuses on these three countries to investigate contexts, where a political transition occurred which briefly inspired hopes for a significant regime change. In doing so, it specifically considers the challenges to digital activism in such a transitional phase. Admittedly, many other countries such as Yemen, Libya and Syria deserve to be studied from a similar angle. However, these other cases raise a broader range of questions, which would involve accounting for the history of local civil conflicts alongside geopolitical parameters. The same reasoning applies to monarchies like Morocco, where the first wave of the Arab Spring led to a referendum on constitutional reforms in 2011. Studying these other political environments would introduce a broader reflection on the very notion of regime change. It is for this reason that I will limit the scope of this research to these three already fairly ambitious case studies. That being said, I will argue that many of the case-specific findings presented in this book are relevant to many other countries in the Middle East and North Africa. I will for example demonstrate that the dynamics at play in the political economy of media development manifest themselves in similar ways across the region. The book also highlights similarities between local media activists seemingly opposing different kinds of political forces. It describes the securitization of digital media as a global trend while drawing analogies between distinct practices of online activism. Most importantly, by comparing and contrasting evidence from Tunisia, Egypt and Lebanon, I intend to illustrate how the discursive tools of the revolution were reappropriated by different types of counterrevolutionary forces.

In Tunisia, a Constituent Assembly was democratically elected in October 2011, thanks to which the main opposition parties gained representation and a new constitution was adopted in 2014. In the followings years, the revolution had introduced more freedom of speech, while stimulating the development of a vibrant civil society sector. These changes were achieved in spite of the economic crisis and the contentions resulting from the reconfiguration of the political landscape. In Egypt, the military body of the Supreme Council of the Armed Forces (SCAF) remained in control of the electoral system during the post-revolutionary transition. The candidate of the Muslim Brotherhood Mohammed Morsi was nevertheless able to win the 2012 presidential election and his party managed to secure the majority of seats in parliamentary election. However, the debate became increasingly polarized in the context of the subsequent constitutional referendum, during which Morsi tried to impose his controversial constitutional decree. This paved the way for the 3 July 2013 military coup, when President Morsi was removed by army chief General Abdel Fattah al-Sisi. As I will demonstrate in light of my empirical research, the particularities of these distinct political contexts have also shaped the local media environment in different ways.

I will for example stress the fact that, in the Tunisian case, the revolution initially introduced opportunities for the development of an independent media sphere as well as better legal framework for the freedom of the press. However, my research also highlights common denominators between these cases, identifying similarities in the rapid politization of the social media sphere. It will also argue that in both countries, the national media market continued to serve the interests of the political leadership, through mechanisms of either state control or clientelism.

This introduction also calls for a brief overview of the Lebanese case and a discussion on the limitations of this comparative framework. Political analysts are often tempted to argue that the Lebanese environment is radically different because of ethnic conflict and the history of sectarian politics. In Lebanon, both the national media and political landscape were historically fragmented and divided between Sectarian elites. Like in Tunisia, a number of independent media outlets gained exposure thanks to the revolution. However, the Lebanese post-revolutionary debate also presents interesting similarities with the Egyptian case, because of the growing polarisation opposing the political camp of Hezbollah and the right-wing party of the Lebanese Forces, which secured the majority of seats in the general elections of May 2022. I will further outline the context around these tensions, and show how it impacted on the social media sphere. However, as I outline these particularities, I will also work towards demystifying the myth of a Lebanese exceptionalism that tends to focus on the issue of sectarian conflict. The 2019 revolution demonstrated that the young opposition sees all the actors of the political leadership as part of the same corrupted system. In essence, the Lebanese revolution intended to challenge the same neoliberal forces as in other cases of civil movements around the world. As was the case elsewhere in North Africa, the political landscape was also dominated by a conservative discourse that was in part tapping into insecurities rooted in the history of colonialism. To quote a young pro-revolutionary activist I interviewed:

> It is extremely important to overcome the narrative of Lebanese exceptionalism and use Lebanon as a case study that can derive lessons worldwide. We have one of the most violent forms of neoliberalism and one of the most extreme cases of economic collapse. The conservative discourse takes the same shape here as in other parts of the world, and this is also a country that was created as a colonial product.
>
> (Pro-revolution activist, Beirut, March 2022)

As much as I am planning to acknowledge the particularities of these contexts, my objective is also to highlight their commonalties from the perspective of the pro-revolutionary youths. This should allow me to reflect on the power dynamics at play in a revolution. I will be using the terms 'revolution' and 'revolutionaries' in ways that relate to the initial project of the uprisings as well as to the ideal of political change that these young activists have in common. Admittedly, the use of the terms 'revolution' and 'Arab Spring' is disputed, because they often obscure the complex realities of these opposition movements within local contexts. Yet this research precisely aims to deconstruct some of the common interpretations of these terms, and consider how their meaning has evolved in recent years. As was the case for our experience of digital technologies, the framing of the Arab Spring considerably changed in the last decade. Over time, the memory of the 2011 uprisings began to inspire the same feelings of disillusionment, as the ones associated with digital media. As I will argue, the representation of the Arab Spring was eventually altered by global public concerns over the political stability of the region. In recent years, the international audience became increasingly more preoccupied with issues of global security and migration. Foreign media eventually presented a defeatist take on the Arab Spring and its outcome. Their coverage ultimately focused on civil wars and terrorism, implying that there was not much hope left for democratization in the Middle East. In fact the original representation of 2011 uprisings has undergone the same changes as the utopian vision of technological revolution that supported the emergence of digital media. Over the last decade, these two ideals have conjured up similar feelings of hope, fear and disillusion.

The next chapter (Chapter 2) starts by exploring how these conflicting tropes have evolved in the case of digital technologies. It comments on the fears that came to be associated with these communication tools now that they are officially treated as another form of mass media likely to spread populist rhetoric. This chapter will also challenge today's academic debate on the rise of populism by drawing on the work of theorists who formulated a feminist and postcolonial critique. It argues that this new body of critical theory invalidates the Eurocentric argument of recentralization that is invoked to justify the increasing securitization of these communication platforms.

Chapter 3 introduces the conceptual framework of my research. It contemplates on the process through which a media evolves from the emergent to the mainstream and argues that our relationship with media remains very dynamic. The chapter will then posit that the same process applies to the counter-discourse of a revolution and explain how this approach can be used to understand the discursive power dynamics that unfold in the context of a revolution.

Chapter 4 dives into the case of the Tunisian and Egyptian uprisings, drawing on the first empirical strand of the research I conducted between 2012 and 2014. This part of the book comments on a large sample extracted from the Tunisian and Egyptian blogosphere to show how social media activism evolved during the post-revolutionary transition. The chapter reports on the testimonies of prominent bloggers and activists who witnessed the mainstreaming and politization of the online debate. The evidence presented demonstrates that this intellectual elite had to rethink its role, once social media became the new mainstream.

Chapter 5 focuses on the case of Egypt's 2012 presidential election. It shows how leading political players began to campaign on platforms like Twitter, illustrating how the social media sphere became politicized and rapidly polarized. The chapter compares the campaigning styles of these different political actors and argues that counterrevolutionary forces simultaneously capitalized on retail politics to reclaim ownership of the street. This empirical strand ultimately demonstrates that many of these well-established political actors applied a 'mass media' communication strategy when running their 2012 social media campaign.

Chapter 6 further examines the evolution of the online debate in post-revolutionary Egypt with an emphasis on the highly contentious debate surrounding the 2012 constitutional referendum. It provides an overview of the context around this constitutional debate and reports on the study of an e-deliberation platform, which was set up to communicate the constitutional draft. In doing so, this chapter argues that, due to the disconnect with the political praxis of the street, the vocabulary of the revolution soon lost its meaning and was easily hijacked to serve the agenda of the counterrevolution.

Chapter 7 covers the findings of my 2014 ethnographic fieldwork in Egypt, quoting from interviews with Egyptian activists and young members of the leftist opposition. It describes the challenges faced by the pro-revolutionary youth after the military coup of July 2013 and examines how this community came to formulate its own introspective critique of digital activism.

Chapter 8 expands the scope of the discussion to explore how the discourse on digital technologies changed in the mid-2010s, and comments on the implications for the market of media development. This part of the book demonstrates that this debate became largely informed by negative or pessimistic assessments of online political engagement, which is increasingly viewed through a security lens. It argues that these debates have opened the door for tighter media regulations and state surveillance policies, limiting opportunities for media pluralism and independent journalism in the MENA region. In addition, the chapter emphasizes the fact that the agenda of global security has shifted the priorities of international donors in the market of media development, which local media activists, along with other civil society actors, depend upon. Two subchapters will consider evidence from Tunisia and Egypt to show how the imperative of national and global security affected the independent media sphere in each of these specific contexts.

Chapter 9 follows on from the preceding one, while introducing a discussion on the Lebanese case. It looks at the consequences of this security lens in the Lebanese context and argues that this discourse allowed political elites to create an illusion of legitimacy in the years preceding the 2019 revolution. The chapter then considers how the young opposition was initially able to rely on the political praxis of the street during the early days of the mobilization. Finally, it analyses how counterrevolutionary forces here again attempted to regain control over social media and the public space prior to the general elections of May 2022.

The concluding chapter (Chapter 10) will provide an overview of these different findings and empirical strands. It will reconsider the significance of a political message designed to engage the grassroots and consider how a progressive intellectual elite can interact with a broader range of social actors and rely on a more informal type of political power when competing with populists in a mass media environment.

2

From utopia to dystopia

In recent years, the rise of populist rhetoric and conspiracy theories has introduced a general sense of apprehension with regard to informal communication (Groshek and Koc-Michalska, 2017; Pomerantsev, 2019). These insecurities specifically pertain to the alarming popularity of the far right and the anti-vaccine movements, which revealed a growing climate of public distrust in Europe and the United States. Communication scholars have extensively researched the cases of the 2016 US election and the Brexit referendum, which, they have argued, have manifested the crisis of liberal Western-democracies (Bennett and Livingston, 2018; Howard et al., 2018). Since the Cambridge Analytica scandal, we have become increasingly aware of the data-driven campaigning practices used by populists to target an audience via informal communication channels (Mazzoleni and Bracciali, 2018). The issues raised have been reemphasized in the context of the 2020 'infodemic', which have led communication experts to predominantly focus on the topic of disinformation (Ball, 2017; Bergmann, 2018; Boler and Davis, 2018; Thorson, 2016). Many of them seem to have embraced the controversial phrase 'fake news', which President Trump ironically popularized in an attempt to discredit mainstream media outlets (Levinson, 2017). This new body of literature appears to be primarily invested in explaining why Western audiences would suddenly become so receptive to these anti-establishment narratives (Masood and Nisar, 2020; Mejia et al., 2018).

Within this academic debate, concerns over disinformation originally centred around a very Eurocentric perspective. It is indeed the case of the Western public and its polarisation that has been considered as the most problematic, as if populism and public distrust were to be expected in the Global South (Wahby, 2017). A common assumption was perhaps that there was more of a grounds for disinformation under political regimes characterized by evident infringements of media freedom (Bennett and Livingston, 2018). In any case, it is clear that its dissemination was somehow treated as a priority concern in the context of neoliberal democracies. In fact, this argument has already been raised by the postcolonial critique of the discourse on far-right populism. By shifting focus away from the North West, postcolonial thinkers (Masood and Nisar, 2020) already challenged the double-standard of this scholarship, highlighting its Orientalist undertone:

> In fact, the entire contemporary rhetoric about the far-right populism is based on the fundamental assumption that the 'normal' North West is becoming 'abnormal' (or at least going through a change). The question of such changes in the Global South East is not taken up because for the always-assumed-to-be uncivilized, the undeveloped South East, the question of 'abnormality' is already foreclosed.
>
> (Masood and Nisar, 2020: 163)

By problematizing disinformation in reference to the Western experience of populism, the latest academic research in political communication came to overlook a couple of important parameters. First, it often implies that informal communication is somewhat detrimental to the democratic process of deliberation. The emphasis is commonly placed on the need to fact-check and monitor content as well as the imperative of tighter media regulations. Besides, this tradition often endeavours to provide applicable policy recommendations, which advocate for the recentralization of the public debate. As for the broader political discourse surrounding the issue of disinformation, the aim is often to restore the credibility of mainstream and official news sources, without investigating the root causes of public distrust (Ball, 2017; Pomerantsev, 2019). As a result, communication practices that originate from the realm of emergent media are increasingly viewed with fear and scepticism. In fact, another parameter worth mentioning is that this Eurocentric lens is likely to distort one's appreciation of grassroots communication in other parts of the world. Yet beyond the conventional scope of the Global North, these other forms of informal practices may be the last resort for inclusive deliberation or public expression.

There is indeed much confusion about how to define informality in the realm of communication. As I will define it, 'informal communication' pertains to the creative forms of public expression that one comes to experience at the peripheries of the public sphere. It relates to the processes of disruption and appropriation through which minority voices gain agency over hegemonic narratives. It involves the use of new genres and experimental media practices that may be limited to a niche audience. In essence, it revolves around subaltern counterpublics and their ability to leverage emergent media (Fraser, 1990). The field of Cultural Studies reminds us that these processes may occur in the private sphere as well as in the context of informal politics. It admits that audiences can reinvent *the order of discourse* (Foucault, 1971), ascribing a new meaning to mass media narratives or popular culture (Hall, 1993; Jenkins, 2006a and 2006b). It is this particular approach, which I will refer to when using the term 'informal'. This type of communication points to a broad range of unconventional, creative and sometimes-subversive practices that contribute to channelling the voices of civil society, regardless of the medium or technological tools applied. I will come back to this definition and show how this concept features in the larger context of the 2011 and 2019 uprisings.

Before getting to the heart of the matter, it is crucial to acknowledge some of the parameters that may obscure our understanding of 'informal communication' in the current media environment. This brings us to untangle some of the insecurities and feelings of disillusion that came to be associated with emergent media (Gerbaudo, 2018; Mejia et al., 2018). Besides the postcolonial critique, other theorists have deconstructed today's conventional wisdom on populism and public distrust. They have suggested that the fear of populist rhetoric, however legitimate, has generated a binary typology of information sources. Media content is now categorized along the lines of a clear-cut distinction between the elitist mainstream of the political status quo and the anti-establishment rhetoric of the radical fringe. Most cases of political contention have now been reduced to the perceived contrast between a blind faith in liberal values, on the one hand, and a conservatism disguised as anti-conformism, on the other. Such a normative interpretation of the debate contains an element of self-fulfilling prophecy, which is not always helpful when it comes to making sense of the relationship between media and populism (Krämer, 2018). Indeed, we may be unwillingly feeding into polarisation, by over-simplifying the terms of these antagonisms.

The work of Benjamin Krämer (2018), amongst others, indicates that such a binary framework can be dangerously misleading when it comes to explaining the rise of populist rhetoric in the media. More specifically, Krämer (2018: 458) examines the interplay between 'anti-populist media' and 'anti-media populism'. He argues that the two are often bounded in a mutually 'parasitic' relationship. A similar thought was formulated by Nancy Fraser (2017) with regard to what distinguishes populism from the rhetoric of progressive neoliberalism; using the case of the 2016 US campaign, Fraser (2017) proposed that the latter insidiously paved the way for the former. Though her perspective was yet again centred on the Global North, it is very much in line with her feminist critique of the bourgeois 'public sphere' (1990). In her earlier writings, Fraser had significantly influenced the field of political communication by introducing the notion of 'subaltern counterpublics'. She drew attention to those 'members of subordinated social groups', who act as 'alternative publics [...] to invent and circulate counterdiscourses' (1990: 67). She demystified the normative concept of 'public sphere', which philosopher Jürgen Habermas had originally modelled on the experience of the European Enlightenment. Her critique was precisely seminal in acknowledging alternative forms of expression and civic engagement, beyond the scope of the male-dominated bourgeoisie.

In her recent work (2017), she continues to challenge the way we think about deliberation and public trust, by engaging with the debate on populism. The author interprets the liberal discourse of the 1990s with the rise of what she calls 'progressive neoliberalism'. She proposes that, while this form of American politics appropriated the progressive values of the 1960s, it was eventually redirected to serve a strictly neoliberal agenda. Over time it became clear that, behind the rhetoric of progressive neoliberalism, American liberal politics would not commit to bringing long-term structural change. Those who advocated progressive values in the political sphere continued to implement neoliberal policies, widening the social inequalities that the civil movements of the 1960s initially intended to resolve. Ultimately this distorted the very meaning of these progressive values, paving the way for the success of the far right. According to Fraser (2017), this explains the public's disillusion with progressive neoliberalism that became visible in the context of the 2016 US election. Her theory ultimately demonstrates that – in the absence of a viable alternative – reactionary populism and progressive neoliberalism engaged in equally pervasive styles of rhetoric in a symbiotic relationship:

> (…) seen analytically, liberalism and fascism are not really two separate things, one of which is good and the other bad, but two deeply interconnected faces of the capitalist world system. Although they are by no means normatively equivalent, both are products of unrestrained capitalism (…) Left to fester in the absence of an alternative, those sentiments fuel authoritarianisms of every sort, including those that really deserve the name fascism and those that emphatically do not. Without a left, in other words, the maelstrom of capitalist 'development' can only generate liberal forces and authoritarian counter-forces, bound together in a perverse symbiosis.
>
> (Fraser, 2017: 4)

Along with the postcolonial critique, this feminist perspective shows how we came to exclude a broader of range of voices, by reducing the debate to these two mutually reinforcing political forces. It is this particular bias that is likely to affect the way we understand informal communication and its potential benefits for civil society in other parts of the world. That is not to say, of course, that we should dismiss the problem of disinformation or populist rhetoric. On the contrary, evidence clearly demonstrates that these issues dramatically harm civil society around the world (Masood and Nisar, 2020; Wahby, 2017). Yet the spread of these narratives is often initiated and incentivized by well-established political groups, rather than grassroots communication networks. Therefore, in order to effectively tackle this issue, we need to start by overcoming the trope of 'post-truth whiteness', which transpires from the political discourse on disinformation (Clennon, 2018; Mejia et al., 2018). As I will argue, this trope reveals a desire to control and recentralize the public space. It feeds into our feelings of disenchantment with communication technologies, whilst creating more grounds for disempowerment through surveillance and media regulations. The intricacies of 'post-truth whiteness' have, in other words, tinted our understanding of informal communication with a certain cynicism. In doing so, they may have also altered our memory of the 2011 uprisings and exacerbated the scepticism which has been expressed about the second wave of the 'Arab Spring'.

During the first wave of the 'Arab Spring', social media was still emerging and viewed as a potential driver of democratization. The Egyptian uprisings were framed as a 'Twitter revolution' and international commentators primarily focused on the role of social media (Castells, 2012; Lim, 2012; Lotan, et al., 2011; Meraz and Papacharissi, 2013). Like the printing press in the eighteenth century, digital tools were regarded as having introduced a new *Habermassian* public sphere. They were described as the product of scientific and industrial progress, and were thus expected to serve modern society by fostering pluralism and freedom of expression (Flichy, 2011; Fuchs, 2012; Turner, 2008).

Just like the *public sphere* of the European Enlightenment, online activism was pioneered by an intellectual elite from the highly educated bourgeoisie. The analogy seemed to deliver a reassuring sense of familiarity to the Western gaze, evoking an idealized vision of linear progress towards freedom and emancipation. The representation of the revolutions accordingly centred around the urban youth within the tech-savvy middle class. But this perspective was skewed by what Christian Fuchs later described as a 'cyber-utopian' (2012) form of technological determinism. This romanticized vision of online activism did not last once social networks became the new mass media. In contrast, new communication technologies are now increasingly viewed through a dystopian lens (Bessi, et al., 2014; Flaxman et al., 2016; Groshek and Koc-Michalska, 2017; Webster and Kiazesk, 2017). Yet, I will argue that this 'techno-pessimism' is just as technologically deterministic and equally misleading.

In fact, the dystopian view that prevails today is revealing of many Eurocentric assumptions about the communication practices that should contribute to democratization. In the current context, disinformation has become a primary concern. The realm of emergent media is broadly associated with information warfare and the neo-concept of 'post-truth' politics (Boler and Davis, 2018; Greenberg, 2019). One of the prevailing arguments in the ongoing debate around the crisis of public trust revolves around the need to (re)centralize the public sphere by regulating alternative communication channels. The emphasis is placed on 'countering disinformation' by restoring the legitimacy of official news sources. This approach is hardly ever informed by a critical reflection on the reasons for public distrust within particular contexts. It draws on a body of social theory that tends to portray mass audiences as a liability likely to jeopardize the proper functioning of public deliberation (Lippmann, 1998; Tarde, 1969). Influential theorists within the field of political communication have traditionally advocated for a public debate credited with an aura of impartiality, which is centred on expert knowledge and professionalized media practice (Habermas, 1962, 2006). They have disconnected the idea of an emotionally driven mass audience with that of a well-informed and highly educated elite, deemed capable of rational thinking (Fraser, 1990). This started with early research on social psychology, long before Habermas theorized the emergence of the public sphere amongst the enlightened intelligentsia of the bourgeoisie. In the late nineteenth century, sociologists Gabriel Tarde (1989) and Gustave Le Bon (2009) initiated research on crowd psychology (Borsch, 2006). They postulated that the crowds (or masses) were deprived of critical thinking when acting under the influence of a charismatic leader. They stated that the members of a crowd would lose sense of their individual will to conform with the rest of the herd by a process of *imitation* (Tarde, 1962). In its early stage, the study of crowd psychology was very much part of a national state's critique of socialism (Le Bon, 1982). The aim was to control popular mobilizations viewed as a threat to national sovereignty. Its pioneers had associated a number of gendered negative connotations to the concept of crowd, which they described as emotional, irrational and unpredictable. In their view, this notion presented a number of stereotypically feminine attributes. It contrasted with the ideal of an educated and well-informed public, considered as far more *civilized* because of its ability to express itself through institutionalized channels, away from the perceived vulgarity of the streets. Today, these theories are admittedly very controversial, which is why they have been extensively disputed in contemporary social psychology (Stäheli, 2011; Stort, 2017). Yet some of the concepts that underpin later research on political communication draw on the same assumptions. For instance, Habermas's public sphere (1962) and the work of Lippmann (1998) on public opinion arguably apply a very similar perspective. The Habermassian public sphere is also limited to the normative framework of the modern state in ways that resonate with crowd psychology, because it argues that public deliberation should be primarily driven by rationalism.

This scholarship implies that mass audiences may not have the media literacy nor the intellectual capital required to make a well-informed judgement. In addition, we can also find these arguments referenced in more recent academic debates. There is, for example, an interesting analogy with the neo-concept of 'post-truth' that became central to communication studies (Ball, 2017;

Boler and Davis, 2018; D'Ancona, 2017). Digital audiences came to inspire the same fear as the rebellious crowds of the late nineteenth century. In the post-utopian regime of the digital age, they have been described as deprived of their own agency, versatile and easily manipulated. Once again, these anxieties are admittedly understandable insofar as they are founded on the legitimately alarming rise of far-right populism (Bergmann, 2018; Pomerantsev, 2019). However, the consequence of our disillusion is that it ironically brings us to essentialize the idea of the masses in the same way populists essentialize the idea of the people. Here is another interesting conundrum, which resonates with Fraser's critique of progressive neoliberalism.

Those who have embraced the neo-concept of 'post-truth' suppose that the audience is driven by impulsive emotions or blind conformism (Ball, 2017; D'Ancona, 2017; Pomerantsev, 2016). This sentiment is only exacerbated by today's dystopian take on communication technologies. Experts have drawn attention to the effects of these social media echo chambers called 'filter bubbles', which they believe to be primarily responsible for online polarisation (Flaxman et al., 2016; Groshek and Koc-Michalska, 2017; Webster and Kiazesk, 2017). They have considered how these might affect information consumption, by generating more confirmation bias. They have also argued that social media users feel the need to position themselves by performing 'virtue signalling' (Ball, 2017). Many of these theories implicitly blame the psychology of the audience for the social media sphere being perverted by inter-group conflict and identity politics. By doing so, they tend to dismiss the perspective of the audience, which is viewed as inherently tribal, to focus exclusively on the structural issues at play in the political economy of the tech industry (Ball, 2017; Boler and Davis, 2018). As is often the case, the academic debate tends to overlook the perspective of the audience. It fails to explain how audiences navigate the hegemonic framework of this media to gain agency in creative ways. Even the Marxist critique of the media is not immune to this paternalistic approach, which implies that audiences are defenceless, helpless and vulnerable (Fuchs, 2010). Mass audiences are still viewed as ill-equipped and deprived of media literacy, which suggests they will need to be educated by those deemed capable of reason and critical thinking. These assumptions draw on the same tropes as early crowd psychology, whilst endorsing the neo-concept of 'post-truth' (Pomerantsev, 2016). It is generally presumed that these audiences, which are increasingly exposed to disinformation, are naive, inexperienced and vulnerable. This implies that they will have to be guided and supervised. In response to the issue of disinformation, the educated middle class will invoke expert knowledge, reclaiming its intellectual leadership over the public sphere. It is as if the only remedy to the so-called outbreak of 'post-truth' politics is the reaffirmation of age-old gatekeeping processes, designed to keep these erratic audiences under control. Such arguments reinforce the idea that we have no alternative but to choose between the camps of anti-elitism or anti-populism. Yet this very notion is precisely the bedrock of populist rhetoric.

Mejia et al. (2018) address this conundrum in their essay on the racial history of '(post)-truth'. The authors demonstrate that communication research romanticizes a time when public discourse was allegedly more reliable and inclusive. Those who appear to benefit from this 'post-truth' narrative seemingly refer to an idealized golden age, when minority voices supposedly had more opportunities for inclusion and representation (Mejia et al., 2018: 110). In contrast, minority voices have always experienced a struggle, remaining well aware that there have always been competing representations of the truth. In essence, there is nothing new about 'post-truth'. Looking at the recent critique of far-right populism in the United States, the authors show that communication theorists somehow hope to restore the same type of leadership over public discourse, which historically excluded minorities. This conundrum has been referred to as 'post-truth whiteness' (Mejia et al., 2018). Once we become aware of this trope, we can demystify two common assumptions. The first one lies in the idea that dominant and exclusionary narratives have only just resurfaced in the (Western) model of liberal democracies. From the perspective of race, feminism or postcolonialism, it is clear that minority voices have always struggled for inclusion and representation. Those who interpreted the re-emergence of far-right populism as a paradigmatic shift were simply lured by their own privilege.

The second assumption is that one can only prevent polarisation, hate speech and identity politics by institutionalizing the avenues and practices of public deliberation. Media scholars, practitioners and legislators often rely on this approach when trying to elucidate the question of (post)-truth politics. As argued earlier, such assumptions evoke early crowd psychology and the desire to control popular means of public expression. It implies that informality in communication is detrimental to the democratic values of pluralism and freedom of speech. Whilst there is much concern about diversity and the media representation of minorities, the political discourse surrounding these questions often fails to put the legacy of cultural studies into practice. This is because policymaking, as well as a considerable part of the scholarship (D'Ancona, 2017), advocates for securitization and re-centralization. Indeed, it implies that decentralized communication networks represent a threat to public trust (Bontcheva and Posetti, 2020; European Commission, 2018). And yet both cultural studies and postcolonial theory clearly show that the real struggle for representation happens in the peripheries (Appadurai, 1996; Fraser, 1990; Hall, 1997, 1993).

They demonstrate that, in order to feel more included, peripheral audiences continuously reinvent new tools and practices of communication. When creative process unfolds organically, it is likely to deliver a great sense of empowerment. Well-established populist leaders occasionally capitalize on these experiences, by creating a deceitful sense of informality. What is to blame, in this case, is not so much the success of these informal communication networks, but the fact that they are being politicized and re-centralized. In reality, discussions around public trust and populism often shy away from an important consideration: the fact that audiences are expressing a legitimate interest in a radically informal approach to political communication.

You may be wondering what this has to do with the case of revolutions and transitional politics. Well, these questions simply condition the way we think about the voices of social change. They also pertain to the strategic aspects of a revolution, in terms of political communication. In fact, the characteristics of decentralized networks have been extensively discussed in relation to the social movements of the early 2010s (Bennett and Segerberg, 2012; Castells, 2012; Gerbaudo, 2012). Along with contemporary cases of civil mobilizations, the first wave of the Arab Spring was often associated with a new type of public engagement. This form of political action was considered as horizontal, connective and deprived of institutional structure (Bennett and Segerberg, 2013). A number of scholars suggested that these new forms of digital activism would be more spontaneous and inclusive as traditional partisan politics. However, this realization led them to express concerns about the long-term efficiency and sustainability of these movements (Bennett and Segerberg, 2011: 201). Some researchers contested the lack of organizational structure, calling for a more robust institutional framework to consolidate a clear agenda in the realm of formal politics (Tufekci, 2016). This argument became all the more convincing in light of the rapid transition of digital media from the emergent to the mainstream. These once decentralized practices of communication were increasingly intertwined with surveillance capitalism and a logic of consumerism (Dean, 2005; Fuchs, 2010; Zuboff, 2019). In this context, online activism is no longer expected to foster an authentic spirit of resistance. Today, the conventional wisdom is that political dissent is in fact more likely to be affected by the mainstreaming of digital media.

In this context, the political communication scholarship often calls for the restoration of an intellectual leadership over the public sphere. It reaffirms the importance of expert knowledge and institutional credibility. When faced with the shortcomings of online activism, we are tempted to resort back to traditional forms of partisan politics. The emphasis is then placed on the political literacy of an intellectual elite, which is considered as well-placed to provide the opposition with an ideological framework. The subtext of this debate comes down to the same question, which has been discussed in relation to populism, of whether informal networks can successfully lead the way towards organic social change, or whether they will alternatively need to engage with formal politics. In some cases, the media research applied to the first wave of the 'Arab Spring' gave a naively idealist twist to the core principle of crowd psychology. Some argued that networked communication facilitated the creation of civil movements based on the expression of feelings and affects (Papacharissi, 2014). The emotional charge of powerful hashtags and slogans was supposedly instrumental to the sense of belonging that audiences would experience when promoting the online message of the movement (Breuer, 2012; Meraz and Papcharissi, 2013). Such theories presented intriguing similarities with the work of Tarde, almost suggesting that this kind of public engagement was populist in nature (Gerbaudo, 2018). In retrospect, it appears that the historically gendered power relations that we ascribe to the roles of the masses and the elite have significantly conditioned the way we understand informal communication. Even those who claim to explore this topic from the perspective of the grassroots do not always consciously overcome this duality.

Some expect the formation of new political elites within opposition voices, while others continue to essentialize the idea of the masses, as hopelessly driven by their affects and emotions (Boler and Davis, 2018).

Another conceptual weakness of media research is that it focuses on the technological tools we use to consume and produce information. The emphasis is commonly placed on the design of communication infrastructures, their affordances and their implications for the broader political economy of the media. Accordingly, research on grassroots communication has been considerably influenced by the idea that the medium is the message (McLuahn, 1994). The tools we use to communicate are thus treated as a key parameter when it comes to understanding the outcome of communication. In fact, this approach underpins the assumption of technological determinism, which has been so vividly criticized in the aftermath of the 2011 uprisings (Fuchs, 2012; Hirst, 2012). My intention is to (re)define 'informal communication' as a practice, which is not circumscribed to any particular medium or technology, so as to reconsider its limitations and potential benefits for civil society. Another way to look at the case of the 2011 uprisings is to explore the role of grassroots informal networks as a flexible and more resilient type of social infrastructure. These networks continuously evolve and adapt to their environments, involving different media, depending on the technical challenges and limitations to one's freedom of expression. This approach allows us to shift perspective away from the hardware of the technology to focus on the software of social interactions. Informal communication is not so much about the affordances of technological tools, as it is about the process of reinventing a new medium. It is this creativity that we find amongst 'subaltern counterpublics' (Fraser, 1990) and communities that proactively experiment with emergent media. I argue that it is more useful to think about informal communication as a constantly regenerating process, because the emergent media of today is most likely destined to become the mainstream media of tomorrow. Stuart Hall beautifully described this cycle when studying the history of discourse and representation, stating that 'yesterday's deconstructions are often tomorrow's orthodox clichés' (2000: 91). Arguably, this also applies to media, which is both a product as well an enabler of discourse.

The evolution of online activism over the years that followed the 2011 uprisings perfectly illustrates this transition. In Tunisia and Egypt, the 2011 civil movements channelled genuine feelings of exclusion within youths and the working class. A number of influential online activists witnessed and documented police brutality. They engaged with a more organic and decentralized form of public engagement. Street mobilizations and alternative communication channels were meant to redirect attention to the peripheries of the public sphere, which would be more inclusive and representative of civil society. These alternative spaces and communication practices initially resonated with the pro-revolutionary civil opposition, because they appeared to contrast with the national public discourse. However, over the course of the political transition that followed the uprisings, digital media was increasingly used as a traditional communication channel for political campaigning. The blogosphere and social media sphere became highly polarized, fragmenting the pro-revolutionary opposition in favour of leading political forces and institutionalized parties (Lynch, 2011; Lynch et al., 2017). In Egypt, many pro-revolutionary online activists from the urban middle class concluded that the social media sphere had failed to produce a political narrative that would speak to the rural working class. They became nostalgic about the earlier phase of online activism, during which social media was still playful and emergent. In retrospect, it was clear that the *mainstreaming* of digital media had instigated polarizing echo chambers, while generating more exposure to state surveillance.

The experience of online activism was, however, part of a broader media ecology. Over the years that preceded the 2011 uprisings, the activist blogosphere was only one out of many possible avenues for informal communication (Abaza, 2013; de Souza and Lipietz, 2011; Kanna, 2012). Each specific medium would provide access to its own relevant audience, involving different skills as well as various degrees of risk and exposure. It is perhaps one's ability to navigate these complex parameters that would account for their level of agency under the authoritarian regimes of Mubarak and Ben Ali. Informal communication thus allows us to account for a broader range of communication practices that relayed opposition voices long before the events of 2011.

Let us remember that amongst the political groups that presented themselves as part of the revolutionary opposition were the Tunisian Ennahda party and the Egyptian Muslim Brotherhood. In this early phase of the political transition, they were seen as legitimate alternatives, having suffered years of repression under the previous regimes. Naturally, they each gained the majority of seats in the 2011–12 elections of the Egyptian Parliament and Tunisian Constituent Assembly. By the time of the first post-revolutionary campaigns, the two political groups were operating as well-structured organizations that were about to enter the arena of institutionalized politics. Yet one can argue that the legitimacy they benefitted from on the eve of the uprisings stemmed from years of experience in grassroots communication.

The study of political movements in the Middle East and North Africa shows that these actors became popular thanks to an informal approach to campaigning (Whaby, 2017; Wolf, 2017). It is when non-state actors are banned from the formal political sphere that they become well implemented in the informal community network of local associations. Within the realm of informality, they build interpersonal interactions within the grassroots and remain well aware of their realities and grievances. It is in this context that the largest opposition groups historically gained popularity, engaging in non-profit community work to provide the services that the public sectors would fail to deliver. Researcher Noura Whaby (2017) reminds us that:

> In Egypt, for example, [the Muslim Brotherhood] had long provided healthcare, education, and food supplies both in urban slums and provincial villages. They were able to bank this support when they launched their successful parliamentary and presidential campaigns after 2011.
>
> (Whaby, 2017: 140)

Compared to the leftist pro-revolutionary youth, Ennahda and the Egyptian Muslim Brotherhood both appeared to be closer to the grassroots. This was the result of a long history of engagement in local charity work and associative networks. Their involvement in civil society over the years that preceded the revolution later allowed them to frame themselves as a credible alternative to the political status quo of the previous regimes. They had built a large community network in disfranchised neighbourhoods and rural regions, which enabled them to mobilize an electorate amongst those whose voices were hardly ever relayed in formal politics. On the one hand, local charity work involved interpersonal communication practices that resonated with the priorities of the grassroots and contrasted with large-scale political campaigning. On the other hand, alternative approaches to communication would sometimes enable these opposition groups to circumvent censorship and political repression. In fact, the history of these local opposition movements offers multiple examples of informal communication networks. In her research on the Tunisian Ennahda party, Wolf (2017) shows how years of exile and incarceration under Ben Ali led Islamists to interact closely with leaders of the left-wing opposition. This may have encouraged a cross-fertilization of ideas when debating over the ideological foundations of the movement. Another interesting example comes to mind when we think about the role of women in the history of the Ennahda party. Under the former regime, women were well-placed to circulate information. The fact that they remained, in all appearance, circumscribed to the private sphere paradoxically placed them in a somehow strategic position. It enabled them to keep the movement alive in spite of the measures enforced to exclude their male counterparts from the realm of formal politics. These examples suggest that in a political environment where tight media regulations are in place, inventiveness and informality have been instrumental to political dissent. This idea resonates, in fact, with a famous argument already formulated by Nancy Fraser (1990) in her feminist critique of the public sphere: peripheral communication practices have just as much – if not more – potential to translate into substantial socio-political change. The creativity one demonstrates in a context of scarcity and oppression reveals a high level of political awareness. Further, this political awareness does not come with high education nor with an institutional experience of politics. It is part of the skills and empirical knowledge developed by those who find themselves excluded, marginalized or misrepresented in the official public discourse and formal political sphere.

Of course – relating back to Stuart Hall's quote – history tells us that these experiences of agency are usually short-lived. In spite of their initial journey of political resistance, these parties eventually evolve to promote rigid and institutionally framed narratives, which often do not relay the perspectives of the grassroots at the policy level. This was also the case for Ennahda and the Muslim Brotherhood. As well-organized structures, they came to embrace the political game, by compromising on the ethos of dissent to impose a normative ideological identity strategically branded to compete in national politics. This arguably resulted in a significant decline of the credibility they had originally gained from the organic practice of informal communication. The Egyptian

Muslim Brotherhood quite naturally lost its popularity after former President Morsi announced his 2012 constitutional decree. This led to the success of the counterrevolution by legitimizing the 2013 military coup led by chief General Abdel Fattah al-Sisi. As for the Tunisian Ennahda party, it became increasingly disconnected from its support base, failing to bridge the gap between traditionalists and the political establishment (Boubeker, 2017; Cavatorta and Merone, 2013; McCarthy, 2018; Wolf, 2017). Its progressive decline in popularity amongst the grassroots was already perceptible in 2016 when the organization decided to give up the 'Islamist' label, rebranding itself as a national and civil political party. In order to enter the political game, Ennhada would have to compromise for political legitimacy, which meant that it would lose its relevance in the eyes of the disfranchised youths (*mouhamishin*) (Cavartota and Merone, 2013: 862; Cavatorta, 2015; McCarthy, 2018). One could even argue that, over time, the politicization of the movement contributed to pave the way for the election of Kais Saied, the anti-establishment candidate of the 2019 Presidential Campaign.

We are thus left to wonder if there is a point in its evolution, where informal communication ceases to be genuinely empowering. It seems that, over time, what is left of it is either invoked to establish a new power institution or redirected to manufacture consent around the pre-existing status quo.

Nevertheless, besides the question of its perennity, informal communication needs to be studied as a process that serves the inclusion and self-representation of minority voices across socio-political environments. These informal practices involve a broad range of non-state actors, ranging from opposition groups to diasporas, human rights defenders or civil society organizations. They appear to be intrinsically linked to social capital and community trust, which makes them worthy of attention in social sciences (Houston, 2018; Houston et al., 2015). Unfortunately, this perspective on informality is too often absent from the contemporary debate on both populism and political activism. Some have suggested that this question is typically associated with the Global South, because it points to the importance of informality in the absence of social welfare:

> The informal sector in the Global South is described as the illustration of how communal networks can support jobs, housing, service provision, social welfare, and others with minimal state interventions.
>
> (Whaby, 2017: 141)

Comparatively, 'an informal sector in the North seemingly does not exist' (Whaby, 2017: 141). But such a comparative approach is not always useful when it comes to overcoming Eurocentrism. It fails to explain how the Western experience of populism limits our understanding of informal communication in other parts of the world. As I will show, its practices were arguably instrumental to the consolidation of a counter-discourse in the years preceding the 2011 uprisings. Yet communication studies have overlooked the creative skills applied by political dissidents during exile and imprisonment. The inventiveness required to circulate sensitive information under the regimes of Ben Ali and Mubarak is a precursor of the ingenuity that civil activists later demonstrated when applying social media as a resistance tool. Today, activists continuously reinvent new codes and applications of communication devices to avoid online surveillance and automated censorship.

To name but a few examples, this was the case in May 2021, when pro-Palestinian voices found creative ways to document the unlawful evictions of civilians living in the neighbourhood of Sheikh Jarrah in East Jerusalem. In that case, pro-Palestinian activists simply reverted to ancient Arabic, removing all dots (diacritics) from the modern alphabet in order to trick the content moderation used by mainstream social media platforms (Erhaim and Mahlouly, 2023). Informal communication is also likely to have played a role in the impressive longevity of the Algerian Hirak, and the sustained momentum of its peaceful Friday protests. Further, the young Lebanese pro-revolutionary opposition also engaged creative forms of informal communication to reclaim ownership of a historically fragmented public space. And, as I will demonstrate in the last chapter of this book, they also had to develop a more organic and dynamic approach to media literacy, in order to fact-check the online disinformation spread by counterrevolutionary forces. These various examples illustrate the fact that informal communication is a bottom-up process of communicative resilience and social creativity, which is not specific to a particular medium or communication technology.

From the emergent to the mainstream:
The cycle of discursive power

We have now established that informal communication is a short-lived process through which grassroots networks experiment with emergent media. It involves the creative use of different art forms and popular genres, engaging a broad range of tools and social skills. The question that remains is how informal communication evolves, once it reaches the mainstream. Is there a critical mass of interactions where the media is no longer emergent? How do these practices grow to become the new norm and at what point do they cease to be genuinely informal? Finally, and most importantly, is this shift likely to diminish the sense of empowerment they produce?

These questions come with the realization that media conveys both dominant and counter-hegemonic voices. By relaying narratives and visual representations, the media has always been a vehicle of *discursive power*. On the one hand, it is used to impose, maintain or reinforce cultural hegemony. On the other, it provides us with a sense of agency as an interactive form of expression. As such, it also supports the creation and circulation of counter-discourse. Communication theorists are usually too quick to dissociate these two sides of the same coin. Yet when it comes to the evolution of our communication practices, the tensions between hegemony and counter-power are not as linear as we might think. They often appear to unfold in a cycle, punctuated by different turning points that mark the transitions from the emergent to *the new* mainstream. As different actors compete for discursive power, our mediated representations of the world constantly evolve through various processes of disruption, adoption and reappropriation. It is precisely in the context of this broader cycle that we need to think about the benefits of informal communication. Let me outline this framework in very generic terms

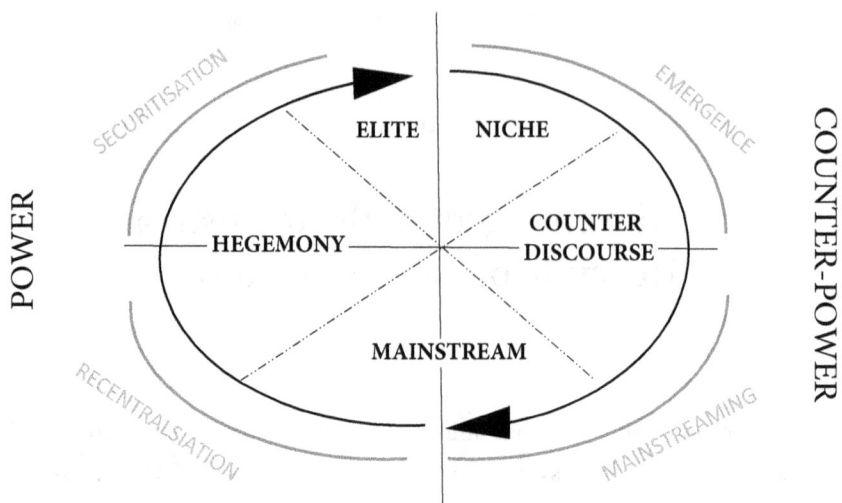

Figure 1 The Discursive Cycle.

before drawing on specific examples. In order to illustrate this concept, I will refer to the model represented in Figure 1, which maps out the evolution of this cycle along two coordinate axes.

Mapping the evolution of media and discourse as a cycle allows us to visualize the moments when alternative modes of interactions emerge. During these turning points, creativity is at the core of informal communication. It has the potential to switch the trajectory of discourse by introducing a 180-degree shift (cf. Figure 1). However, within this cycle, we also need to account for other dynamics, which are detrimental to the development of a counter-discourse. For example, tensions may occur amongst counter-hegemonic voices, once the political value of their message is leveraged and widely acknowledged. Throughout this evolution, we may as well consider situations, in which a counter-discourse is at risk of being hijacked by dominant voices. This typically happens when informal practices of communication are commodified or reappropriated for political purposes. History shows that these processes are just as likely to reverse the trajectory of *discursive power* and that is the reason why they can be mapped out as part of the same cycle. The field of political communication is traditionally structured around a binary distinction between a *top-down* and a *bottom-up* approach. Theory often fails to explain how these dynamics intersect in a holistic way. In practice, everything however indicates

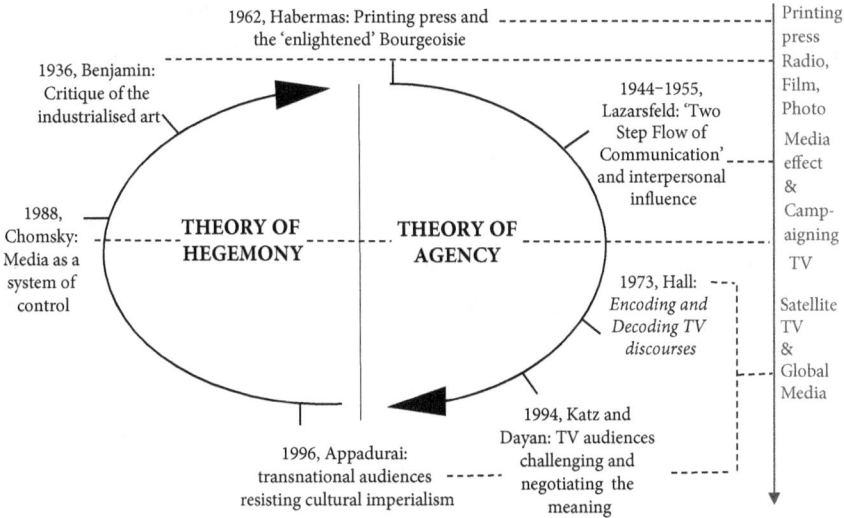

Figure 2 A Mapping of Media Theory: Between Agency and Hegemony.

that the double-edged sword of the media is used by competing players to serve different agendas. That is why media theory continuously alternates between arguments of *agency* and *hegemony* (cf. Figure 2). To a certain extent, the history of communication studies perfectly mirrors the cyclic evolution of media as a driving force of discourse.

With the arrival of every medium deemed significant, new theories come along, which only document a short window of time in the grand cycle of discursive power. In the early twentieth century, the School of Frankfurt produced a structural critique of mass media to make sense of its influence in the era of nationalist state-propaganda (Benjamin, 1936). This Marxist perspective was still relevant in the late twentieth century, when media scholars described the development of globalized media as a form of cultural imperialism (Dorfman and Mattelart, 2019; Tomlinson, 1991). Around the same period, however, audience reception studies introduced a different take on global media. It argued that satellite TV, for example, also had the potential to engage diasporas and transnational communities. Postcolonial theorists proactively contributed to this scholarship, laying the grounds for the field of Cultural Studies (Appadurai, 1996; Hall, 1993). They revisited the role of media from a bottom-up perspective to show how women, minorities and the working class had gained informal power by subverting and negotiating the codes of popular culture (Jenkins,1992; Morley, 1986, 1992). These examples show how we came to oppose theories of *agency* and *hegemony* to describe different phases in the evolution of old media (cf. Figure 2). Over the last two decades, we have seen the same debate unfold with regard to the development of digital technologies.

In the 2000s, communication experts saw the Internet as an emergent media that would support the decentralization of the public sphere (Rushkoff, 2003; Turner, 2008). The conventional wisdom was that online tools created more opportunities for public engagement. In the field of Cultural Studies, it was argued that Internet had introduced a 'participatory culture', allowing audiences to reinvent popular genres in creative ways (Jenkins, 2006). Fandoms were thriving across the Internet and users had just started to experiment with the meme culture (Jenkins, 2006). In political communication, a large body of research was produced, which suggested that online audiences were able to set their own agenda (Meraz, 2009; Wallsten, 2007). They would not only consume but also produce on-demand content, giving saliency to the news topics relevant to their own interests. In the fields of development and public policy, digital technologies were viewed as an opportunity to facilitate access to public services (Saebo et al., 2010; Saltanat, 2010). The assumption was that the application of online platforms in the realm of governance (e-governance) and citizenship (e-deliberation) would help reduce corruption, restoring trust in public administrations (Semetko and Krasnoboka, 2003). With the rise of social media as we know it today, it was later argued that digital technologies contributed to the relative success of the 2011 uprisings. Commentators associated the Arab Spring with other cases of civil mobilizations like the London riots, the Spanish Indignados and the Occupy Wall Street protests (Mason, 2011). They drew analogies with the 1990s anti-globalization movements, with an emphasis on web activism as a key logistical tool for civil movements (Khondker, 2011). In other words, within the conventional framework of modernity, it was generally assumed that these technologies designed in the West would bring freedom, equality and prosperity to the rest of the world.

That early phase of cyber-utopianism arguably seems to have ended around the mid-2010s. Scholars developed a range of new theories, which intended to explain the ongoing transition from emergent to mainstream. Other concepts like 'convergence' (Jenkins, 2006b) or 'hybrid media' (Chadwick, 2013) gained relevance. They pointed to the tensions between grassroots and institutional actors, both competing for discursive power across the social media sphere. This shift of perspective marked a turning point in the evolution of the media that corresponds with the lower pole (cf. north axis, Figure 1) of the discursive cycle. Over time, we came to demystify cyber-utopianism and began to understand its long-term implications. We can see, for example, how these utopian narratives have allowed foreign investors to capitalize on big data, in the global race for artificial intelligence. We also become increasingly aware of the trade-off between privacy and security. Along with the 2013 revelations of Edward Snowden, the Cambridge Analytica scandal shed light on the alarming scope of state and corporate surveillance. Filter bubbles proved to increase audience fragmentation, creating more grounds for polarisation and identity politics. The creative meme culture born out of platforms like *4chan* has been flooded with conspiracy theories and far-right content (Merrin, 2019; Tufekci, 2017). Finally, the concerning issue of algorithmic bias revealed that today's challenges to inclusion and diversity are perhaps greater than the ones posed by traditional media (Noble, 2018). Digital communication is now viewed through a dystopian lens as we find ourselves in a position of helpless subjugation to technology, which raises constant fears and anxiety. Accordingly, the media theories that have gained popularity in recent years are the ones that expose the downfalls of social media (Tufekci, 2017; Zuboff, 2020). One could in fact argue that it is our apprehension of digital technologies – more than the technology itself – that has become *the new mainstream*.

This dystopian lens remains nonetheless infused with its own technological determinism. It is clear, for instance, that the current political debate on disinformation continues to focus predominantly on technology. Policymakers and the tech industry conveniently resort to new technological tools, while disregarding important sociological parameters. Automated content moderation has been invoked as the best remedy against hate speech. With the uncertainties related to deep-fakes and machine learning, public resources are invested in the development of software designed to authenticate content (Thakor, 2019). As for the privacy-security dilemma, some are hoping to resolve it by relying on blockchain cryptography (Bindra, 2018). Indeed, blockchain technology recently generated a lot of enthusiasm as an alternative system of data management. In contrast to the increasingly centralized Web 2.0, it bears the promise of a transparent data history, recorded through highly secured information chains. As such, it is expected to succeed where the Internet has failed, by ensuring 'distributed trust' across a network. In other words, technology remains, once again, central to the argument. Meanwhile, there is not much interest in re-evaluating the definition of 'distributed trust' from a strictly sociological perspective.

Ultimately, as much as we find ourselves disillusioned with these tools, we seem to continuously fall into the trap of technological determinism. And that is the reason why I suggest rethinking the evolution of media, on the basis of the framework presented above. The objective here is to understand media as a social practice, regardless of its technological infrastructure. What drives the evolution of media through this cycle is the power dynamics at play in a particular context. The aim is to shift focus away from the technology to consider how the media is used, by whom and for what purpose. This approach admits that a communication channel is nothing but the theatre of complex power relationships. I will thus rely on this model of a discursive cycle to study the evolution of emergent media. Simultaneously, I will apply this framework to deconstruct the trope of technological determinism.

I propose that informal communication practices involve various forms of emergent media and narratives that continuously evolve, following the course of this discursive cycle. This model is certainly not meant to be applied as a standardized framework. My objective is, on the contrary, to redefine communication as a dynamic process rather than an endpoint with tangible outcomes. By relying on the idea of a cycle, I hope to highlight the nuance and complexity of what drives the regeneration of discourse.

Such a holistic framework is also helpful when it comes to distancing ourselves from today's intense climate of polarisation. We tend to assume that there is such a thing as a binary opposition between the anti-conformity of self-proclaimed counter-cultures and what is viewed as *the mainstream*. Yet, as mentioned in the previous chapter, it may be the case that these polar opposites are insidiously bounded in a symbiotic relationship. If so, relying on a strictly binary overview of the public debate is likely to reinforce polarisation. Bear in mind that, like in the case of quantum physics, communication theory is influenced by the observer effect. Social scientists inevitably alter the conditions of the phenomenon they claim to study as external observers. When we label something as a counter-discourse, or casually debate as to what is mainstream, we become part of the discursive cycle. Therefore, it is all the more important to acknowledge the complex interplay between power and counter-power, in an attempt to better understand the role we all play in this process.

On another level, the idea of a discursive cycle is particularly relevant when it comes to studying revolutionary movements. When a revolutionary counter-discourse gains popularity, it will generate deep sociocultural and ideological changes. In the case of a successful revolution, it will presumably become the new hegemony, establishing a new political elite in power. Alternatively, if the revolution fails, the narrative of the counterrevolution will become existential to the old hegemony. In that case, the discourse of the political status quo no longer has a legitimacy of its own but is reasserted as the *de-facto* alternative to the revolution. Hannah Arendt indeed reminds us that 'counter-revolution (…) has always remained bound to revolution as reaction is bound to action' (Arendt, 2016: 18). The history of revolutionary movements reveals how much the sphere of power and counter-power remain interconnected. This arguably applies to all revolutions, whether they introduce radical regime changes or gradual sociocultural transformations. By definition, they are the result of a regeneration of discourse.

In this regard, one could argue that every revolution marks the end and the beginning of a discursive cycle. Within this cycle, informal communication is what makes a counter-discourse resilient enough to survive in the peripheries of the public sphere. But after a long period of gestation in the margins of society, it will eventually mature. Once this counter-discourse grows in momentum, it may no longer be as flexible and responsive. The same logic applies to revolutionary movements once they reach a critical mass of followers. Over time, the counter-discourse gains inertia, inevitably spreading into the realm of institutional power. At that point, it will be granted a political value because it is an existential threat to the status quo. As such, it will be inevitably politicized, whether it is hijacked by its opponents or destined to compete in the sphere of formal power.

According to the Foucauldian definition of 'discourse', language is at the core of discursive power. Therefore, a revolution arguably starts by challenging the meaning of language. By conveying different frames and narratives, the media is simply one of the means through which the authorship of language can be maintained or challenged. When revolutionaries mobilize in the name of 'freedom', 'dignity' or 'equality', they simply capitalize on the power of language. In response, a counterrevolution is also likely to fight over the actual meaning of these terms in an attempt to regain legitimacy. Hannah Arendt (2016) describes this process as part of the dialectic between revolutions and counterrevolutions. She stresses the fact that revolutionary ideals – such as the concept of *freedom* – have remained very flexible over time. 'Freedom', in this sense, has always acted as a fluid component of discourse. As much as it remains a revolutionary leitmotiv, it is recurrently used to legitimize a new institutional order as in the context of warfare. Through the circulation of discourse, the *revolutionary cause of freedom* is succeeded by *freedom as a justification of war* (and vice versa):

> (…) it has become almost a matter of course that the end of war is revolution, and that the only cause which possibly could justify it is the revolutionary cause of freedom.
>
> (Arendt, 2016: 17)

This only shows that there is an ironic symmetry in the way meaning evolves through the natural course of the discursive cycle. Rethinking the role of the media in terms of discursive power only reminds us that political actors are competing over the meaning of the same language. As it circulates from *emergent* to *hegemonic* media, language remains fluid. It is this characteristic of language that explains the circulation of discursive power as well as the logic of informal communication. Indeed, it is by applying a creative approach to language that counter-hegemonic voices demonstrate resilience in the face of repression.

I began to think about the cyclic evolution of discourse when investigating the activist blogosphere and the development of online campaigning in post-revolutionary Tunisia and Egypt. While I was studying these particular types of political mobilizations, I became interested in the evolving application of the media as well as the struggle for the reappropriation of the public space. In order to describe evolving practices of online engagement, I relied on a model designed to illustrate the cycle through which counter-hegemonic voices eventually gain recognition within the mainstream.

My first research project contributed to mapping the evolution of emergent media used by pro-revolutionaries as part of a broader range of informal practices. Based on interviews with activists and a combination of both fieldwork interviews and online research, I examined the reappropriation of channels initially used by the civil opposition, during the 2012 Presidential and constitutional debates. It is in this context that I came to associate the history of revolutionary movements with the idea of a discursive cycle. On the one hand, it allowed me to retrace the growth of revolutionary narratives through various forms of emergent media. On the other hand, it illustrated the nuanced juxtaposition of hopes and disillusion associated with the memory of the Arab uprisings, as well as with the coincidental so-called revolution of digital technologies.

I proposed that this cycle could be divided in four quarters illustrating different phases in the evolution of counter-hegemonic voices. The first quarter represents the very early phase of the revolutionary movements, during which the activist blogosphere was limited to a niche audience. If we had to visualize it, this phase would start at the north axis of the discursive cycle (cf. Figure 1). The creativity of informal communication was born out of a repressive environment and a very centralized media market. In the early 2000s, activists were able to leverage the blind spots and weaknesses of hegemonic media to mobilize a community of bloggers and citizen journalists. In Egypt, for example, some of the policies implemented by Mubarak's former administration had encouraged the emergence of web-activism in the years that preceded the uprisings. Gamal Mubarak – who was considered to be the most likely successor to his father Hosni – had been very active in promoting new communication technologies. The جيل المستقبل[1] (*Gil al Mustaqbal,*) association he founded in 1998 encouraged the adoption of digital technologies by young university graduates to stimulate entrepreneurship and economic opportunities (Sobelman, 2001). Before the Internet was subverted by revolutionary voices, it was already promoted by the ruling party with the aim to perpetuate the economic leadership of the military elite through modernization. Over time, these initiatives also contributed to the formation of a young tech-savvy intelligentsia that became part of the opposition. This shows that, within the first generation of Egyptian online activists, some had gained access to new technologies thanks to their sociological proximity with the former elite of the

National Democratic Party. Although such projects intended to serve the interests of the military regime, they eventually provided the opposition with technical skills to build on the momentum of the first civil mobilizations that took place between 2005 and 2006. This perfectly illustrates the transition that occurs at the north axis of the discursive cycle. Another parameter to consider is the fact that many of the pioneers of online activism in Egypt had been directly involved or closely interacting with the formal political sphere. Young revolutionaries – such as Amr Hamzawy[83] – had been part of social environments or families, whose members were either part of the military elites, or had common interests with the former National Party.

Other revolutionaries, including noteworthy figures such as Alaa Abdel Fatah and Wael Ghonim, who were independent from any political party in 2011, were originally affiliated with the Muslim Brotherhood, one of the most well-structured organizations within the opposition. In other words, many of the prominent figures of civil activism in Egypt – who promoted an alternative form of political engagement on the eve of the revolution – had previously been affiliated with well-established political groups. This suggests that the sphere of institutional powers indirectly contributed to the emergence of a new form of political activism.

This is important to acknowledge in view of the fact that digital activism has often been described as deprived of a well-rooted political identity. It has been in fact argued that these new forms of 'connective action', which became prominent in the early 2010s, presented themselves as an alternative to old-style partisan engagement (Bennett and Segerberg, 2012). This new type of civil movements introduced a 'do-it-yourself' approach to politics, involving loose network associations and sporadic issue-based campaigns, which were supposedly free from organizational structure. At the time, scholars like Tufekci (2017) or Bennett and Segerberg (2012) questioned the efficiency and sustainability of these mobilizations, because of their apparent lack of institutional framework. In doing so, they failed to account for some of the political cultures upon which these various forms of activism were based, and the fact that their communication tools and practices often originated within the sphere of institutional power. In the case of Egypt, prominent figures of online activism actually had a history of partisan engagement, which arguably contributed to shape the culture of political dissent within the opposition.

Most importantly, the left-wing and liberal voices of the young civil opposition that became active online were often part of a rather highly educated urban middle class. As I will argue, this partly explains why this community was not always viewed as a fair representation of the grassroots and did not receive as much popular support as the Islamists in the context of the 2012 elections. One of the most striking examples of this is the campaign led by the prominent Egyptian activist Mahmoud Salem, alias Sandmonkey, when he ran in the late 2011 parliamentary election. In spite of a relatively large Twitter audience (close to 45,000 followers at the time[2]), the candidate only secured 5,000 votes in the district of Heliopolis, which was one of the most tech-affluent parts of the country. One has to wonder if these figures of online activism really had the potential to position themselves as legitimate representatives of the grassroots, when they were no longer interacting with them on the streets. Then again, this intelligentsia was well-placed to leverage resources that were otherwise limited to the tech-savvy and politically literate circles of the youth.

This suggests that some of the skillsets and communication tools inherited from the sphere of power had been transposed into the realm of counter-power. Conversely, once they had organically evolved to serve the voices of political dissent, they were once again reappropriated to manufacture consent around the restoration of the political status quo. In fact, as I will argue in the next chapters, these tools ended up being extensively used by well-established political groups, during the presidential and constitutional debates that followed the uprisings.

This was afforded by the expansional growth of these informal networks, which I situated in the second quarter of the discursive cycle (cf. Figure 1). At the time of the 2011 protests, the commodification of digital media became perceptible, which led to a rapid transformation of online pro-revolutionary networks and the blogosphere. During this period, the penetration rate of social media significantly increased, which accelerated the formation of online political clusters. In retrospect, many activists stated that this shift was detrimental to the cross-fertilization of ideas they had experienced, when these online platforms were still limited to a niche audience. The revolutionary agenda became compromised by the fragmentation and polarisation of these online audiences. Revolutionaries were now directly exposed to the formal political sphere and under the spotlight of national and international media.

Shortly after the 2011 uprisings, Tunisian bloggers received Nobel Prize nominations and were asked to serve as interim ministers. Around the same time, well-established political actors affiliated to the old parties started to proactively campaign on social media, applying a 'one-to-many' approach that was similar to that of the traditional mass media. It is this phase of institutionalization that I identified with the third quarter of my 'discursive cycle'. The very last stage of this cycle referred to the reframing of revolutionary narratives by the actors of the counterrevolution. That part of the framework evokes the securitization of digital tools by political elites and the use of these technologies as a means of state surveillance. Overall, my model was designed around these four phases, each related to processes of: disruption, adoption, reappropriation and (re)centralization.

On another level, this cycle does also account for the evolution of the discourse around technology. Over time, we come to express different hopes and apprehensions about our technological environments. That interpretation of the discursive cycle simply indicates that our relationship with communication technologies is also very dynamic. Every time a new technology starts to feel 'colonized' by the mainstream, another one comes along, which promises to be more ground-breaking and disruptive. Besides the example of blockchain technology, this was also the case with the application of encrypted platforms. In the mid-2010s, users massively adopted encrypted messaging applications like WhatsApp, Signal or Telegram to circumvent state surveillance and censorship. However, many of these platforms have since been exposed to new regulations imposed under the banner of global and national security. In response, users have drifted away from the mainstream and newly regulated communication tools to keep experimenting with the latest forms of emergent media. This suggests that the reappropriation and mainstreaming of new technologies are only part of a broader cycle, a complex ecology of which informal communication is part. In the next chapters, I will thus rely on this framework to outline the findings of my research on media activism in post-revolutionary Tunisia and Egypt.

Before we go any further, I should make it clear that the interplay between revolutionary and counterrevolutionary voices played out very differently in these two countries. To begin with, there is a debate as to whether the Egyptian case qualifies as a revolution, given the backfire of Morsi's constitutional decree and the subsequent coup that led to the restoration of the military regime. In contrast, Tunisia has until recently been depicted as the success story of the 'Arab Spring'. The Tunisian uprisings certainly led to important constitutional reforms, a significant empowerment of civil society and the liberalization of the public debate. However, after the dissolution of the former ruling party, some of its former members had re-entered the political game. These 'feloul'[3] figures would sometimes rebrand themselves as reformists to regain legitimacy in the post-revolutionary landscape. This introduced a gradual and perhaps more subtle counterrevolutionary process, as 'the [...] networks linked to the former parties [ultimately] survived in the economical field, by means of a reshaping' (Steuer and Doron, 2020: 129). In spite of what had been achieved in terms of freedom of expression, many young Tunisians felt disillusioned with the formal political sphere, manifesting more interest in soft news topics and informal politics. This partly explains why the legitimacy of the partisan elites was once again challenged on the eve of the 2019 campaign, when the anti-establishment rhetoric of Kais Saied struck a chord with the young electorate.

Prior to the 2011 uprisings, Egypt and Tunisia were each ruled by the National Democratic Party (NDP) and the Constitutional Democratic Rally (RCD). Following the Tunisian revolution, the leaders of the former RCD were not allowed to run for the 2011 election of the Constituent Assembly. However, no further regulations were imposed to prevent their involvement in the subsequent campaigns. Ben Ali's former Minister of Defence Kamel Morjane was in fact able to found his own party – *Al Moubadara* – to promote the reconversion of former RCD members, now campaigning in the name of a liberal democracy. In 2012, the late Prime Minister Beji Caïd Essebsi, who then became President in 2014, formed the Nidaa Tunis coalition. In an attempt to present a consolidated front against the Islamist Ennadha party, Nidaa Tunis contributed to blur the lines by bringing together former RCD members along with old left-wing and liberal opponents to Ben Ali's regime. However, new alliances were formed in preparation for the 2014 legislative elections, as Ennahda and Nidaa Tunis came together to form a multi-party coalition government. The conservative Ennahda party compromised, re-labelling itself as a civil party aligned with the progressive right-wing. This decision was perhaps made with the hope of avoiding the climate of polarisation that had been so detrimental to the Egyptian Muslim Brotherhood. Yet this raised questions as to whether Tunisian traditionalists would still be fairly represented. As for Nidaa Tunis, its rapprochement with Ennahda would conveniently 'remove suspicion about its alleged status as heir of the old order, [and contribute to] normalize relations with the opposition forces that struggled against the repressive state under Ben Ali' (Jamaoui, 2015).[4] Over the following years, former RCDists like Abderrahim Zouari and Abir Moussi joined the Free Destourian Party (Parti Destourien Libre, PDL). This political group capitalized on the compromise made by Nidaa Tunis to position itself as the adversary of Ennahda, reaching third place (6.63 per cent) in the legislative election of 2019 (Steuer and Doron, 2020). Overall, former RCD figures continued to play an important role in the post-revolutionary debate. This was still the case in 2019, when Kamel Morjane was delegated Prime Minister instead of Youssef Chahed, who was now running in the Presidential election. Some have in fact argued that the persistence of 'the elites born out of the former RCD was at the heart of the [2020] crisis opposing President Kais Said to his Prime Minister Hicham Mechichi' (Steuer and Doron, 2020: 7). Besides the diffusion of the Tunisian counterrevolutionary forces in the political landscape, the elites of the previous regimes also maintained their privilege through the transposition of old clientelist networks into the private sector. Those who initially had ties with the 'clan Trabelsi' continued to benefit from executive functions and strategic access to the same profitable businesses, over which the previous political elite previously had a monopoly. These networks of clientelism had operated in a very centralized regime prior to the revolution and would now remain active in a deregulated market.

In Egypt, counterrevolutionary forces were outwardly visible during the course of the post-revolutionary transition. The SCAF remained in control of the electoral system, setting the rules of the 2012 elections. As I will argue in following chapters, the candidate of the military Ahmad Shafiq most certainly benefitted from the largest infrastructure available to run his campaign during the 2012 presidential race. Even after the success of the Muslim Brotherhood in both the parliamentary and Presidential elections, the judiciary predominantly remained in favour of the military elites. This added to the challenge of drafting the first constitution as the Supreme Judicial Council proved to be very responsive, calling for a national strike to oppose Morsi's controversial decree. The 2012 constitutional referendum took place in a climate of intense polarisation, as many leaders of the civil opposition joined forces with the military to contest the authority of the Muslim Brotherhood. An alliance called the 'National Salvation Front' was formed, which brought together prominent political dissidents like Mohammed El Baradei. This reconfiguration of the political landscape allowed the military to restore its legitimacy, blurring the lines between the military and the pro-revolutionary civil opposition. After military coup, 3 July 2013 was instituted as the historical date marking the victory of the Egyptian people against the *Muslim Brotherhood*.

This brief overview of the Tunisian and Egyptian contexts highlights the interplay between revolution and counterrevolution. The tensions admittedly manifested themselves very differently in each of these two contexts. However, it is fair to say that, in both cases, these power dynamics generated a contentious environment, in which former regime figures were able to reposition themselves and maintain their political influence. With this in mind, I will now examine how the climate of polarisation introduced by the 2011 uprisings became perceptible online. I will quote from a sample of the activist blogosphere in post-revolutionary Tunisia and Egypt to show how the practice of online activism was disrupted by contentious politics. In doing so, I will demonstrate that this young community of bloggers and activists came to reconsider the value of online engagement, once digital media became mainstream.

Emergent media in post-revolutionary Tunisia and Egypt: A study of the blogosphere

In this chapter, I will explore the tensions that may occur between the first and the second quarter of the discursive cycle. I will examine what marks the transition from the emergent to the mainstream, when the informal networks that support the consolidation of a counter-discourse reach a critical mass. To illustrate this process, I will refer to the evolution of the activist blogosphere in post-revolutionary Tunisia and Egypt, drawing on a sample extracted from the activist blogosphere, which covers a period of two years following the uprisings. Prior to the first wave of the 'Arab Spring', the blogosphere proved to be a powerful form of emergent media, which had brought together a range of activists with different political backgrounds across the opposition. Bloggers would document cases of corruption, police brutality and human rights violations. This new genre of informal communication would focus on first-person accounts and relatable anecdotes. It enabled opposition voices to talk about politics in a vernacular language, drawing on everyday life experience of political struggles. It placed the emphasis on individual subjectivities and the politically charged reality of the mundane. Bloggers were, in other words experimenting with an innovative style of social commentary and a new angle, which was absent from the national media and political discourse. As expressed by Egyptian blogger Behayya, cyber-activism was in other words part of a broader range of revolutionary channels that facilitated informal practices of public engagement:

> As many commentators have pointed out, the revolution reversed Egyptians' forced alienation from politics. It put politics back in its rightful place, in people's daily lives where it belongs. And not just in the form of freer political speech and expression, but more importantly in the form of political praxis.
>
> (Behayya, May 2012)[1]

The autobiographic perspective was perhaps one of the most liberating aspects of the activist blogosphere. Bloggers would address politics from a layman's perspective, by drawing on their everyday life. In the early stages of the post-revolutionary transition, self-narration was a distinctive feature of the blogosphere, which characterized the writings of prominent Egyptian bloggers like Zeinobia or *The Big Pharaoh*. This was in some cases incorporated to new forms of investigative citizen journalism, which provided new opportunities for self-expression and continued to relay the perspective of the civil opposition in the months following the uprisings. In October 2011, *The Big Pharaoh* published the testimony of a Christian protester witnessing the Maspero massacre, which took place on 9 October. In order to thoroughly report the story through the eyes of the protagonist, the blogger relayed his account in a single blog post, leaving the article written in the first person. In another instance, *The Big Pharaoh* reported on 24 July clashes that took place in the neighbourhood of Abbasyah, when demonstrators were injured by attackers as they marched towards the Ministry of Defense. In this other first-person account, the blogger once again provided an insider perspective of the protests in a style that contrasts with the conventional norms of journalistic writing:

> I arrived in Tahrir at around 3:30 pm. The sun was blazing and the square looked a bit empty. 'If this number will go on the march to the MOD, the square will be very vulnerable to attackers,' I told my friend who accompanied me to the square. An hour later the numbers started getting bigger and we were ready to embark on the long march to the MOD. The numbers leaving Tahrir were very good and I was quite confident that with such numbers, the army would think twice before attacking us. Besides, we just wanted to reach the MOD, deliver our message and then head back to the square. Our march was peaceful, just like all our marches.
>
> (The Big Pharaoh, 2011: Ref. 49)[2]

In some cases, bloggers subverted journalistic norms by adopting a sarcastic tone. Such a stylistic device allows them to tackle sociocultural taboos, while lampooning the official political discourse. Conversational witticisms and political satire play an important role in the informal channel of the blogosphere. Amongst others, the Tunisian blogger and cartoonist _Z_ used the art of parody to comment on the drama of the post-revolutionary transition, ridiculing prominent figures as they try to re-position themselves in the new political landscape. In cases where bloggers operate under the cover of anonymity, this also allows them to test the evolving boundaries of freedom of speech. In February 2011, _Z_ went as far as to mock the support base of Ennhadha's leader Rached Ghannouchi, who was returning to the country after a long period of exile. In one of his drawings, the blogger represented Ghannouchi like a rock star waving at a crowd of groupies dressed in conservative outfits, but baring their breasts in an idolatrous frenzy. The cartoonist then engaged in a conversation with his audience, outlining the intention of the message – which was to formulate a critique of personality politics through humoristic references to popular culture:

> I took inspiration from a scene in which the Beatles meet an overjoyed crowd of young girls, who throw their bras at them and cry at the sight of the British stars. What I wanted to emphasise was not the boobs of this woman wearing hijab, but rather [my] criticism of this sudden adulation for the leader of the Islamist movement Ennahda. (…) do not interpret this drawing as an attack to women wearing hijab, to Islam or to Ghannouchi. My caricatures (…) are a provocation against the low spirit of adulation.
>
> (_Z_, 2011: Ref. 155)[3]

In Egypt, bloggers like *The Big Pharaoh* applied satire and irony to document the late 2011 parliamentary election. In a post from December of that year, they imagine how Cairo's districts of Heliopolis and Nasr City would claim their independence and found their own federation after electing non-Muslim-Brotherhood/Salafi MPs. The story draws on common Egyptian in-jokes about the different populations of Cairo's suburban localities. Overall, the subculture of the early activist blogosphere appears to be similar to a broader range of emergent media, such as the first generation of Arab YouTube influencers. An activist I had interviewed in 2014 in fact stated that early social media users playfully engaged in the same practices, subverting the norms of journalistic writing, using the language of the street in online posts, expanding the scope of informal communication into the public sphere:

> On Facebook I write whatever I want, whatever comes to my mind, I'm not apologizing, I use harsh language, even mixing, even creating a new type of writing where formal language is combined with Egyptian dialect or slang. This is available to a broad audience and those who contribute do not have

any particular credentials. There is no expectation of political correctness and we do not have to conform to any academic standards; on Facebook we speak like we would speak on the street. When I write an article for a newspaper, I have to think twice about the words I choose, it's a form of inner control.

(Mukhtar[4], writer and social media activist; research interviews, September 2014, Cairo)

Before social platforms were politicized or securitized by counterrevolutionary forces, they still had the potential to operate as an emergent media for informal networks. As such, they were used – along with other grassroots environments – to initiate more inclusive practices of public engagement. Over the course of the post-revolutionary transition, the activist blogosphere continued to report on political controversies. Bloggers commented on partisan campaigns, election boycotts, union demonstrations, rallies, street clashes and nominations of interim officials. In doing so, they deconstructed some of the disputed narratives around the revolution, which lay at the core of the struggle for discursive power. During this period, testimonies from the blogosphere revealed how pro-revolutionary activists experienced the politization and growing polarisation of their once-informal communication network. Over time, many dissidents found themselves having to redefine the revolution by the negative, having to debunk the pseudo-revolutionary narratives of well-established political groups.

Whereas the counter-discourse was initially directed against the ruling elites of the former regime, it would now have to account for a broader range of political players, who would reposition themselves and shift political alliances. This included officials, who had served under the previous regime, well-established syndicates with political leverage and coalitions of independent opponents to the Islamist parties. During this period, the counter-discourse of the blogosphere retained the same primary function as prior to the 2011 uprisings. However, in addition to denouncing corruption and human rights violations, activists decried the systemic reappropriation of the revolution. They described how the public debate shifted away from revolutionary demands to focus on the drama of contentious politics. This turning point precisely corresponds with the south axis of the discursive cycle, when the very meaning of the revolution is disputed as well as deliberately distorted.

In his writings, Tunisian blogger *UnderAshes* argues that the revolutionary project will suffer from this competition over discursive power, as leftists, conservatives and liberals mutually label each other as the enemies of the revolution:

> Almost every sentence circulating in the media does not have the same meaning for the speaker as for its reader or listener; to begin with, of course, the term 'revolution', as well [what pertains to] (…) its consolidation, martyrs, (…) enemies and [its project of] transitional justice. You should use a term wisely and rely on evidence, or you might create more grounds for misinterpretation. [...] Everyone has agreed on the fact there is a conspiracy theory [amongst political groups], but nobody agrees as to who the conspirators are. Meaning is not determined by 'logic' in the Aristotelian sense (…) but on the basis of political allegiance. (…) In this confusion, everyone is desperately eager to belong to the group that would reaffirm their own interpretation, even if that means sacrificing on freedom of speech (…) This search for meaning follows a quasi-sectarian logic, which is natural in a society that suffered serious obstacles in the determination of its identity for decades (…)
>
> (Under Ashes, 26 December 2012)[5]

To some extent, this phenomenon is to be understood as part of the natural circulation of discourse. The revolution was continuously reframed and informal practices of deliberation became instituted as the new mainstream. This also generated internal divisions within the pro-revolutionary camp. Whereas some members of the opposition were ready to enter the political game, others remained fundamentally attached to the principle of revolutionary action. This was very elegantly described by the Egyptian journalist Ibrahim Issa in his verse 'high in the sky, the revolution flies; while politics walks on the ground'.[6] These internal tensions created confusion at a time when the ideological framework of the revolution was yet to be determined. The informal counter-discourse was entering the formal sphere of politics but remained fluid in nature, ever more likely to be misappropriated.

What I will refer to as the *institutionalization* of the revolution is the process through which dominant political institutions and their leaders – such as the former RCD, the SCAF and the partisan Islamist organizations – claimed credit for the achievement of the 2011 uprisings. In this case, the term 'institution' designates long-established political groups, as opposed to fluid networks of independent activists. Such a process does not only apply to the revolutionary counter-discourse *per se*, but also to the technological tools used by the revolutionary opposition. That is to say that Internet and social media, originally applied by a minority of activists, started to be used by leading political organizations in an attempt to compete against the civil opposition made of informal youth networks. As mentioned above, this phenomenon is highly problematic for the pro-revolutionary debate, since it creates confusion by conveying divergent perspectives of the revolution. Bloggers find themselves exposed to smear campaigns and personal attacks, having to deny or justify every statement in this increasingly polarized environment.

Tunisian bloggers like Lina Ben Mhenni, who was now recognized as a prominent figure of the revolution, found herself having to correct false information about her, which circulated on partisan Facebook pages and news articles. The function of web activism had in other words shifted from informing the opposition, to fact-checking formal networks of communication. Web activism had no choice but to interact – whether directly or indirectly – with the traditional media sphere. Bloggers would find their messages re-framed to serve different political agendas, in ways that contrasted with the initial experiment of informal politics. This is what brought Ben Mhenni to decry the politicization of the social media sphere and the many conspiracy theories intended to discredit figures of the pro-revolutionary opposition in January 2012:

> It is not because 90 per cent of the Tunisians, who are on Facebook claimed to be (…) members of the cyber police or State security (…) and like to imagine that bloggers and cyber-activists are all CIA agents, Zionists and freemasons, that I shall respond to each and every one of them (…). I don't have time to lose with conspiracy theories that have so much success among the Facebook youth (administrators of Facebook pages created after the 17th December 2010 (…)). I don't have to respond to the mockery of traitors, who are paid to discredit cyber-activists (…) following the orders of certain political parties (…) nor the delirium of so-called revolutionaries eaten away by jealousy and envy.
>
> (Ben Mhenni, 2012)[7]

Similar to Lina Ben Mhenni, Tunisian blogger Yassin Ayari contested the fact that well-structured campaigning strategies are run in the name of the revolution to promote long-established parties. He specifically drew on the example of the 15 August 2011 demonstration organized by the syndicate of Tunisian workers (UGTT).[8] Indeed, the Tunisian union founded in 1946 had not been proactive in supporting the January mobilizations, but was now competing with the UTT,[9] a new trade-union organization for workers' memberships. On the eve of the demonstration, Ayari argued that the union's leaders promoting the event intended to increase their popularity like most of the registered parties that saw the revolution as a new opportunity to advertise themselves:

> So the UGTT is calling for a demonstration on the 15th of August to restore its image and position itself as the leader of the revolution and bla bla bla! A real caricature. And the other parties then? (…) It's simple, they just want to be present, they don't want to miss the event, it's like a wedding, every party wants to make sure not to miss the pictures! even the parties that once supported and are still supporting the government (…) or those that got disengaged from the streets after spreading just a few political messages.
>
> (Ayari, August 2011)[10]

Initially, the main assets of the communication practices that underpinned the revolution had to do with resilience, flexibility and malleability. It was thanks to the lack of a rigid structure that diverse and organic networks could thrive, experimenting across languages and ideological frameworks. As soon as the revolution became mainstream, the field of informal communication was exposed, encroaching upon the sphere of formal politics. Those who mastered the political game were then able to leverage the fluidity of the revolutionary counter-discourse for their own advantages. For a period of time, the revolution became a political label, which was continuously reframed, leading to the fragmentation of the debate. As a result, informal networks of pro-revolutionaries no longer enjoyed the feeling of social cohesion they had experienced in the early days of the uprisings.

Bloggers witnessed how this politization of the revolution created strong social divisions, conveniently limiting policy-makers' ability to negotiate and reach consensus. In Tunisia, blogger Fares Mabrouk deplored the polarisation of the debate following the election of the Constituent Assembly. Due to the overwhelming tensions opposing the Tunisian union of the UGTT to the secular elites and the Ennahda party, deliberations about the future of the country were briefly reduced to the idea of a conflict between secularists and Islamists:

> By all means, the political sphere recomposed, or – shall I say – became polarised again. The interests of the corporate circles, composite middle class and the most disfranchised (…), which used to be commonly shared, are diverging again. In this regard, the conflict between UGTT and the party in power Ennahda is a revealing prism. (…) On the political level, the pro-State movement, which is fundamentally secular and constitutionalist, refuses to consider Ennahda as a properly Tunisian emergence (…) I consider this position as nonsensical. Why shall we deny our history in such a way (youssefisme, islamo-destourisme, [Ennahda]) and deny our Arabic Muslim identity?
>
> (Mabrouk, 27 May 2013)[11]

In Egypt, political leaders previously engaged in the Presidential election formed the united coalition of the National Salvation Front, with the aim to defeat the Muslim Brotherhood. This paved the way for the restoration of the military regime, reducing the notion of 'opposition' to the fight against Islamists, while failing to address revolutionaries' demands.

In late 2012, Egyptian blogger Baheyya already suspected the project of the National Salvation Front to be opportunistic in nature. Instead of seeking negotiation and compromise, opponents would focus on discrediting Morsi's democratically elected government, which inevitably benefitted the army in the aftermath of the constitutional decree. It is precisely thanks to this political reshaping that the subsequent 30 June coup (2013) was strategically invoked as a substitute for the 25th of January revolution (2011):

> I'm stunned at Morsi's opponents' failure to act like a credible opposition ever since his November 21 decrees. They could barely contain their glee at his cascading failures, outdoing each other in branding him a dictator and clambering atop the rising tide of popular protest (…) Morsi's critics turned into shrill Cassandras, prophesying doom and impending civil war. Most significant, they resolutely refused to meet with the president when the crisis worsened, treating him like an enemy who must be brought down. (…) The sight of politicians refusing to negotiate with an elected president but then agreeing to the military's 'we're all family' shindig is beyond pitiful.
>
> (Baheyya, 13 December 2012)[12]

The same criticism applies to the Muslim Brotherhood, as they gained a monopoly on the political scene in 2012 and started distancing themselves from the youths close to the civil opposition. As stated by *The Big Pharaoh* in late October 2012, divisions arose between the conservative party and its younger support base.

After young members of the movement joined clashes in Tahrir Square, the party denied its involvement on its official Facebook page, which antagonized its youth, resulting in internal tensions and a long feed of negative comments (The Big Pharaoh, 20 October 2012).[13] At the time, what appeared to be the only influential partisan movement with the potential to represent the opposition already had too much institutional inertia to reconcile its agenda with the informal politics of the streets. The real dilemma that the civil opposition was facing related to the compromise between the realm of informal communication and what the blogger referred to as a well-structured and 'viable political alternative' (The Big Pharaoh, 20 October 2012)[14]:

> The last presidential elections, especially round one, proved that there are millions of Egyptians who are willing to vote for an alternative to the MB. A viable alternative though. (...) We don't have an alternative that is 1) organized 2) has money 3) and can convince people.
> (The Big Pharaoh, 20 October 2012)[15]

Pro-revolutionary activists continued to witness the distortion of the revolutionary counter discourse in the realm of institutionalized politics. This appeared to defeat the purpose of an informal approach to communication, rooted in the reality of the streets. Some activists wondered, for a little while, if structural change would only be achieved through old school partisan politics, once again hoping for 'a viable alternative'. And while the revolutionary camp split in trying to navigate this compromise, the Egyptian counterrevolution dramatically progressed, regaining control over the channels of informal politics.

In Tunisia, the blogosphere became divided as to how activists should position themselves during the post-revolutionary transition. Some influential bloggers called for a boycott of the first post-revolutionary election, while others briefly joined the interim government. Tunisian blogger Slim Amamou was named Secretary of State for Sport and Youth in January 2011 and served under the transitional government before resigning in May of the same year.

A year later, he published a new blog post, in which he commented on the fact that references to the Tunisian revolution were now visible in popular culture products, such as video clips of internationally well-known music artists. In his view, this media exposure marked the success of the revolution and its recognition amongst a large international audience:

> The revolution would never have dreamed that much exposure; the revolution [is] mainstream. In good French: la révolution populaire. Pure genius.

> (Slim Amamou, 31 May 2012)[16]

Mainstreaming is to be distinguished from the other process of politization described above, through which the revolution becomes an object of political controversy. Whereas the latter is driven by partisan politics, the former is simply due to the natural expansion of a counter-discourse. It occurs when informal communication networks grow beyond the peripheries of the public sphere. Once the online community of pro-revolutionary activists is under the spotlight of the national and international media, bloggers come to question the validity of the tool. At this stage of its evolution, digital media becomes central to the official public discourse and is just another form of mass media, in which one can easily manufacture consent, creating an illusion of public legitimacy. In that context, bloggers often start to reflect critically on the relevance of this communication tool. They question the extent to which social media remains valuable to their experience of political dissent, if it no longer qualifies as an emergent media. This brings them to formulate an introspective critique of web activism. Bloggers express a nostalgia for the early days, that time when the Internet was still just emerging. Along with the political narratives surrounding the revolution, the informal channels of communication associated with it have been hijacked. This is precisely what the blogger Fares Mabrouk suggests in a blog post, where he recalls the history of Tunisian web activism:

> Today on the Internet, which charms the crowds of commentators, and whose revolutionary role shall not be underestimated (…) the beautiful story of this genesis proves to be wrong. Because the story has evolved. Because the Tunisians, witnessing and being active on the Web obstruct the official story with their personal experience, distorting the enlightenment of the emerging ideals. (…) The poetry is affected. The 'spring', [is] less than an

event [...]. Romantically referred to as Jasmine39, '2.0' by foreign media, the Tunisian revolution has been reversed over a period of two years.

(Fares Mabrouk, 27 May 2013)[17]

Through the mainstreaming of the revolution and its association with digital technologies, activists became the victims of their own success. Due to both media and political exposure, the blogosphere was increasingly polarized and activists were labelled into different camps, sometimes accused of jeopardizing the revolutionary agenda out of sheer opportunism. Bloggers themselves formulated this introspective critique of web activism, longing for another *behind-the-scenes* setting for interaction and self-expression. This shift was already perceptible in late 2011, when Tunisian blogger and cartoonist _Z_ commented on the downside of public recognition:

> The Internet under Ben Ali was good! We were nice and innocent and Ammar 404[18] was our only enemy. We didn't take ourselves too seriously and we knew how to remain united, when unfortunately one of us was caught. But here we are, after the so-called 2.0 revolution, things have slightly changed. Cyber-heroes have emerged from the crowd and became very serious people. Some have been appointed as Secretaries of State,[19] others host TV shows and others publish books.[20] Before January 14th there was a minimum level of decency between cyber dissidents, and we would have polite arguments through our blogs. Today, a small conflict and the law gets involved. Just like this stupid fight between the 'star of the web' Yassine el Ayari and the 'blogger celebrity' Sami ben Adbdallah (...) This is without mentioning the Facebook administrators, who have become millionaires by prostituting their pages for the political parties.
>
> (_Z_, 11 September 2011)[21]

In another instance, this climate of online polarisation was described by Yassin Ayari in a tribute to the late blogger and martyr of web activism Zouhayer Yahyaoui. Yahyaoui, one of the first Tunisian cyber-dissidents, died in 2005 after being prosecuted, imprisoned and tortured under the former regime. By invoking his memory, Ayari draws a distinction between what he describes as the golden age of cyber activism and a later generation of bloggers, increasingly mindful of their public image. As a result of contentious politics and media exposure, activists were, in his view, primarily driven by their egos, failing to demonstrate the abnegation required for sustained political resistance (Ayari, December 2011).[22]

As part of this introspective critique, activists from the blogosphere drew attention to the increasingly perceptible fragmentation of online platforms. These echo chambers – also called 'filter bubbles' – were in their view responsible for the isolation of the young civil opposition. Social media activism led them to interact within a limited sphere of influence made of like-minded people from the same urban middle-class background. Communicating within their own echo chamber led them to assume there was a commonly shared interpretation of the revolution:

> The revolutionaries are still living in their own self-created bubble. They only talk to themselves, they rarely talk to the people on the street. They are all cocooned in their own meetings, Facebook pages and on Twitter. There has been very little attempt to burst this bubble and talk directly to the public (…) When I raise this point, fellow revolutionaries often confront me with this rationale: revolutions are done by the minority and we can never expect the majority to support us; they will only cheer when we win just as they did when Mubarak stepped down last year.
>
> (The Big Pharaoh, 8 May 2012)[23]

Those who had pioneered the emergent media of the blogosphere represented a minority that was hoping to set new rules for public deliberation. They were experimenting with political cultures involving their own codes and references, which were inspired by different ideologies and experiences of political resistance. In its early stages, this form of 'connective action' (Bennett and Segerberg, 2012) was composed of an intelligentsia that was well-placed to leverage and deconstruct the mechanisms of power. This provided some activists with a sense of intellectual leadership over the counter-discourse of the opposition. Yet this intellectual leadership was dramatically compromised, as soon as digital media grew to become the new mainstream.

Unlike the media itself, the political language of dissent was still limited to a niche and perhaps not yet accessible to the masses. As it was described across the Tunisian and Egyptian blogosphere, this sense of intellectual leadership faded once the emergent media of the intelligentsia reached a mass audience. However, by that time, the counter-discourse of the young civil opposition was not yet fully formed, and not always relatable to the most disfranchised, because it was rooted in the intellectual capital and political literacy of a privileged demographic amongst the youth.

This brings me to challenge the idea that civil movements involving online activism were entirely deprived of organizational structure. As a premise of political movement, it was still evocative of the skills, resources and formal political knowledge that characterized the sphere of power. Activists engaged in the post-revolutionary blogosphere were now facing a dilemma, which I would situate on the east axis of the discursive cycle (cf. Figure 1). At that point, opposition voices had to consider whether it was more strategic to speak the political language of the elite, or that of the masses. It is this dilemma, which transpires from the idea mentioned above of a revolution led by 'a minority' (The Big Pharaoh, 8 May 2012).

In fact, this dilemma explains why pro-revolutionary bloggers appear to be divided with regard to how digital activism should contribute to the revolutionary agenda. Whereas some of them see it as a way to raise awareness about the revolutionary cause, others contest the fact that digital activism deviates media attention from the streets to the sphere of institutional politics. And yet, within the field of political communication, many have suggested that the early 2010s civil movements, which involved networked communication, lacked ideological frameworks and organizational structures (Tufekci, 2017). It was said that social media contrasted with traditional forms of political engagement, because it presumably operated like a more inclusive and horizontal social structure, channelling affects and feelings of injustice (Bennett and Segerberg, 2012; Papacharissi, 2014). Many scholars described this form of communication as fluid, versatile and lacking a well-defined political project. Such 'connective action' was, in other words, assumed to be almost populist by nature (Gerbaudo, 2018; Meraz and Papacharissi, 2015). However, in some regards, the most proactive and engaged voices of the opposition came from well-defined ideological backgrounds and a privileged understanding of political theory. Over the course of the post-revolutionary transition, many activists were still learning how to formulate a counter-discourse that would relate to a broader audience. At this stage of the discursive cycle, the opposition had to reconcile the skills, resources and political theory inherited from the sphere of power with the perspectives of the grassroots, which was alternatively grounded in the political praxis of the streets.

The scholarship on civil movements and digital activism does not always help us to overcome this challenge, because it tends to advocate for old school partisan engagement. By reducing the debate to the realm of institutional politics, it continues to dismiss the potential benefits of the informal practices that have historically supported public trust and social capital in the absence of a welfare state. In doing so, it also overlooks the importance of informal communication networks as a bottom-up stream of political dissent.

In the aftermath of the 2011 uprisings, activists engaged in the blogosphere had just started to express the premises of what could have been an ideal middle ground: a relatable revolutionary discourse phrased in the informal language of the streets, which would have been informed by the different ideological cultures that composed the young civil opposition. This would have bridged the gap between the top-down structural critique of a young, educated middle class and the voices of the most disenfranchised as long as the former remained – one can hope – self-conscious about its own privilege. Of course, in order to succeed, the experiment of online activism required this elite to part with this notion of intellectual leadership, the very same notion that is still considered as a characteristic of the Habermassian public sphere, and an essential component of any liberal democracy. In Egypt, however, these challenges were never resolved nor fully explored, because of the external parameters that interfered with the informal practice of online activism. The mainstreaming of the revolution led activists to lose intellectual leadership and, in doing so, facilitated the politicization of the revolution. Although digital media democratized the political debate, it turned the vocabulary of the revolution into an increasingly polysemic object of controversy, which could no longer relay the perspectives of the grassroots. As they were witnessing this phenomenon, some attempted to recreate the conditions for intellectual leadership, by interacting within the same demographic of like-minded web activists. Yet this only emphasized the polarisation of the debate, making the opposition even more vulnerable. These are some of the internal tensions that occur throughout the first half of the discursive cycle, as the informal practices that may support the consolidation of a counter-discourse gain momentum. In the following chapters, I will focus on the case of the 2012 Presidential election and the constitutional debate that took place in post-revolutionary Egypt. This will bring me to consider the external parameters at play, and the ways in which counterrevolutionary forces further instituted digital media as the strategic campaigning tool that it is today.

Mass media campaigning on Twitter: Egypt and the 2012 presidential election

Among the events that punctuated the post-revolutionary debate in Egypt, the 2012 Presidential elections marked the return of traditional parties and formal institutions on the political scene. It is also in the context of the 2012 presidential race that well-established parties and political leaders started to proactively campaign on social media. It is more specifically in this context that the rising politicization and polarisation of the social media sphere became perceptible.

Following the roadmap and the electoral laws promulgated by the SCAF, the 2012 Presidential Campaign took place between 23 and 24 May (round 1) and 16–17 June 2012 (round 2). In accordance with the conditions for candidates' nomination announced by the electoral committee on 30 January 2012, future candidates were required to be supported by thirty members of the parliament or 30,000 eligible voters. They were expected to have been Egyptians for at least two generations and to be born in Egypt. Citizens married to a foreigner or with a dual nationality were not eligible for Presidential election. Candidates' registration officially took place between 10 March and 8 April 2012. On 14 April 2012, the Supreme Presidential Electoral Commission (SPEC) disqualified ten people among the twenty-three candidates originally registered. Some of the most influential and controversial political leaders were removed from the Presidential contest. Among them were the prominent figure of the Muslim Brotherhood Khairat El Shater, former intelligence chief of Mubarak's administration, Omar Suleiman and the popular Salafi leader Hazem Abou Ismail.

Five leaders – Abdel Moneim Abu al Futuh, Ahmed Shafiq, Amru Mussa, Hamdeen Sabahy and Mohammed Morsi – shared more than 90 per cent of the votes in the first round of the elections. Although some of the leading candidates had been involved in the opposition against the former regime, others had strong connections with the previous government and had completed most of their political career under Mubarak's administration.

Among the five leading candidates, the independent liberal Amru Mussa had served as Minister of Foreign Affairs between 1991 and 2001, and represented Egypt as secretary general for the League of Arab states between 2001 and 2011. Mussa had also been appointed as permanent representative to the United Nations between 1990 and 1991. Independent candidate Ahmad Shafiq had served under Mubarak's administration as Minister of Aviation from 2002 to 2011 and had previously been Commander of the Air Force for six years. Ahmad Shafiq stood out as a supporter of the SCAF and was perceived by all the factions of the opposition as the representative of the military elite as well as an agent of the counterrevolution. Candidate of the Freedom and Justice party (Muslim Brotherhood) Mohammed Morsi as well as the left-wing Nasserite Hamdeen Sabahy had been elected in 2000 to serve for five years as independent members of the parliament.

The pro-revolutionary youth contested the set-up of the Presidential race and the regulations imposed by the military council. However, there was agreement among members of the opposition that Sabahy and Abu al Futuh would be more aligned with the views of young leftists and moderate Islamists, who had joined the pro-revolutionary civil opposition. Both candidates had become leaders of the opposition, by mobilizing civilian movements for social equity and contesting acts of repression against the Muslim Brotherhood. As a co-founder of Kefaya (Egyptian Movement for Change), Hamdeen Sabahy had publicly condemned corruption and nepotism under Mubarak's government. He was involved in Mubarak's previous government as an independent member of the parliament for ten years prior to the revolution, representing the Al-Karama (Dignity) party, which only formally recognized in August 2011.

Abdel Moneim Abu al Futuh had become famous in the 1970s for his critique of former President Anwar Sadat and his support of the Muslim Brotherhood. The candidate was well known for his moderate position within the conservative wing, being considered as particularly progressive on issues relating to gender equity and relationships with the Christian minority.

Although he competed as an independent, he had gained experience as a member of the strongest political organization within the opposition. By the first round of the Presidential Campaign, each of these five candidates had reached a significant suffrage ranging from 11.13 per cent to 24.78 per cent. Abu al Futuh and Mussa, each ranked 17.47 per cent and 11.13 per cent – the lowest scores out of the top five candidates – in spite of being the only ones taking part in the first TV Presidential debate. Sabahy came third, with a fairly decent suffrage of 20.72 per cent. The victory of the military candidate Shafiq (23.66 per cent) and the Muslim Brotherhood Morsi (24.78 per cent) was interpreted as the sign of a growing polarisation between Islamists and the counterrevolutionary forces of the military establishment. The public space, which had been reclaimed by Egyptian revolutionaries, was now becoming a strategic field for conventional political campaigning.

Digital media was only part of a broader range of communication channels and social environments that were reappropriated to serve distinct political agendas after the revolution. Across these different platforms, many of the leading candidates had capitalized on the age-old practice of retail politics, which was often more successful in the streets and beyond the circles of the urban middle class. It was perhaps this approach that was arguably missing from the arsenal of the young civil opposition. Compared to rallies, public events, official interviews and the televised debate, social media platforms still offered a relatively limited reach. A 2011 study conducted by Dubai School of Governance indicated that the penetration rate of Twitter – which international media had presented as the main channel of the revolution – was still relatively low in Egypt. The platform was also not the most strategic campaigning tool, due to the initial lack of Arabic interface and the concentration of Twitter users in Cairo (Salem and Mourtada, 2011: 24). Yet aside from the conventional approach to retail politics, most candidates launched official Twitter campaigns, which marked the beginning of mass-media communication strategies transposed to the social media sphere. Most successful candidates, who benefitted from the support of the largest political groups relied on professional teams in charge of administrating their online campaigns. Sabahy proved to be the only candidate to proactively use Twitter as a way to interact with his electorate, a presumably younger, tech-savvy audience within the pro-revolutionary left.

While creating a facade of online engagement through sheer visibility, the military counterrevolution was also able to divert attention away from the online space, thanks to its monopoly over the mainstream media and its systemic control of the public space. This allowed well-established political leaders to achieve something that the left-wing civil opposition was unable to sustain after the uprisings, by portraying themselves as interacting with the population on the ground. Shafiq's campaign had to mobilize his electorate in Delta, while Morsi was capitalizing on his support base in Upper Egypt. These audiences did not centre around internet-affluent voters active on social media, but instead a large-scale top-down mass media approach was applied, which included social media amongst other communication channels. It is this dynamic that interfered with the informal practices of political dissent, which were initially limited to a niche within the opposition. Once the Internet operated as a traditional tool of campaigning, it became detrimental to pro-revolutionary voices.

In order to illustrate this process, I will now outline the findings of a study I conducted in 2012[1] comparing the campaigning strategies of the five leading candidates. This research relied on the data visualization tools and large Twitter dataset made available through the R-Shief open source project[2] (cf. Figure 3; appendices, Figure 9). My mapping of the online campaign was then cross-examined with a dataset of national media outlets covering the Presidential race, extracted from the private NexisLexis archive (cf. Figure 6; appendices, Figure 11). These resources allowed me to assess the media visibility of Presidential candidates, and examine the evolution of the social media sphere in relation to mainstream media. As a quantitative indicator of online visibility, the sheer volume of tweets associated with each of the five leading

| Candidates | #hashtag | Tweets archived in the R-Shief data base | | | |
		Number of tweets	days collected	Start date	End date
Abu al Futuh	#ابوالفتوح	81991	423	14.04.12	11.06.13
	#حمدين	141342	395	12.05.12	06.11.13
Hamdeen Sabahy	#صباحي	113630	396	11.05.12	11.06.13
	#مرسي	3157356	396	11.05.12	11.06.13
Mohammed Morsi	#مرسي_الاستبن	2447	422	15.04.12	11.06.13
Amru Mussa	#موسى	49259	396	11.05.12	11.06.13
Ahmad Shafiq	#شفيق	703354	341	01.05.12	07.04.13

Figure 3 Dataset Extracted from the 2012 R-Shief Database.

candidates provided a basic description of the social media landscape during the first round of the election. The data collected were later contextualized in the big picture of the broader national media. It was also re-examined through a qualitative analysis of the communication strategies used by the two most proactive Twitter campaigners.

The dataset sampled for this study indicated that Ahmad Shafiq had gained more visibility on Twitter than his opponents, with a significantly higher average and total number of tweets (cf. Figure 5). Additionally, as shown on the graph below (cf. Figure 4), the number of tweets referring to Morsi and Sabahy considerably increased during the three days that preceded the election. However, despite the success of Mohammed Morsi's campaign, Hamdeen Sabahy reached the second place in terms of Twitter visibility, with a considerably high number of tweets displaying hashtags assigned to his name and campaign (cf. Figure 5). The data extracted from the R-Shief dataset revealed a fall of tweets relating to candidate Abu al Futuh, which correlates with the date of the Presidential TV debate, featuring Abu al Futuh and Amru Mussa, on 10 May 2012.

These findings coincide with Laila Shareen Sakr's study (2012), which applied R-Shief's sentiment analysis tools to investigate a broader set of hashtags reporting the 2012 campaign. While the volume of tweets per hashtag was used as an indicator of Twitter visibility, sentiment analysis was also used to infer the degree of popularity for each candidate. The sentiment analysis computed by Sakr (2012) demonstrated that Sabahy, Morsi and the latecomer Khaled Ali

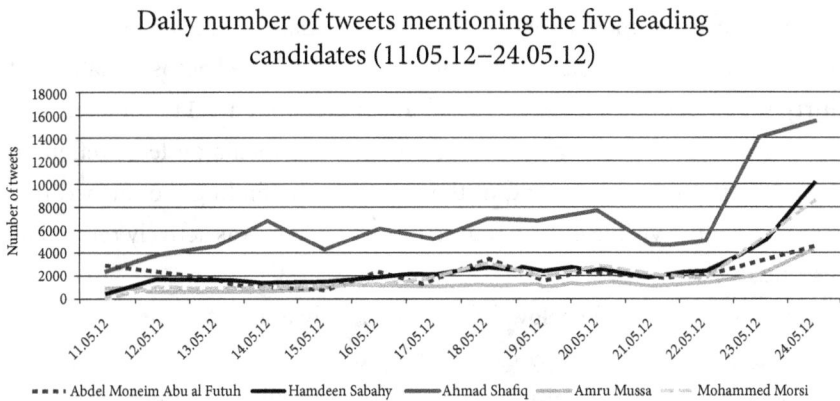

Daily number of tweets mentioning the five leading candidates (11.05.12–24.05.12)

Figure 4 Visibility of the Leading Candidates across the 2012 R-Shief Twitter Dataset.

Tweets mentioning the five leading candidates between 11.05.2012 and 24.05.2012					
Trending hashtags referring to candidates	Hamdeen #حمدين Sabahy #صباحي	Ahmad Shafiq #شفيق	Mohammed #مرسي Morsi #مرسي الأسـئن	Amru #موسي Mussa	Abdel Moneim Abu al Futuh #ابوالفتوح
Minimum number of tweets in a day	466	2,395	74	611	851
Maximum number of tweets in a day	10,085	15,492	8,484	4,181	4,529
Total number of tweets	38,080	94,669	33,179	19,589	32,287
Average of tweets	2,720	6,762	2,370	1,399	2,306

Figure 5 Visibility of the Leading Candidates across the 2012 R-Shief dataset.

had reached a higher percentage of positive sentiment than Shafiq amongst the young Twitter audience. And yet the agent of the counterrevolution Shafiq was recurrently mentioned, standing out as one of the most visible candidates on the extracted R-Shief dataset. Hashtags mentioning Shafiq dominated the sample extracted for the dataset 41.51 per cent covering the first round of the campaign, whereas mentions of other candidates ranged between 7 per cent and 13 per cent of tweets (cf. Appendices, Figure 12; Sakr, 2012).

Admittedly, Twitter campaigning was only part the wider media ecology. Beyond the social media sphere, mentions of Shafiq and Morsi dominated the national media. In fact, a content analysis conducted across a dataset of thirty-seven periodic newspapers (cf. appendices, Figure 11) revealed that the visibility of the two candidates in mainstream media outlets prefigured their victory in the first round of the election. The findings confirmed that Morsi was more visible offline and that his campaign was actively relayed by the press.

As shown in the table below (cf. Figure 7), only four out of the five leading candidates had been actively campaigning on Twitter over the months that preceded the first round of the Presidential race. No official Twitter account was administered on behalf of Mohammed Morsi prior to his election in June 2012. This can partly be explained by the fact that, as the representative of the Muslim Brotherhood, his campaign already benefitted from the large communication infrastructure of the Freedom and Justice party. Whereas Morsi could rely on the network and resources of his organization, independent candidates were dependent to a greater extent on social media's facilitation of a more direct engagement with their electorate. The appeal of personality politics afforded by social media campaigning was, in some regards, irrelevant to Morsi, who could rely on the communication channels of the party as the official figure of the Muslim Brotherhood. During the course of my fieldwork, it was suggested to me that the charismatic would-be candidate Khairat al Shater, who had been disqualified by the SPEC, might have made better use of social media. Presumably, his persona and grassroots popularity might have been used to develop an influential online profile and stimulate social media engagement in favour of the organization. The same can be said about the Salafi leader Abu Ismail, who had a large Twitter audience but was also prevented from running in the Presidential race. Ultimately – due to the military council's strategic engineering of the election – none of the other political actors involved in the race represented a significant threat to counterrevolutionary forces in terms of social media presence. As the largest political organizations involved in the campaign, the military and Muslim Brotherhood successfully banked on mainstream media visibility and a monopoly over the means of traditional retail politics (cf. Figure 6).

Candidates	Visibility score among all political leaders mentioned [%]
Ahmad Shafiq	24.8
Mohammed Morsi	22.8
Hamdeen Sabahy	12.6
Abu al Futuh	22.2
Amru Mussa	9.6
Hazem Salah Aby Ismail	8

(Sample collected from a selection of 37 Egyptian newspapers extracted from the Nexis Lexis archive)

Figure 6 Visibility of the Main Political Leaders Campaigning in the 2012 Election, Egyptian Press. First Round of the 2012 Presidential Campaign (1 March–22 March 2012).

Aside from the sheer question of visibility, the candidates that proved to be the most proactive online also applied different campaigning styles, which clearly distinguished the pro-revolutionary left from the actors of the counterrevolution. A more qualitative analysis of the official Twitter campaigns in fact revealed that the pro-Shafiq military forces were now transposing a large-scale mass media approach to the social media sphere. The increasing presence of counterrevolutionary voices on social media further illustrates the transition that occurs at the south axis of the discursive cycle (cf. Figure 1). While they gained more reach online, military agents also altered the informal practices of communication that had been initiated on this once-emergent media. That is indeed what came out of an in-depth thematic analysis comparing Shafiq's Twitter campaign to that of the independent leftist Sabahy. Unlike Mussa and Abu al Futuh – whose Twitter campaigns were administered by supporters – the official accounts of Shafiq and Sabahy relayed personal statements. They also delivered more content than other candidates, whose official Twitter channels[3] would simply post links to other websites, news articles and YouTube videos featuring the main offline events of the campaign. Unlike their opponents, Shafiq and Sabahy developed a particular Twitter communication strategy. Their posts revealed an attempt at reappropriating the informal practices of communication initiated by the technologically literate middle class. However, while Sabahy consistently tweeted in the first person, Shafiq's official account simply relayed quotes extracted from public speeches and interviews. Further, although they both engaged with the channel of the urban middle class, the two candidates employed very different approaches to political communication.

Candidate	Twitter account	Date of first tweet	Number of tweets (Round 1)	Daily tweet average (Round 1)	Number of tweets posted by the end of election round 1 (23.05.2012)
Ahmad Shafiq	AhmadShafikEG	18.05.12	93	10.2	93
Amru Mussa	moussacampaign	25.06.11	205	22.6	606
Hamdeen Sabahy	HamdeenSabahy	08.06.10	39	4.3	240
Abu al Futuh	MaadiCampaign	05.04.12	150	16.5	150

Figure 7 Inventory of the Candidates Twitter Accounts (2012 Presidential Campaign).

As part of the counterrevolutionary strategy, Shafiq's online campaign intended to invoke the need for a powerful alternative to the Muslim Brotherhood. The arguments of gender equality and the fight against sectarianism were suddenly weaponized to portray the actors of the counterrevolution as the advocates of progress, modernity and political stability. The pro-military campaign was also centred on the narrative of national security, whist invoking modernization and industrialization as the ultimate answer to the challenge of economic development. Unlike his opponents, Ahmad Shafiq called for citizens' trust in the military council and argued that the SCAF's involvement in electoral regulations and infrastructure would not affect the democratic process. Shafiq's Twitter campaign reported his visit to Nag Hammadi – in which several Copts were massacred on 7 January 2010 – advocating peaceful and strategic relationships with the United States, neighbouring Arab countries and the Gulf region. Meanwhile, candidates Sabahy, Abu al Futuh and Morsi would publicly address the need to renegotiate the peace treaty with Israel. Shafiq's campaign reported on his economic plan intended to tackle youth unemployment by focusing on industrial development in the Delta region. However, these aspects of his political programme stand out from our Twitter data set, inasmuch as they characterize Ahmad Shafiq's entire campaign. In other words, Shafiq's Twitter account was used to amplify a discourse that had been strategically framed by campaigners, rather than as an interactive communication channel between the candidate and his electorate.

In contrast, Hamdeen Sabahy's tweets offered complementary statements and provided his followers with exclusive reactions to everyday news. Unlike his opponents, Sabahy did not use Twitter to report the highlights of his Presidential Campaign, but positioned himself amongst regular Twitter users by posting personalized comments on the most topical issues. On 10 April 2012, Sabahy expressed his supports to the workers, who protested on 2 April in front of the State Council to contest the government's decision to renationalize the companies of Ghazl Shebeen, Tanta for linen, El Nasr for steam boilers and El-Nil for cotton ginning. On 11 April 2012, Sabahy paid tribute to the Algerian revolutionary socialist Ahmad Ben Bella on the anniversary of his death, referring to him as a leading figure of the mobilization for freedom and social equity. The following week, the candidate reacted to Sheikh Ali Goma's controversial visit to the Al-Asqa Mosque in support of the Muslim community of Jerusalem, calling for the resignation of the Al-Azhar scholar. This allowed him to reaffirm his position with regard to a potential renegotiation of the peace treaty with Isreal, by commenting on current events, while engaging with his Twitter audience. On 20 April 2012, he personally addressed the latest developments of the campaign, expressing his condolences to candidate Ahmad Shafiq for the loss of his wife. On 22 April and 4 May, he contested the arrest of the Egyptian citizen Ahmed Al-Gizawy in Saudi Arabia, which had led to several protests in Cairo. A few days later, Sabahy once again positioned himself by reacting to international events, and celebrated the election of the French socialist candidate François Hollande, which reemphasized his alignment with the pro-prorevolutionary left. Finally, on 15 May 2012, he referred to the death of former Egyptian Prime Minister and member of Gamal Abdel Nasser's administration Zakaria Mohieddin.

By shaping his postings more immediately around everyday news, Hamdeen Sabahy afforded a certain currency to his political message, adopting the same perspective as his audience. Inevitably, this brought him to articulate his political campaign in relation to the controversies that punctuated the Presidential debate in a way that reflected prorevolutionaries' application of social media. His ability to communicate with the pro-revolutionary youth not only manifests itself in the style of his tweets, but also in the issues he raises from his Twitter account. Over the first round of the campaign, Sabahy continued to pay tribute to the martyrs of the revolution and expressed his support to activists protesting in front of the Ministry of Defence. He called for the right of the youth opposition to protest peacefully, holding military authorities responsible for their safety. He recurrently formulated scepticism about the way traditional mass media reported the campaign, which coincided with one of the most important criticisms of the revolutionary opposition. For these reasons, Sabahy clearly stood out as the only candidate, who applied social media in a way that was arguably more representative of the pro-revolutionary left.

Analysing Twitter both quantitatively and qualitatively shows that among the top five candidates running for the 2012 election, Shafiq and Sabahy were most active and visible on social media. The sample of tweets collected from the R-Shief database suggests that these two were the subject of a significantly larger number of tweets than their opponents.

The sentiment analysis computed by Laila Shereen Sakr (2012) as well as the volume of tweets mentioning the names of the five political leaders both suggest that Mohammed Morsi's Twitter popularity also increased in the days that preceded the election (cf. appendices, Figure 12). However, the candidate did not reach as much Twitter visibility as Shafiq and Sabahy, presumably due to the fact that Morsi's campaign did not primarily rely on social media and digital communication tools. On the other hand, the sample of Egyptian news articles collected from my NexisLexis corpus included a large number of references to the Muslim Brotherhood candidate. Consequently, the success of Morsi's campaign is more likely to be explained by his exposure in the press and in broadcast media. Admittedly, it is very unlikely that Twitter in itself, along with the entire social media sphere, played a significant role in the outcome of the Presidential Campaign. The fact that the most visible and popular Twitter campaigners were among the top three candidates would rather suggest that they benefitted from a strong infrastructure and a successful campaigning strategy overall (both online and offline). However, the dynamics of the Twitter campaigns is revealing of a shift in the evolution of social media, amongst other types of informal communication networks. More specifically, the significant Twitter visibility of Shafiq and Sabahy suggests that both the revolution and counterrevolution were now competing for exposure in the same media environment. Yet while Sabahy engaged in communication practices, which were similar to that of the young leftist opposition, Shafiq strategically distorted them to reproduce a one-way-stream standardized style of mass media campaigning.

These findings illustrate how the tools as well as the semantics of the revolution had been employed to serve different political agendas. Each candidate ultimately capitalized on a different aspect of what the revolution could have been. Some distorted the argument of gender equality to portray themselves as a shield against the Islamists, while others focused on imposing an ideological framework to the revolutionary concept of dignity. As predicted by Arendt in *On Revolution* (1963), 'freedom' is also repeatedly invoked across the political spectrum. While the revolution was redefined in the political sphere, the informal practices of communication were rapidly altered to create an illusion of consensus around the pre-established political status quo.

Making sense of the revolution: Debating online over the 2012 Egyptian constitution

Following the 2012 Presidential election, the Egyptian constitutional referendum generated further political controversies and confusion as to how one should interpret the ideals of the revolution. Despite the fact that the referendum was now administrated by the first democratically elected government, it revealed deep conflicts of interests between the new elite and the judicial administration. The constitutional debate ultimately highlighted polarisation, creating confusion as to how the unifying slogans of the revolution should materialize in policymaking. By the time Morsi's administration started drafting a new constitution, a broader range of citizens, who were initially not involved in politics, were now publicly expressing their views online. Some of the public profiles and social platforms that had been created with the intention to consolidate a revolutionary strategy for the opposition simply became part of a divided market for political campaigning. This was also the case with the Dostour Sharek project, which was designed on the occasion of the 2012 constitutional referendum to stimulate voters' participation. This e-deliberation platform was intended to circulate the new constitutional articles drafted by the Constituent Assembly, and enable citizens to post their comments and suggestions.

Research interviews revealed that, prior to the revolution, the Middle East branch of Google initially introduced an independent team of software engineers to the government, while providing financial support to develop new applications intended to facilitate voters' participation. After January 2011, the government appointed the company in question to create a functional voters database in order to handle voter registration and inform citizens of the location of polling stations. This team of independent software developers was now in charge of creating a voter database in preparation for the first post-revolutionary referendum, in March 2011. In the midst of the political transition, the contractors delivered the services required on very short notice, temporarily working on a volunteering basis or for late remuneration. Inspired by the increase of online public engagement, this independent team of developers then suggested the creation of an e-deliberation platform designed to provide an up-to-date public assessment of the constitutional draft. According to anonymized research interviews, the Constituent Assembly was particularly interested in the possibility of conducting sentiment analysis to assess participants' appreciation of the drafted constitutional articles. As per the original plan, the outcome of the analysis would have been presented to the Assembly in the later stage of the drafting process. However, the precipitation with which Morsi's administration submitted the constitutional draft in early December put an end to the final stage of the project. Due to the many political controversies surrounding the 2012 referendum, the administration became progressively more reluctant to publish late articles. Most importantly, the commissioned administrators of the platform did not have the opportunity to turn user input into genuinely interactive feedback for the Constituent Assembly.

A number of descriptive statistics were produced, along with highly informative posts and comments, in which most users demanded a clearer phrasing of the constitutional laws. In many regards, the case of the Egyptian Dostour Sharek initiative can be seen as an allegory of what was happening elsewhere in the Egyptian social media sphere. Indeed, the project was originally envisioned by a group of skilled computer engineers, who would identify or sympathize with the young civil opposition in spite of operating within a market that remained close to the political sphere. Instead of reforming the communication practices applied in the realm of formal politics, it only created a facade of political consensus, which granted more power to the centralized networks of public bureaucracy. In this chapter, I will set the context in which the 2012 constitutional referendum took place and demonstrate that this event announced a new stage in the cycle that led to the success of the counter-revolution. I will rely on fieldwork interviews with stakeholders involved in the implementation of the constitutional referendum and refer to a study of users' participation in the 2012 Dostour Sharek initiative.

First and foremost, I should outline the context of the controversial constitutional referendum that paved the way for the success of the counterrevolution. The first Constituent Assembly was elected by the parliament in March 2012 and dissolved in April 2012, after civil party members withdrew from the drafting process, calling for a boycott of the new constitution. Liberals, and left-wing and secularist parties, who formed the opposition against the Islamist majority, claimed that the panel was unconstitutional and failed at representing Egyptian youths and minorities. Consequently, the first Assembly was dissolved by court order, although Islamist parties argued that this decision did not conform to the SCAF's original constitutional declaration (2011). Indeed, although the original set of regulations did not state how the Constitutional Assembly should be appointed, members of the military council argued that article 60 of the original constitutional declaration was too vague to guarantee a fair representation of the Egyptian population within the Assembly and should be reviewed. A new Constituent Assembly was formed in June 2012, which included delegates from the armed forces, representatives from the judiciary and trade unions as well as members of the Coptic Church. The new Assembly was intended to include both Islamists and representatives of the civil parties. However, the liberal opposition stated that traditionalists still represented the majority of seats and parties such as Al-Masryeen Al Ahrar kept calling for a boycott of the constitution.

The first Constituent Assembly, which was formed in January 2012, was composed of members of the House of Representatives who had been elected by the Egyptian people during the parliamentary elections. The second Constituent Assembly included thirty-nine seats of MPs, who had been elected by the people. Other blocks of seats were allocated to other representatives of the religious institutions, workers' unions as well as members of the armed forces, the police and the judiciary. During the process of drafting the constitution, the Assembly was divided into five committees assigned to the five different chapters of the constitution. Additionally, a sixth committee – composed of members of the Assembly – was in charge of ensuring participation and consultation. In the early stage of the deliberations, the committee in question hosted hearing sessions in different governorates' city halls and public universities to collect feedback and input from citizens. Supporting staff were in charge of collecting all suggestions and enquires from citizens and reporting feedback to the Assembly after analysing it. All meetings of the Constituent Assembly were broadcast by national TV channels.

A first constitutional draft was issued on 10 October 2012, after which the Constituent Assembly implemented a nationwide campaign promoting the constitution via mainstream media channels. Additionally, supporters of the constitution hosted consultation meetings and information centres in order to stimulate participation. The Freedom and Justice Party launched its own campaign advertising, 'yes' to the constitutional referendum. In reaction, opposition groups, such as the 6 April Movement and the now-defunct National Democratic Party publicly contested the fact that the new constitution maintained the privileges of the elite in power, while restraining the rights of religious minorities. Following the resignation of a few of the members of the Egyptian Bloc alliance, liberal leaders, including former candidate Amru Mussa, requested a better representation of the Christian minority. Hamdeen Sabahy and the opposition figure Mohammed El Baradei called for the mobilization of left-wing and revolutionary organizations – such as the Kefaya movement – to boycott the Constituent Assembly.

Strong criticism was expressed regarding article number 2 of the constitutional draft, which established the sharia as the basis of Egyptian law. Opponents of the constitutional draft stated that the text did not fairly represent pluralism of opinion within the population and restricted the rights of the Coptic minority. They contested the fact that the new constitutional text remained extremely vague, which potentially enabled ruling elites to circumvent the law or promulgate new regulations that would serve their interests. Various protests and demonstrations took place over the course of the drafting process as well as when the final draft had been submitted for referendum.

By the end of the drafting process, 236 articles had been produced, for which 320 had been originally drafted. However, most of the changes made to the original draft did not substantially improve the formulation of the articles. New parliamentary elections were expected within three months of the referendum, if the constitutional draft was to be accepted. Alternatively, a new Constituent Assembly would have to be formed within the same period of time. The polemic intensified in the days that preceded the referendum scheduled on 15 December, as opponents condemned Islamists for attempting to influence voters. Leaders of the opposition, who had previously been involved in the Presidential debate, such as Mohammed El Baradei, Hamdeen Sabahy and Amru Mussa formed the National Salvation Front, which intended to consolidate the opposition against the Islamist majority and called Egyptians to vote 'no' to the constitutional referendum. Members of the 'no campaign' primarily focused on two criticisms of the Muslim Brotherhood, which had been already raised by the Shafiq campaign – namely the concerns over the rights of women and Christian minorities.

On 22 November, President Morsi issued a constitutional decree, in which he granted himself ultimate power over the parliamentary chambers, allowing him to promulgate new laws by decree and to annul on-going adjudication. In this constitutional declaration, the President assigned a new prosecutor and extended the period of time originally set for the activity of the Constituent Assembly, which was limited to fifteen days between the issue of the final draft and the date of the referendum. The decree also prevented the Shura Council from being dissolved by the judiciary and established the predominance of the Presidential administration over the military council.

Morsi's decree was interpreted as an attempt to control legislative powers and stimulated a wave of protests. At that moment, the tension reached its peak outside as well as within the political circles represented in the new government. Judges in charge of supervising the polling stations went on strike to contest Morsi's constitutional decree and manifest their discontent regarding the appointment of the new prosecutor. The strike considerably affected the organization of the referendum, making it impossible to administer the poll in one round.

This was likely to alter the results of the vote, given that citizens voting in the second round could have been influenced by preliminary results. Demonstrations, sometimes leading to violent confrontations took place across the country, contesting the fact that the new President intended to hold all executives and legislative powers. On 5 December, clashes occurred between members of the Muslim Brotherhood and protesters conducting peaceful demonstrations in front of the Presidential palace. The event led to six deaths and 400 people being injured. The constitutional decree was eventually revoked in early December. However, after considering the possibility of postponing the suffrage, Morsi confirmed his intention to hold the referendum. By doing so, he conformed to the SCAF's 2011 constitutional declaration, stipulating that a referendum should take place fifteen days after the President receives a final draft from the Constituent Assembly. Secretary General Zaghloul al-Bashy and Vice President Mahmoud Mekki both resigned in December. In spite of the overwhelming discontent, the referendum eventually took place on 15 December 2012 and the constitution was technically approved by 63.8 per cent of eligible voters, with a 32.9 per cent turnout.

Over the weeks that preceded the 22 November decree, the person in charge of supervising the work conducted to promote the drafting process and its transparency resigned. The interview conducted with participants involved in the implementation of the project revealed that the participative dimension of the constitutional draft reached a critical point at this stage. Due to the polemic of Morsi's decree, Islamist parties regained control over the constitution and the company in charge of administering the Dostour Sharek platform did not have the opportunity to present an overview of participants' input to the Assembly.

In December 2012, designers released the statistics of the project, which indicated that 653,718 contributions from 68,130 participants had been made to the draft of the constitution, among which 12 per cent were posted comments and the other 88 per cent were ratings (thumbs-up versus thumbs down). According to this statistical report, the large majority (89 per cent) of ratings assigned by users were 'likes' (thumbs-up). The most commented-upon articles addressed the themes of public authority, rights and freedom, and the number of contributions increased between September and November 2012. Most participants were located in the largest Egyptian cities, such as Cairo, Giza, Tanta, Port Said, Alexandria, Mansoura and Suez. Outside Egypt, more than 5,500 participants originated from Saudi Arabia, Kuwait and the Emirates. 1,313 visitors were located in the United States. Only 14 per cent of participants were women, who were on average aged twenty-four to forty-four. The majority of male participants were aged twenty-four to thirty-four. The data sample used for this research was retrieved and archived between September and October 2013, as the web design company in charge of editing the Dostour Sharek platform was launching a new version of the project to cover the January 2014 referendum. The company in question provided me with access to all the comments posted on the 2012 version of the constitutional draft, which would no longer be publicly available via the official Dostour Sharek webpage.

The first phase of the project was described to me as chaotic and experimental. Administrators had to decide how user-generated content would be moderated and were soon asked to design a code that would filter 'inappropriate language'. In a later stage, they decided to remove copy-pasted comments that might skew the findings of their report on citizens' feedback. The issue presented itself after the influential Salafi leader Hazem Salah Abu Ismail, who had built a very large audience of followers on social media, called his supporters to copy-paste the same comment in response to draft article 2 of the constitution. The article in question, which referred to Islam as the main source of Egyptian law, was indeed contested by a large majority of pro-Salafi participants, who insisted that Islam should in fact be described as the one and only source of law in the constitutional text. This proved to be the most disputed draft article, according to the statistics released by the platform. After the incident, the developers ensured that the exact same comment would not be recurrently posted for a single article. Interviewees, who had liaised with the Constituent Assembly reported to me that, whereas members were initially reluctant to communicate draft articles, they later took consideration of the feedback reported from the supporting staff in charge of analysing users' input. Some of the most commonly posted comments were discussed before redrafting the articles. Yet, the consultative infrastructure implemented to draft the constitution was threatened in late November 2012, due to the struggles generated by the constitutional decree. Despite the conjunction of communication channels applied to involve citizens in the drafting process, the debate remained highly polarized. As mentioned above, it resulted in a relatively low turnout and in the opposition's call to boycott the referendum.

The climate of contentious politics surrounding the referendum thus invalidates a common approach in research on e-governance, which seeks to evaluate evidence of success in terms of interactivity. In early Internet studies, the potential benefit of such an e-consultation project was often associated with the volume and reciprocity of interactions occurring between citizens and the public administration, as well as amongst citizens themselves (Chatfield and Alhujran, 2009). Yet the quality and efficiency of social interactions are hardly measurable. Besides, they vary considerably depending on the particular context and purpose of deliberation. This essentially comes down to how we understand consensus. Are there ever reliable signs indicating that a consensus has been achieved through public deliberation? The same question in fact applies to the social settings that are regulated or controlled by other entities, outside of the field of governance. One has to consider whether the interactions that occur in these environments are part of an organic process of legitimation, or if they are used to manufacture consent by creating an illusion of consensus. At the time of the referendum, theorists like Emma Murphy (2009) and Jodi Dean (2003) had already referred to the age of 'informal' or 'communicative' capitalism as detrimental to citizenship. According to Dean (2003: 108), communicative capitalism introduced a form of 'neodemocracy' by altering one's ability to spontaneously grant legitimacy or question the authority of those in power. Dean (2003) argued that this framework for public deliberation, which was expected to serve participative democracy, was indeed driven by a logic of consumerist entertainment. By creating an illusion of consensus, it deprived ordinary citizens of the informal power of legitimation, which is the primary function of the public sphere.

In the case of the 2012 constitutional referendum, one has to wonder if the experience of the Dostour Sharek platform did not ultimately act as a means of legitimation (Hart, 2003; Maboudi and Nadi, 2014). The project offered limited opportunities for consultation through social interactions. The Constituent Assembly only responded to citizens' comments by reviewing the constitutional draft accordingly. Offline interactions occasionally took place as part of the infrastructure implemented during the drafting process, such as the committees in charge of collecting citizens' suggestions in local districts. However, the online platform was certainly not designed to facilitate interactions between users. Although participants' accounts linked to their social media profile (Facebook), the interface did not provide an opportunity for peer-to-peer conversations, nor did it include functionalities for replies to other users. Participants were only able to post individual feedback and rank the articles by using a thumbs-up or thumbs-down option. Some participants posted the same comments for different articles, no matter the object of the articles in question. In most cases, these inputs addressed the entire constitutional draft, calling for electors to vote yes or no to the referendum. Most of these generic comments did not specifically address the content of the articles below which they had been posted. Therefore, in the absence of a genuinely interactive space for deliberation, each participant's input appeared to be very isolated and disconnected.

Yet one can easily argue that, as a centralized public space for deliberation, the platform delivered a misleading sense of consensus. In fact, in spite of the public's overwhelming discontent, the draft had received a large proportion of positive feedback (89 per cent), according to the official Dostour Sharek statistics. This number did not reflect the generally negative sentiment expressed in the comments. A qualitative analysis revealed that there was, in fact, not much of a consensus on the revolutionary ethos that was expected to transpire from the new constitution. People had diverging interpretations of the great ideals that had been invoked during the uprisings, such as the notion of 'dignity' and the means through which one hoped to achieve 'social equality'. To many, the term 'democracy' encapsulated the sense of an ideological conflict between Islamists and the camp of the civil opposition, creating more grounds for contentious politics. Many of these equivocal concepts, which were initially charged with revolutionary hopes, had to be redefined in legal terms.

Beyond the practice of deliberation, it was the semantics of the revolution that was used to create an illusion of consensus. Beneath the surface, the comments however conveyed diverging interpretations, raising more questions about the actual meaning of these hopeful ideals. Overall, the experience of deliberation that came out of this e-consultation project did not involve so much interactivity as it did *intertextuality*. In a literary sense, *intertextuality* refers to the common themes and shared references we use across different sources of writings. This was certainly a feature of the early post-revolutionary debate. Political actors did not miss the opportunity to capitalize on the rhetorical power of revolutionary leitmotivs, such as 'justice', 'freedom' and 'dignity'. However, the first post-revolutionary constitution would no longer hide conflicting interpretations, raising questions about the actual meaning of these terms. An in-depth analysis of the comments indicated that participants were seeking clarity, actively trying to elucidate the confusion around revolutionary semantics in a climate of intense polarisation.

To a large extent, the most recurrent criticism, which was formulated on the Dostour Sharek platform, pointed to the vagueness of the articles. Participants agreed on the fact that many of the concepts stated in constitutional laws should be clearly redefined. In response to article 5, which stated that national sovereignty belonged to the people, comments requested clarifications as to how people's sovereignty should be exercised. In some cases, contributors explicitly condemned the fact that the ambiguity of the draft would grant too much power to the legislators in charge of introducing further regulations. This clearly stood out from the comments analysed for articles number 14 and 18 of the draft, which both stated that further regulations and potential exceptions would be applicable by law.

Article 14 asserted that economic developments should support social justice and solidarity, by improving standards of living, preserving the rights of the working-class and allowing a fair distribution of wealth. Additionally, it briefly addressed the question of minimum salaries, establishing that minimum wages and pensions should be sufficient to allow decent living standards. A final statement instituted that a maximum wage would be determined in the public sector, while permitting potential exceptions that would be justified by law. Most of the criticisms expressed in the comments underlined the fact that none of the concepts mentioned in the article had been appropriately defined. Among them, 21 per cent of the contributions claimed that the amount or proportion of minimum wage should be specified in the article and that its value should be determined in relation to inflation. A considerable number of comments – 37 per cent – argued that the article should not include any potential exception that might enable policymakers to circumvent this regulation.

Article 18, which established the responsibility of the State for preserving and managing public resources, received similar feedback. In this case, the draft stated that natural resources should be preserved and administered for the sake of public good and that no concession should be granted by the state to exploit these resources, unless it might be justified by law. Close to 25 per cent of the posts analysed in the thread of comments contested the exception formulated in the article. Vague articles would require further legislation before becoming fully applicable, which would inevitably limit citizens' consultative power, while providing the parliamentary chambers with more room for manoeuvre.

Participants also recurrently questioned the meaning of concepts, which they perceived to be loaded with ideological value. This only highlighted the extent to which revolutionary demands had been strategically reframed by different political groups over the course of the post-revolutionary transition. One of the most striking examples came from draft article 6 of the constitution, which defined the Egyptian system as 'democratic'. Participants engaged in a debate on the Islamic concept of Shura, which was viewed by many as a more culturally appropriate interpretation of democratic governance. As in the case of article 2, these views pointed to the widening divide between Islamists and the civil opposition, which paved the way for the success of the counterrevolution. The most recurrent response generated by article 6 of the draft regarded the article stipulating that no political party should be based on discriminatory criteria of distinctions between citizens, such as gender, origins or religion. Since the terms 'non-discriminatory' and 'democratic' were commonly associated with secularism, reactions to article 6 only heightened the sense of an existential conflict between Islamists and civil parties. Twenty per cent of comments analysed for this article questioned whether Islamist parties would still conform to their ideology if they complied with the law. Some of these comments came to question the legitimacy of the Muslim Brotherhood and Salafi Noor party, while others requested to remove this reservation in order to avoid any formulation that might discredit Islamist movements. On one hand, the article failed at clarifying to what extent Islamist parties might conform to this particular definition of a discriminatory ideology. On the other hand, it did not provide any clear definition of what should be considered as democratic versus discriminatory, allowing every reader to interpret those terms from their ideological perspective.

Article 8, which referred to notions of 'social justice, equality and freedom' (ConstitutePorject.org, 2022: 5), generated the same confusion. The draft stipulated that the state should ensure social solidarity and aim at providing 'sufficiency for all citizens' (ConstitutePorject.org, 2022). A large majority of comments considered how sufficient means of living could be achieved, enquiring into the notion of a welfare state. As much as the terms 'dignity' and 'social justice' (ConstitutePorject.org, 2022) evoked the slogans of the revolution with a touch of romantic lyricism, they were too equivocal to materialize in policymaking.

The 2012 draft was the first legislative output of the revolution. As such, it was expected to ensure the applicability of the revolutionary language, which was initially formulated via informal communication channels of the uprisings. However, unlike the innovative genre of the blogosphere, constitutional laws failed to provide tangible and relatable definitions for the concepts of freedom, dignity and social justice. The Constituent Assembly had overlooked the more pragmatic concerns of the grassroots, the realities of the streets and the implications of the law in citizens' everyday lives. Meanwhile, the same criticism was directed at the young leftist middle class, who – in spite of operating within an isolated echo chamber – had nevertheless tried to relay the voices of the grassroots while engaging in street mobilizations. That process illustrated the dynamic at play in the third quarter of the discursive cycle, to wit the hijacking of informal communication channels by well-established political institutions.

By the time of the 2012 constitutional debate, this process of reappropriation was primarily initiated by formal political organizations and their assimilation of revolutionary narratives. Although freedom, equality and social justice delivered a sense of consensus, the indefinite meaning of these terms benefitted those who competed for legitimacy in formal politics. The reappropriation of the revolutionary language in partisan politics had contributed to fragment informal communication networks while discrediting the pro-revolutionary youth. Once the revolutionary language had been politicized, it became devoid of its potential meaning and was left imbued with an aura of populism. The comments posted as part of the e-consultation project however demonstrated that ordinary citizens expected the constitution to offer tangible and applicable solutions, which would resonate with the political *praxis* of the street.

Article 7, which called for the preservation of national security and mandatory military conscription, generated two sets of reactions. 25 per cent of the comments analysed argued that the draft should include further regulations on military service. The most common criticism concerned the fact that no additional information was given about the duration of the conscription, the wage of recruits and the potential conditions for exemption. Participants insisted on redefining the conditions for dignity in the context of military conscription, as well as in relation to the military's treatment of civilians. Once again, contributions reflected the will to be involved in a more engaging form of policymaking that would ensure the realization of revolutionary demands, with regard to the primacy of civil power over the military.

In another occurrence, participants reacted to the wording of article 26, which introduced tax regulations, by referring to the concept of social justice: 'Social justice is the foundation of taxation and other public finance duties' (ConstituentProject.org, 2022: 7). Participants argued that social justice should not essentially depend on the administration of public finance, but on a broader set of laws. They also requested from the Constituent Assembly to elaborate on the relationship between taxes and social justice. Once again, these two examples manifested the desire to assess and improve the applicability of revolutionary semantics.

An examination of the way the revolutionary vocabulary was received in the context of the first constitutional draft in fact shows the public was still eager to engage in a genuinely informal deliberation to reconsider the scope of the revolution. Beyond the polarisation of the debate, citizens proved to be very critical with regard to the marketization of revolutionary concepts in the realm of partisan politics. In spite of the polarisation, the Egyptian public was not fooled, and often demonstrated a high level of citizen engagement by addressing the confusion around the terminology of the revolution. The momentum of the revolution was, in that sense, still perceptible across citizen reactions to the constitutional draft. Many intended to pursue the process of proactive social enquiry that had started prior to the uprisings in the peripheries of the public sphere. In spite of the disillusionment that came out of Morsi's constitutional decree, participants continued to demonstrate civic engagement. It is for this reason that they often challenged the misleading doublespeak which came to be associated with the revolutionary leitmotivs of freedom and dignity.

Some fascinating questions were raised, which implicitly enquired into the potential ideological underpinnings of the revolution. For example, a number of draft articles introduced a rather philosophical reflection on the definition of private versus public interest. Articles 24 and 29 generated a discussion about the distinction between private and public good, suggesting that the limitations of those two concepts should be explicitly stated in the constitution. Article 22 of the Constitution, which regulated the preservation of public finances, stimulated similar reactions. The large majority of participants insisted that the law should name the actors in charge of administering public resources, clarify the role of civil society and stipulate the penalties for fraud. In addition, contributors challenged the fact that the wording itself did not emphasize the responsibility of the state in ensuring the preservation of public finances.

Apart from the ambivalence of the constitutional text itself, users of the e-consultation platform pointed out that the draft applied a confusing vocabulary and failed at providing comprehensive measures. In addition to the feedback to article 22 cited above, reactions to articles 21 and 23 mainly related to the aspects of the law that were missing from the original draft. Paragraph 21 of the constitution confirmed the state would protect the rights and 'legitimate ownership of all kinds of public, cooperative and private property' (ConstituentProject.org, 2022: 7), administered in compliance with the law. 15 per cent of the comments analysed in this thread argued that the law should explicitly prevent foreigners and foreign investors from owning such private cooperatives. 7 per cent of the comments sampled claimed that the article should include a definition and further regulation on intellectual property. Finally, 35 per cent of the reactions to article 23 of the draft, which ensured the support and sponsorship of the state to all forms of 'cooperatives' (ConstituentProject.org, 2022: 7), claimed that the cooperatives in question should be clearly defined. These reactions indicated that participants had been sensitive to the fact the constitutional draft failed at defining the conditions for *freedom, justice* and *equity*. They however expressed the desire to rethink and understand public good, private interest and civil society engagement from not only a legal, but also a social and more philosophical perspective.

In other circumstances, this could have been the continuation of the revolutionary counter-discourse through public channels of deliberation. However, due to the limited timeframe imposed for the submission of the referendum, citizens' input was hardly considered. If anything, the tool was used as an experiment under Morsi, before being re-applied by Sisi's government as part of the 2014 constitutional referendum. In both cases, one can easily argue that it acted as a means of legitimation. Many were eager to participate in a collaborative and constructive discussion to further explore the meaning of revolutionary leitmotivs. However, these concepts conveyed different visions and representations of the revolution, due to their marketization in the political sphere. Everyone was certainly interested in justice, social equity or freedom, and certainly concerned with the application of Islamic law as well as the distinction between civilian and military powers.

However, revolutionary narratives remained highly divisive, after being strategically reframed for campaigning purposes. This phenomenon is of course very common in a climate of contentious politics. As suggested by Arendt (2016), it appears to be a key feature of language as a driver of discursive power. I am here referring to the polysemy and fluidity of language, which may significantly alter the course of discursive power. As much as it allows peripheral voices to shift public attention in creative ways, it also benefits those who have a monopoly over public discourse and the means of public deliberation. This characteristic of language explains why the media – in its multiple forms – may serve different agendas, acting like a double-edged sword. On the one hand, language may be deconstructed to challenge discursive power. On the other, it can be devoid of meaning and subsumed to its symbolic value in a specific context. Populism as a style of political rhetoric precisely corresponds to that latter scenario. Indeed, it has been argued that, across the ideological spectrum, populism tends to rely predominantly on redundant symbolism. It is the symbolic value of the language, which is often used to essentialize the identity of an in-group, while discrediting opponents by means of political othering. Yet one would be mistaken for believing, as has often been suggested, that this was initially the case with the emerging language of the revolution. As mentioned above, the history of web activism shows that pro-revolutionary voices were influenced by different ideological cultures of resistance. Amongst the young leftist middle class, the opposition would also leverage the political literacy of the elite. This suggests that, in 2011, the language of the revolution was a political project in the making, which could have continued to benefit from informal practices of communication at the grassroots level. Its organic growth was however aborted by the interference of well-established political actors, who attributed different symbolic values to the revolutionary agenda in an attempt at regaining legitimacy. My study of the 2012 online constitutional debate reveals that many participants were still interested in a constructive exploration of revolutionary semantics. However, this process was jeopardized by the rhetoric of the largest political groups, which began to invoke and reframe the revolution as they positioned themselves in relation to the conflict opposing the Muslim Brotherhood to the counterrevolution.

Besides the technological infrastructure of the debate, it was the equivocal language of the revolution that was used as a means of legitimation. In fact, beyond the case of the constitutional draft, the broader developments of the semantic web simply brought to light the dynamics at play in the circulation of discourse. Discursive power was perhaps circulating at a different pace and on a larger scale now that language was encoded into hashtags and algorithms. However, as has been the case throughout history, what was at stake was the contested meaning of the language, as well as the strategic use of language as a means of legitimation.

Looking back at the revolution: Gathering impressions from the field after the 2013 military coup

Three years after the uprisings, the disillusionment of the Egyptian pro-revolutionary youth had reached its peak. This transpired from the fieldwork interviews I conducted between Spring and Autumn of 2014, after the reinstated military regime had launched its crackdown on the Muslim Brotherhood. As it stood out from the blogosphere, members of the young leftist opposition had undergone a critical introspection. This was also the case for those who had been involved in partisan politics – such as active members of the pro-revolutionary Dostour party – as well as independent activists involved in parliamentary elections. They had witnessed the distortion of revolutionary narratives and the rapid politization of the social media sphere. They would also reflect on the self-segregating elitism of the urban middle class, which was also rooted in the practice of online activism. Many of the participants interviewed as part of my research described at length how the semantics of the revolution had been reappropriated by political leaders as well as the national media outlets covering the presidential and constitutional debates. In their view, the rapidly evolving social media sphere mirrored the intense polarisation that was already perceptible offline as well as in the mainstream media and broader political landscape. These various attempts at hijacking the revolution resulted from a context of contentious politics. They were, in other words, caused by other factors besides digital technologies. That being said, social media was often described to me as a magnifying glass, and was said to have simply accelerated the *mainstreaming* and *politization* of the revolution.

Due to their exponential growth, online networks were no longer suitable for informal communication. This became ever more evident in light of the interference of mainstream political campaigning. In the months following the 2013 military coup, digital media had contributed to the spread of rumours, conspiracy theories and smear campaigns designed to discredit members of the pro-revolution opposition. Many activists, some of whom had been proactively engaged on mainstream social platforms, confirmed that online deliberation was not only increasingly centralized but also applied as a means of legitimation. Moreover, as I will show, interviews further illustrated the fact that left-wing and liberal revolutionaries felt progressively deprived of intellectual leadership when attempting to consolidate the opposition. Due to the 'filter bubble' effect of social media, their audience was often limited to a minority of supporters, amongst Internet users, whose perspective and life experience did not always reflect that of the grassroots. Social media had, in this regard, led many web activists to believe that they would easily find support beyond the circles of the urban middle class.

Overall, fieldwork ethnography further illustrated the cycle of discursive power, accounting for the history of web activism in Egypt. As mentioned earlier, visualizing the circulation of discourse allows us to understand how different communication tools and practices may transition from the realm of counter-power into that of institutional power (cf. Figure 1). In that respect, this research mainly focuses on the lower pole of the discursive cycle. Yet interviews also outlined the fact that some of the policies implemented by Mubarak's former administration had encouraged the emergence of web-activism, over the years that preceded the uprisings. In doing so, they demonstrated that institutional powers often create the conditions for the emergence of a counter-discourse. The ethnography also highlighted how leading political institutions had been involved in the earlier development of web activism, as per the upper pole of the discursive cycle.

Interviewees commented on how the revolutionary opposition had initially gained momentum in early 2011, prior to the rise of the Muslim Brotherhood and its weaponization by counterrevolutionary forces. They provided a very reflexive overview of this succession of events, which contributed to outline the shifts of political narratives over the relatively short period of time covering the post-revolutionary transition. The memory of the revolutionary uprisings was recalled with despair and nostalgia, while the repression intensified over the months following the military coup. Between September and November 2014, students' unions and youth organizations, who had tried to remain active within university circles were weakened under the pressure of Falcon, a private security agency mandated by the state. Many students involved in peaceful demonstrations, petitions and associative projects were expelled or personally threatened. The Muslim Brotherhood was disabled, as most of its leaders were imprisoned or had fled the country. Over the course of my 2014 fieldwork alone, human rights activists, such as Yara Sallam and Sanaa Seif were sentenced for taking part in peaceful demonstrations.

In addition to the threat of the regime, the very few people remaining active within the opposition had lost the support of the population, as a result of the conspiracy theories instigated by the military's electronic army. Under the new military regime, the iconic 25 January revolution, in which both the leftist youth and the Islamist opposition took part, was depicted as the cause of the Muslim Brotherhood's success. The propaganda spread by the new military regime convinced many people that the 25 January revolution had threatened national security and led the country in a deeper economic crisis, affecting tourism and power supply.

Once in power, al-Sisi's administration stated that the intermittent power cuts were due to '300 attacks on electricity pylons nationwide, which had deepened the crisis leading to a drop in production by up to 15 per cent' (Ibrahim, 2015). On 2 November 2014, the Middle East Eye reported on the issue stating that: 'State television and private pro-government media have regularly reported such attacks, usually referring to the assailants as supporters and members of the Muslim Brotherhood group of ousted President Mohammed Morsi' (Ibrahim, 2015). Opponents to the military regime, who once were celebrated as the heroes of the revolution, were now considered responsible for the intermittent electricity cuts and gas shortages suffered by the population.

As for young revolutionaries, they had already been portrayed by Mohammed Morsi's previous government as dangerous radical anarchists. Once in power, the military regime maintained this narrative while implementing new laws that would restrict their visibility in the public and political spheres. Among the legislative reforms implemented by President Abdel Fatah al-Sisi that restrained opposition groups was the controversial amendment to article 78 of the penal code, which prevented any organization from acting against the state's interests. The law stated that:

> Anyone who asks for himself, or for others, or accepts, or takes – even through an intermediary – from a foreign state, or those who work for its interests, or a legal person, or a local or an international organisation, or any other entity that is not affiliated with a foreign state and does not work for its interest, cash, or transferred money, or equipment, or machines, or weapons, or ammunition, or items like it or other things, or was promised of any of that (...) With the intention of committing acts harmful to national interest, or acts like it, or acts that breach the country's independence, or unity, or territorial integrity, or committing attacks that disrupt public security and safety, shall be punished.

> (Al Ahram Online, 2013)

In addition to the anti-protest law promulgated in November 2013 (Al Ahram Online, 2013) – which prevented any protests from taking place without formal consent of the authorities – such amendments would considerably limit the room for manoeuvre of any opposition movement. But most importantly, this contributed to the shaping of the narrative according to which protesters and Islamist groups had been threatening national security and should be considered as public enemies. With the emergence of such narratives, the romantic ideals that surrounded the 2011 revolution vanished along with the sympathy of the grassroots for protesters. Simultaneously, the 30 June coup substituted itself to the 25 January revolution as the ultimate achievement of the 2011–13 political transition and the so-called 'fortunate' victory over the Muslim Brotherhood.

Commentators questioned the assumption according to which these two events should be interpreted as revolutions, sometimes suggesting that they both could be regarded as military coups (Stein, 2012; Phillips, 2012). As I demonstrated earlier, the notion of revolution itself – as well as many other crucial concepts that characterized the post-revolutionary debate – was given different meanings, due to the complex interplay of political actors competing for authorship over discourse. As was expressed by one of the participants interviewed in this study, '(...) the narratives about the past are not unified and we are still fighting to determine who will eventually benefit from the revolution as a historical event'. Although interviews were conducted three years after the first revolutionary protests and despite the fact that participants retrospectively commented on the events, these tensions over discursive power were still perceptible at the time of the fieldwork. Until November 2014, participants had experienced different shifts in terms of discursive leadership and were still witnessing the revival of the military discourse.

The large majority of the participants I interacted with expressed the idea that the discursive tools of the revolution had been reused to serve the purpose of the counterrevolution. When they described the evolution of social media usage between 2012 and 2014, most interviewees attested that a broader and more diversified audience became active online and on social media after the uprisings. They agreed that political elites and institutions, as well as the privately owned and mainstream public media channels, were now actively using digital media to reach this new audience. Most participants agreed that there was a mainstreaming of the revolution, a phenomenon I described when analysing the activist blogosphere. In their views, the revolution had generated a liberalization of the political debate, thanks to which all social classes and demographics were able to deliberate. However, this made public deliberations more chaotic and likely to be manipulated precisely when the revolutionary movement needed to rely on strong ideological grounds. Such an argument was however representative of the view that a revolution would have to be guided by a new elite. The implication was that the highly educated youth, amongst the opposition, should continue to exercise some form of intellectual leadership in the hope that this would ultimately provide an ideological framework for the revolution. This idea, which was often expressed by members of the young leftist middle class, precisely resonated with the argument formulated by Tufekci (2017). It implied that, in order to sustain itself, the young civil opposition would have to enter the political game and come together in the form of an organizational structure.

This was envisioned as an alternative strategy, which could have helped the pro-revolutionary youth maintain some form of control over the revolutionary narrative. In retrospect, most interviewees agreed that the challenge was to prevent the reappropriation of a revolution in the making. However, they did not always explicitly attribute this challenge to digital media. Whereas some participants interpreted this as a consequence of the increasing Internet penetration, others saw it as a dispersion of the revolution *per se* – whether technological or ideological. In the former case, it was assumed that the growth of the social media market had fragmented the audience. Alternatively, the latter interpretation suggested that web activists had significantly contributed to the liberalization of the debate. They may have utilized the logic of consumerism at play in the attention economy of social media to relay their message and gain supporters (Tufekci, 2014). In doing so, they overlooked the flipside of this fast-growing market and did not anticipate that public exposure will backfire once the media is re-centralized and securitized.

The uprisings demonstrated how participative communication technologies could be efficient in mobilizing a critical mass of citizens around the equivocal lyricism of 'connective action' (Bennett and Segerberg, 2012). In this regard, the revolutionary movement was also partly responsible for rendering public opinion less predictable and likely to be manipulated. That being said, whether they related this phenomenon to the 2011 revolution or not, all participants expressed the idea the social media sphere became representative of the highly polarized political environment between 2011 and 2014. Moreover, they asserted that leading political groups – most often identified as the SCAF and the Muslim Brotherhood – had become as proactive and visible on social media as independent activists, reversing the bottom-up stream into a rather top-down communication flow. This shows how digital media transitioned from the emergent to the mainstream, transferring the discursive tools of the revolution into the sphere of institutional power. Symmetrically, as mentioned earlier, the interviews also exemplified the north axis of the discursive cycle (cf. Figure 1). Whereas I essentially considered the transition from counter-discourse to discourse, I was reminded that the former military elite had encouraged social media consumption, paving the way to emergent forms of activism. This confirmed the idea that, in Egypt, the practice of digital activism already relied on some form of intellectual leadership in the early 2000s.

While I was focusing on the transition from revolution to counterrevolution, participants drew my attention to the fact that practices of political dissent and peripheral communication were constantly evolving. Counter-power originated from the previous institutional power just like the new dominant discourse emanated from the revolution. One could hardly argue that this was exclusively the result of connective action – in Bennett and Segerberg's (2012) terms. Digital technologies may have simply accelerated this phenomenon.

As for the transition that occurred on the south axis of the discursive cycle (cf. Figure 1), the great majority of the participants interviewed confirmed the idea that both the ideological and technological tools of the revolution had ultimately served the interests of the counterrevolution. When asked to what extent, in their opinion, the tools, arguments or slogans of the revolution had been used by the counterrevolution, only three of the participants formally interviewed for this part of my research answered negatively. A thirty-something candidate in the forthcoming parliamentary elections who I quoted above argued that while pro-revolutionary activists had been very active online, long-established political institutions retained legitimacy by bringing the debate back to the streets.

During the course of the 2012 presidential election, candidates were particularly inclined to interact directly with their electorate in the field, which allowed them to reach the rural areas and working-class groups not present on digital media. This was still the case as he was campaigning for the forthcoming parliamentary election:

> Let's take an example, I'm running for Parliament and one of my arsenals of communication tools is social media (…) This may help me secure a certain number of votes (…) maybe 10 per cent. And that depends on where I am (…) in the greater Cairo, now this percentage will presumably diminish significantly as I we go to the Delta [region] or Upper Egypt (…) Nothing beats political retailing. Shake the hand, kiss the baby, all that good stuff, you know. (…) Having people [on the ground], having a well-oiled machine of campaigners (…)
>
> (Nabil,[1] young independent candidate in Egypt's 2014 parliamentary election, Cairo, spring 2014)

Such an argument suggested that online campaigning was certainly not the main strategy applied by the leading political forces to regain control over the revolution. Yet it was revealing of the fact that political officials were now competing on the same territory as revolutionaries. While protesters had reclaimed ownership of the street and the social media sphere to build the informal networks of the revolution, political institutions later benefitted from the same communication channels. This process of re-centralization operated beyond and independently from social media. It simply manifested itself online as well as in many other aspects of the post-revolutionary debate.

The 25 January uprisings unleashed a desire to be more involved and engaged in the political debate, across social classes. Yet those who ultimately benefitted from this phenomenon were the main political groups, who were better represented in traditional mass media, as well as in the associative networks of local communities and rural regions. As for the broader range of the middle class that had become active on social media after the uprisings, it was now exposed to another form of state propaganda.

This aspect of the interview also led me to further explore the relationship between the ideological and technological revolution and to identify whether social media had, in fact, prevented the success of the revolution in the long run. In order to assess whether the informal communication channels of the revolution had been hijacked, participants were asked to describe the communication strategy of well-established organizations involved in the presidential and constitutional debates. They described how the semantics of the revolution was reframed by the leading political forces and made vulnerable to political hijacking. Yet as much as it characterized the entire media and political environment, the polarizing effect of this politization was not interpreted as a direct consequence of social media activism. Rather, it was perceived to result from the existing polarisation of the Egyptian political landscape and the fact that the national media market was controlled by counterrevolutionary forces.

For this reason, most participants were unable to determine when social media started being used in the sphere of institutional politics. To some extent, political elites always had a certain degree of involvement in the emergence of digital activism, and this was not specific to the post-revolutionary phase. In fact, one could also consider the upper pole of the discursive cycle to illustrate the fact that the Internet already served conflicting political agendas in its early phases of development. When asked when the security apparatus became active online, one participant highlighted that they had attempted to limit the scope of web activism way before the 25 January revolution:

They did not begin on the 25 January; they began the moment we began. I mean on the 6 April, when Wael Abbas and Alaa Abdel Fatah[2] began blogging, at the same time, they developed their own "لجان الكترونى"[3].

(Elias,[4] leftist pro-revolutionary activist, Cairo, spring 2014)

From his perspective, digital media already benefitted the elites in power in the early stage of digital activism. When recalling the beginning of digital activism in Egypt, he emphasizes the fact that first Internet users operated in a similar environment as the elite in power. The opposition had become visible online, while some of the members of the former NDP considered investing in digital media to stimulate the economy and reinforce national security. The confrontation between power and counter-power – or discourse and counter-discourse – was therefore much harder to situate over time than one might think.

My research originally relied on the assumption that the circulation of discourse was divided between the spheres of political activism and institutional politics. The ethnography however suggested that some political actors happened to navigate between those two spheres of powers and that the boundary between discourse and counter-discourse was often hardly noticeable. Even when analysing the transformation of a counter-discourse in a specific historical context, it was hard to identify the exact moment of the transition from counter-power to power. This was precisely representative of the fact that, as argued earlier, discourse is ambivalent by nature, as it has a cyclic evolution.

This precisely outlines the transition that occurred in the upper pole of the discursive cycle (cf. Figure 1), as it shows how institutional powers indirectly contributed to the emergence of a new form of political activism. More specifically, this aspect of digital activism shows how those, who may be more likely to develop and disseminate a critical theory within the opposition, share many characteristics of the elites in power, which puts them in a position of intellectual leadership. A forty-something journalist and web activist in fact suggested that social media, amongst other kinds of political actions, was particularly representative of this form of bourgeois public sphere (Habermas, 1962):

> Social media doesn't have a unique role by itself. Social media, at the end of the day is a reflection of the people, who are on social media. See the revolutionary camp weren't capable to address these slogans into a serious vision. (...) Most of the revolutionary camp, or the main figures of the revolutionary camp come somehow from middle class, (...) so while they want reform, they are part of the class that may be affected by the reform itself. So, there was a moral contradiction. I realise that in April 2011. I told

some people, 'if you want to stop the revolution it's ok, but if you want to
continue, you should know that your personal life will change (…).' People
weren't ready for this. (…) they were able to sacrifice they life, while they
were not able to sacrifice their … [laugh]

(Mukhtar,[5] Leftist pro-revolutionary activist, Cairo, Spring 2014)

Like many of the quotes reported in this chapter, this statement is particularly
representative of the views shared by the leftist opposition. In this case, the
participant embraces a typically Marxist perspective as he claims that the left-
wing intelligentsia was not fully committed to the revolution. He suggested
that digital activism essentially relayed the voices of highly educated pro-
revolutionaries from the bourgeoisie. As such, it reflected the views of a
privileged minority, within the opposition, that remained disconnected from
the working classes. Whereas many revolutionary activists were ready to
sacrifice their lives for the revolutionary cause – by facing the police, protesting
in the streets and openly sharing their views on the military regime – they
were not ready to sacrifice their lifestyle. To some extent, his comment was
revealing of the fact that, once the public space was recentralized in the
aftermath of January 2011 the young middle class could no longer interact
organically with the grassroots. As much as they benefitted from some form
of intellectual leadership, they were unable to communicate informally with
the most disfranchised. This affected their ability to be viewed as credible
representatives, in spite of their desire to consolidate a viable political
alternative. Beyond the role of the media, the sociology of the revolution may
as well be analysed as part of the cycle of discursive power.

What hypothetically constituted the intellectual elite of the online public
sphere should not be regarded as entirely disconnected from the former regime.
This is partly due to the fact that discourses remain, to a certain extent, fluid
by nature, as they unfold in a cycle. As a result, the distinction between power
and counter-power – as well as the divisions between institutional politics and
political activism – may sometimes be hardly noticeable.

With regard to the way the ideological vocabulary of the revolution had
been applied in the post-revolutionary debate, interviews corroborated the
findings of my blogosphere analysis. Participants commonly agreed on the
fact that the revolutionary ideals had no consistent meaning, since they had

been employed in different ideological contexts over the 2011–13 political crisis. For instance, some of the slogans that had been chanted by protesters in January 2011 became proper labels for specific political groups. Among others was the famous 'عيش حرية عدالة اجتماعية'[6] slogan which had found an echo in the Freedom and Justice party founded by the Muslim Brotherhood. Another example can be found in the claim for human dignity (Warkotsch, 2012: 44). This concept activated a different ideological repertoire as it resonated with the name of the party[7] founded by Hamdeen Sabahy in the 1990s. In a similar way to that Bennett and Segerberg described in their theory of connective action (2012), every individual was able to project personal interpretations onto revolutionary semantics. In order to discuss this phenomenon, participants were asked to comment on the way this vocabulary was applied in the post-revolutionary debate. Many participants argued that the concepts of freedom, social justice or dignity were too vague to support a substantial political debate. This aspect of the interviews substantiated the observations I had made when analysing the constitutional debate:

> I believe that a lot of the concepts and ideals used [...] were popular, because they are vague and everyone can see something of themselves in it. You know if you say 'freedom', you know 'freedom' is such a broad term, everyone can say 'I'm for freedom'. So of course, you can use those terms and you will be popular, you will get a following, but you have to realise that it's only popular because it's vague. And the more you go into details, the more you have a very specific program of what you want. (...) You have to have a different policy, you have to advocate freedom in a certain way. You know you can't just say 'freedom' what does it mean? So you can be still in charge of your political message, but then you have to realise that you're paying for that in numbers [of supporters]. You're paying for that and people won't be behind you anymore, once they know exactly what you are advocating.
>
> (Samira,[8] member of the young liberal-wing of the revolution, Cairo, spring 2014)

This criticism was mainly formulated by thirty- to forty-something liberals, who, among the different participants interviewed, appeared to be particularly critical of leftist pro-revolutionaries' strategies. In their views, the vagueness or flexibility of this counter-discourse demonstrated revolutionaries' failure to mobilize their support base around a consistent and sustainable political programme:

> That's where I draw a line between a revolution and a political campaign. Because those are very broad aspects. You can't really start to cut through those and bring them back into planet earth, into actual laws and regulations that would actually make those something worthwhile. And that's the biggest difference between what it takes to be a politician versus what it takes to be a revolutionary. (…) That's the biggest difference, because those slogans can never be translated into anything.
>
> (Nabil,[9] member of the young liberal-wing of
> the revolution, Cairo, spring 2014)

According to the participant interviewed, this phenomenon contributed to the success of the Muslim Brotherhood, which the liberal wing of the civil opposition viewed as the most problematic outcome of the 25 January uprisings. It revealed that the pro-revolutionary youth was, in fact, relatively fragmented, laying the grounds for political hijacking.

In fact, by the end of the fieldwork, I realized that international commentators covering the events had also misconstrued some of the terminology associated with the Egyptian revolution. This led me to approach the field with preliminary assumptions as to the meaning of the terms 'grassroots', 'liberals' or 'revolutionaries'. Eventually, the ethnography shed light on the connotations associated with these concepts; as well as on the Eurocentric tropes embedded in the literature. Simultaneously, hearing participants formulate their own definitions highlighted the scope of the fragmentation within the civil opposition.

Amongst other things, international commentators often failed to acknowledge conflicting interpretations of the terms 'civil', 'secular' or 'democratic' in the Egyptian context. Most of the literature published between 2011 and 2013 would often use the term 'liberal' to refer to the opposition to the SCAF and the Muslim Brotherhood. Yet this terminology denied the divisions between the left and the liberal wing of the civil opposition. Worst of all, it suggested that the civil opposition had always been entirely disconnected from Islamists, although some of the pro-revolutionary youth had also been previously connected with the Muslim Brotherhood.

As mentioned earlier, many pioneers of the Egyptian revolutionary activism were originally affiliated to Islamist movements. Unlike the literature suggests by using this terminology, the opposition had never been homogenously secular. The terms 'secular' and 'democratic' were in fact considered as rather pejorative in the eyes of the general public and could therefore not be used as a self-proclaimed label in Egyptian politics. Consequently, parties and political actors that constituted the alternative against Islamists and supporters of the SCAF, such as the Egyptian Bloc coalition and the National Salvation Front, were qualified as 'civil' parties. Yet international commentators continuously referred to the idea of a binary opposition between Islamist and a secular camp, insidiously blurring the lines between the pro-revolutionary left and the actors of the counterrevolution.

Likewise, the international coverage of the events was also misleading in suggesting that the pro-revolutionary voices of the urban middle class were fairly representative of the grassroots. Among the opposition, young urban activists were more likely to convey a vision of the revolution that would resonate with the way the international community envisioned the democratization process. However, despite the fact that social media activists had made the opposition visible online on behalf of the grassroots, with the aim of relaying their political demands, their ideological perspective remained significantly different. This was precisely the reason why, according to many participants, leftist revolutionaries were unable to successfully engage with the support base of the Muslim Brotherhood.

In spite of its predominantly leftist ethos, the pro-revolutionary youth was sociologically conditioned to operate like a bourgeois public sphere. Three years after the uprisings, this community was still grappling with this notion of intellectual leadership. It came to realize, through an introspective critique, that it had relied on the same elitist framework as that described by Habermas. In both cases, the assumption was that the intelligentsia would have to lay the foundations for political action. Within the limited timeframe of the political transition, this approach proved to be detrimental, because it did not answer the needs of the grassroots, in terms of inclusion and fair representation.

In this context, the practice of online activism also proved to be detrimental. Participants identified a consequence of digital activism, which specifically related to the process through which social media had evolved towards the mainstream. Interviewees pointed out that the Internet had reached a critical mass of users within the middle class, who emerged in the debate without previous knowledge nor experience of politics. In their view, these contributions affected the quality of the debate, erasing any form of intellectual leadership:

> (…) it seems like most of the Egyptian middle class (…) just woke up one day to discover this alternative reality, so they [join the debate] and try to participate without having any [legitimate] background. (…) People who have not been involved in any form of political ideas, or political action just started [to speak up], and are [now] trying [to express themselves]. Meanwhile, they are also external players, who have discovered that this is a huge tool, an opportunity they may benefit from, so everybody is trying to [gain from it]. The political debate on social media is huge these days. (…) I guess after this whole mess settles down, we will have to set some rules.
>
> (Khalil,[10] journalist covering the post-revolutionary debate, Cairo, spring 2014)

Such narrative is perhaps what ultimately paved the way for the rapid securitization of the social media sphere that was undertaken under al-Sisi's administration in the following years. Participants also criticized the fact that the increasing popularity of social media had contributed to compartmentalizing the debate online. Despite the fact that a broader array of citizens became involved in this particular form of deliberation, they constituted distinctive audiences that hardly interacted with each other. In their opinion, this emphasized the polarisation of the debate, preventing the opposition from reaching a consensus on the purpose of the revolution.

Those different interpretations of the revolution evolved separately, after digital media provided the platform and communicative framework required to enable large-scale deliberation. The liberalization of the debate online created a bubble effect, generating a climate of confusion, which extended to people's private spheres. A participant recalled the anecdotal evidence of couples divorcing on the grounds of their diverging political views, sometimes calling for divorce in front of the polling stations during presidential elections. With social media, individuals became exposed to different networks and online news threads, which may have brought the polarisation to light. In contrast, the early days of digital activism, during which revolutionaries benefitted from intellectual leadership, proved to be more efficient in consolidating a unified opposition. As they recalled the beginning of digital activism in the early 2000s, participants described the first community of web activists as ideologically diversified yet very united:

> (…) Abdel Fatah, he was a Muslim Brotherhood member and Amr Eizzat was a Salafist, Wael Abbas[11] was a radical liberal but (…) they were closer to each other than to they were to their [ideological circles], I mean, Amr Eizzat was closer to Wael Abbas than he was to the Salafists. And this introduced this kind of collective power that is not controllable. They are not a political party, they don't need a kind of political permission from the government to work, they had this kind of connectivity that was more advanced than what the government used to track them.
>
> (Elias,[12] leftist pro-revolutionary activist, Cairo, spring 2014)

This sense of belonging to a united opposition was however shattered as soon as each of these different opinion leaders started building their own specific audience on social media. Most participants spontaneously described the evolution of digital media activism by distinguishing the initial phase of the blogosphere from a later stage characterized by the emergence of Facebook and Twitter.

Though very few bloggers were part of the activist community in 2007, they formulated convincing critique of the political establishment supported by sources, evidence and investigative journalism. Increasingly, with the emergence of social media platforms, a lot of bloggers stopped writing blog posts, exclusively using mainstream social platforms like Facebook and Twitter instead. With the mainstreaming of web-activism, these opposition voices felt that online deliberation was becoming more superficial. This new form of communication was characterized by keywords and hashtag trends, which most probably facilitated sporadic campaigns but prevented users from producing lengthy arguments. For many participants this contributed to making the features of the revolutionary counter-discourse meaningless, as it now relied on short statements, which would be easily disseminated but failed to provide a well-structured ideological argument:

> Twitter for example, because Twitter is so limited, the amount of words you can write in one tweet, (…) for example, after January 2011 there were so

many conversations on Twitter between people that were generally interested in politics (...) but the platform does not allow you to go in depth in those issues (...) you can't really go in that much detailed discussion about very specific issues that require numbers, you know, that require statistics, (...) you can take one tweet out of context and it means something different. (...) literally you don't have the space to write something that is comprehensive that is deep enough to be concrete. It's mostly vague. (...) it becomes, really, really difficult to maintain a decent discussion, (...) because they are so many parties involved.

(Samira,[13] member of the young liberal-wing of the revolution, Cairo, spring 2014)

In addition to the fact that social media extended the debate to include a mainstream audience, it was designed in a way that prevented users from formulating a nuanced and complex discussion around one's interpretation of the revolutionary ideals. The impression was that social media posts with limited characters had contributed to make the meaning of revolutionary slogans more fluid, laying the grounds for the intense climate of confusion and polarisation that characterized the 2012 constitutional debate.

Finally, and most importantly, participants pointed out that the social media sphere was put under surveillance, confirming that the digital networks had become an asset for the ruling elite, in the months following the 2013 military coup. Two months prior to the fieldwork, the Interior Minister announced his plan to apply mass surveillance over the most popular social media platforms and mobile phone applications, including Facebook, Twitter, YouTube and WhatsApp (Amnesty International, 2014). This was mentioned several times by interviewees as one of the most problematic outcomes of increasing social media usage. In their views, this indicated that cyberspace had reached the end of its mainstreaming as well as its process of recentralization. It was now comparable to the traditional mass media. As much as broadcast media and the press, the Internet was now censored and used by leading political groups as well as the national security apparatus to spread rumours and discredit the opposition.

Simultaneously, participants referred to another phenomenon, which made any form of social media statement in Egypt very likely to be manipulated. This consisted of private agents – most commonly hired by the government, the army or any other political group – who would create fake accounts, incorporate a platform or join an online debate with the intent of promoting or distorting a specific narrative. These electronic armies – referred to as 'لجان الكترونى' – spread groundless rumours invalidating the credibility of social media as an alternative communication tool. The public agenda was now controlled by whoever benefitted from the resources and the infrastructure necessary to reverse a trend and dictate the dominant narrative. Additionally, the Interior Minister's decision to monitor all social platforms would lead to self-censorship:

> (…) now social media has been corrupted by state surveillance, I believe they got a multimillion contract with an American company to start surveying Facebook. So [activists] are aware of that and they wouldn't start sharing their new ideas on the revolution just like that on Facebook. (…) So I think right now, everything changes. The activists wouldn't use it as naively as they did before.
>
> (Tariq,[14] young supporter of the revolutionary opposition)

Over the course of the interviews, participants came to express their views on both the potential benefits and negatives of social media activism, based on their personal experiences over the course of the 2011–13 political transition. As already stated in previous studies (Breuer, 2012), many argued that the media had essentially contributed to stimulating public deliberations, by facilitating access to information. It constituted a considerable asset for people who did not benefit from the technological infrastructure but could connect to the Internet through Internet cafes. The speed and immediacy of communication were also mentioned as a considerable advantage of digital media, along with the fact that it enabled any user to connect with an international audience. However, the unexpectedly rapid growth of online networks meant that one would have to compromise on the quality of these social interactions to capitalize on sheer quantity:

> I don't know how direct democracy can address the problem of quantity versus quality, I don't know how. They say 'more quantity brings quality' I don't know about that.
>
> (Nadhim,[15] leftist pro-revolutionary activist, Cairo, spring 2014)

Within the restored framework of the mass media, those who were the most likely to succeed were presumably the ones, who mastered the art of populist rhetoric. This was arguably the case for the Muslim Brotherhood and the military, as they each relied on well-constructed narratives of Pan-Islamist and national identity that had been historically designed to reaffirm one's sense of belonging within a mass audience. In contrast, the leftist intelligentsia always operated as a niche. Yet, once the informal communication of the revolution became the mainstream, there was simply not much opportunity for intellectual leadership.

Participant Mukhtar[16] pointed that the mainstreaming of social media had blurred the lines between the public and private sphere. This convergence of private and public spheres created more grounds for controversies. Once under the spotlight, personal conflicts of interests would be attributed a political value or public relevance. Therefore, instead of facilitating the inclusion of peripheral voices, this mainstreaming process simply contributed to a re-centralization of the debate, which was in his view detrimental to the opposition.

These findings confirmed that the media simply was a double-edged sword. As a tool of discursive power, the emergent media of the revolution had followed a cyclic evolution. Those who were proactively engaged in the practice of web activism had sometimes failed to anticipate the challenges involved with the mainstreaming of emergent media. This realization eventually led them to formulate an introspective critique of web activism, and reflect on the extent to which their voices were representative of the grassroots. And yet on some level, many of those who belonged to the leftist intelligentsia were still hoping to exercise a form of intellectual leadership. They would come to argue in favour the same kind of well-structured partisan engagement that communication experts have ever since advocated for (Tufekci, 2017). As much as they supported freedom of speech the rights of the working class, they regarded the fact that the online debate was brought to the masses as a highly problematic, because this meant compromising on intellectual leadership. In their view, the earlier stage of digital activism had proved to be a more favourable environment for the development of a critical theory and to the cross-fertilization of ideological perspectives.

However, the recent evolution of the social media sphere posed new challenged for the young leftist opposition of the urban middle class. On the one hand, they would now have to envision an alternative channel of informal communication that would allow them to build peripheral networks within the working class. This involved breaking through deeply rooted social clusters to interact more directly with the grassroots. The alternative approach was, on the other hand, to apply the same top-down communication strategy as partisan organizations. In that latter case, the young leftist intelligentsia would have been presumably able to capitalize on its formal political literacy, eventually restoring a form of intellectual leadership. When asked about what kind of alternative communication channel could be used to develop a successful and consistent political agenda, interviewees precisely elaborated on each of these two different approaches.

At first, most of them admittedly insisted that an alternative political discourse could hardly ever be expressed in the current context. Under al-Sisi, the scope of political repression annihilated all hopes for a consolidated opposition. However, participants also reflected on the learnings of the revolution in terms of the best possible approaches to grassroots activism and informal communication. Some argued that no consistent political discourse could ever be successful without reverting to an institutional form of politics. In their view, one could only achieve political change by engaging in traditional approach to partisan politics:

> Me, personally, I think people should engage in more institutional forms of politics. That's one form of engagement that I think people should stress on a little bit. (...) I don't think they can immediately do that but I think on the long run, the best form to support direct democracy or support institutions is to have a backbones of institutional bodies, political parties or syndicates, or unions, if you have such a backbone, then social movements, I think, would considerably benefit from it.
>
> (Nadhim,[17] leftist pro-revolutionary activist, Cairo, spring 2014)

Surprisingly, this can also be interpreted as an attempt to recover the intellectual leadership that opposition activists benefitted from in the early 2000s, when Internet was only used by a niche, small community of dissidents. In participants' terms, producing a new institutional discourse would potentially enable revolutionaries to regain the legitimacy they had lost, as social media became part of the mainstream.

All that being said, interviewees also stated that another potentially successful alternative to web activism could be found in organic and interpersonal communication genuinely involving the grassroots. Yet this touched on the need to use a language that could be relatable to the working class. Such communication practices would have to draw on a more informal political knowledge, as well as in everyday life experiences of political dissent. This involved reinventing new settings for informal communication, which would focus on interpersonal community relationships regardless of the medium or technology used for communication:

> We were relying too much on the hardware [of technology] but these ideas, these debates, these initiatives needed to go down on the streets, they needed to be more engaging to the general grassroots, who are mainly not internet users, or even if they are internet users that not entirely engaged in the design process of these initiatives, so we needed the software [of social] engagement and we did not have it.
>
> (Zakaria,[18] leftist pro-revolutionary activist, Cairo, spring 2014)

Similar views were expressed, as interviewees were asked to consider whether social media allowed them to remain in control of their political message. When answering this question, most participants reemphasized the high likelihood of seeing one's comment distorted and misinterpreted. The majority of interviewees expressed great scepticism, arguing that only the most well-established political institutions could hope to remain in control of their online political narrative:

> It depends. I don't think that you can remain in control of your political message as an individual. (...) Maybe, if you are an institution and you are [promoting your message] in the same way as traditional mass media, but then it wouldn't be social media as we know it [today]. It would be just another medium for a similar process so.
>
> (Amir,[19] leftist pro-revolutionary activist, Cairo, spring 2014)

Cyber-activist Yasmeen[20] developed a technique intended to publicly respond to online trolls attempting to discredit her by distorting the meaning of her posts. This involved tracking all false allegations by uploading regular screenshots of her online accounts. This example highlighted the extent to which this new era of cyber-activism would require foresight and long-term vision, as well as an awareness of the different political actors and narratives competing in the new social media landscape. As such, it constituted one step forward towards a more strategic and less spontaneous form of political engagement.

Most importantly, however, the immediacy of communication made revolutionaries victims of their own success. This had led them to overestimate the popularity of their political message among the broader population and created an illusion of social cohesion. By doing so, it stopped them from anticipating the return of leading political groups on the political scene. As a result, they had become aware of the need to constantly ensure the consistency of their counter-discourse and invest in the content rather than the medium of their political message:

> I think [revolutionaries] should have learned to make a distinction between an impression, an opinion and a message, these are three different things. And the fact that the immediacy of social media got all this mixed this up together (…) they still believe that the real problem is (…) that they are not allowed to speak directly to the people. But that's not the case (…) That's a failure and that's primarily a failure of communication.
>
> (Amir,[21] liberal wing of the opposition, Cairo, spring 2014)

In other words, the artificial features of the discourse – the labels and slogans – had been disseminated before its actual meaning and its ideological framework could take shape. The form of discourses was now circulating faster than its content and before the critical theory and ideology that could have consolidated this movement had even emerged. This was the reason why these labels and slogans soon became deprived of meaning, eventually serving different political agendas in the context of the constitutional debate.

In that context, many of those who were not initially engaged in the formal political sphere came to consider this option, which could have allowed them to remain in control of the revolutionary narrative. Even the young members of the Dostour party, who identified with the more radical wing of the revolution, came to advocate for a more pragmatic and strategic approach. Their objective was to enter the political game in order to materialize the demands of the revolution and prevent its reappropriation by the counterrevolutionary camp:

> [If I could go back in time], I'd change the way we did politics, we didn't want to make any compromise, we wanted to achieve all of our goals in just a matter of one year. I think there's two main mistakes that we made. The first one was, after Mohammed Mahmoud[22], we were powerful, much powerful, we could have just asked for whoever we wanted to become Prime Minister.

But we didn't, this is one big mistake. The other [mistake] was 30th June,
cause we went on the street with the counterrevolution. We should have
gone in the streets alone, not with the counterrevolution. [Laugh]

(Mehdi,[23] leftist pro-revolutionary activist, Cairo, spring 2014)

When reflecting back on the early days of the revolution Mehdi described the
euphoria of an activism not bothered by long-term vision, but practiced on
a day-to-day basis. In his opinion, the civil opposition was acting with the
immediacy of digital media and proved to be unprepared for the opportunities
that the fall of Mubarak's regime unleashed. As a result, it did not seem to
rely on the strong ideological foundations that characterized other significant
revolutionary movements throughout history. This allowed commentators to
dismiss the label of revolution in reference to 25 January, reinforcing a climate
of disillusion, which proved to be favourable to the military regime.

As opposed to what one can expect from the natural circulation of
discursive power, the Egyptian uprisings had not substituted one dominant
discourse for another. The new military dictatorship was not comparable to
any other post-revolutionary state. Unlike the Jacobin or communist regimes,
its authoritarianism was not rooted in the ideology of the revolution. Instead,
its legitimacy was built on the distortion of its symbols and the transposition its
discursive tools. The fact that the revolution did not manage to substitute one
ideological framework for another was now partly attributed to the immediacy
and chaotic nature of participative media. Online activism was accordingly
described as a performance-enhancing drogue for political dissent. It appeared
to have significantly accelerated the natural circulation of discourse. As much
as it may have facilitated the logistics of civil movements, it also induced
pernicious side effects. The Egyptian case in fact demonstrated that well-
established political groups were less likely to be challenged, despite the fact
that emergent practices would spread more rapidly into the mainstream. My
2014 research was no different in suggesting that some of the symbolic and
technological tools of the revolution had been hijacked.

All participants, regardless of their age or political background, appeared
to be rather critical with regard to the way social media had opened access to
public deliberation after the uprisings. The mainstreaming of the revolution
coincided with a sudden massification of social media that became visible
in the early 2010s. The general impression was that online deliberation had

reached a mass audience, before the opposition could produce a well-defined political message. Admittedly, the profit-driven incentives of the tech industry were partly to blame for the mainstreaming of these informal communication channels. To a large extent, the marketization of these social networks in the political field resulted from the same neoliberal logics that the leftist opposition intended to tackle, when raising issues of social injustice and inequality. Yet on some level, one is left wondering if the progressive youth of the leftist middle class was willing to apply the same communication strategy as populists to reach a mass audience. Unlike those who were proactively engaged in retail politics, the leftist opposition within the urban middle class did not master the art of populist campaigning. As a progressive intellectual elite, it was somehow ill-equipped to reach out to the masses and design a political message that would survive on the scale of the mainstream.

Beyond the very first days of the 2011 uprisings, the young pro-revolutionary left did not have much opportunity to build community relationships with the grassroots. One can hope that these connections would have spontaneously occurred, if the communication tools of the revolution had continued to evolve organically and perhaps at a different pace. Yet this would have required a high level of self-awareness from the young pro-revolutionary left, as well as an introspective reflection on the limited reach of the intelligentsia within the opposition.

Revolutions, by nature, introduce a more fluid political language in order to successfully complete a transition of power, eventually substituting one institutional discourse for another. Indeed, the language of the revolution remains dynamic, because it is constantly challenged, reframed or reappropriated, as soon as it threatens the hegemony of the status quo. This language is also likely to evolve as a consequence of the internal tensions that might occur within the revolutionary camp. Ideologues are for example primarily concerned with the need to produce a new political theory. Alternatively, those who engage in revolutionary praxis are essentially interested in the tactical moves and decision that will ensure its success. Over time, diverging views are expressed across the revolutionary camp, which might oppose the radical wing to those who will eventually embrace a reformist approach. These different types of political actors come to reconsider their perception of the revolutionary discourse as soon as it is being debated in the formal political sphere. In Egypt, the conflicts that occurred both outside and within the civil opposition are therefore relatively similar to what revolutionaries have experienced in other cases of historical regime change. However, the circulation of discursive power only requires a narrative to be fluid up to a certain point. Yet in the Egyptian case, the culture of online activism added to the fluidity of the revolutionary language, so much so that it seemed to have precipitated the transition of power in favour of the counterrevolution.

Prior to the 2011 uprisings, emerging practices of web activism had only just started to stimulate a cross-fertilization of ideas. For example, the activist blogosphere provided a more experimental social setting to political dissidents, allowing them to share their perspectives from across the ideological spectrum of the opposition. During the street mobilizations of January 2011, their critique also appeared to resonate with the experiences of the grassroots. However, activists only had a short window of time to ensure that what could become the political theory of the revolution would be informed by the political praxis of the street. As soon as the counterrevolution regained control of the public space, the young leftist intelligentsia no longer had much opportunity to interact with the grassroots. By that time, there was no point reverting back to the virtual social settings of the online space. The young progressive left of the middle class was once again limited to its own filter bubble, cultivating a language and political literacy that was ultimately more representative of the elite. Meanwhile, those who had a monopoly over populist communication channels began to thrive on the mainstream social platforms that increasingly resembled a mass media. Unlike the young leftist intelligentsia, they were happy to capitalize on populist rhetoric and identity politics. Despite the fact that this progressive youth was well-placed to produce a political theory, their efforts were jeopardized by the internal fragmentation of revolutionary voices. In some regards, web activism had contributed to the self-segregation of this young intellectual elite that was unwilling and perhaps ill-equipped to speak the popular language of the masses. Besides, as mentioned above, these voices of the opposition became ever more isolated once their communication tool became the new mainstream. In that context, they no longer had the opportunity to produce a political theory grounded in political praxis.

The main challenge of the revolution resided in the crucial intersection between the intelligentsia and the grassroots. Accordingly, the only solution one could envisage was to reproduce the conditions for intellectual leadership. And yet ironically, as they desperately tried to restore some intellectual leadership, many pro-revolutionary activists found themselves ever more isolated within their own echo chambers. Many of the researchers who observed this phenomenon at the time – myself included – applied a perspective which was sympathetic to the left-wing intelligentsia. As a result, they became primarily concerned with the decline of intellectual leadership. Just like the young leftist middle class, they called for the consolidation of well-structured opposition parties, which could have advocated for structural change in the realm of formal politics. This was viewed as the only way to produce a clear political theory. Such a strategic approach to communication was expected to provide an ideological foundation for the revolution, preventing it from being hijacked by counterrevolutionary forces.

This perspective was certainly well-rooted in the field of political communication and resonated with the idea that the masses (or crowds) are a liability rather than an asset. Little consideration was given for the alternative approach, namely the reinvention of a new medium for informal communication. Most communication scholars once again disregarded the possibility of reproducing an alternative type of decentralized channels, which could involve the grassroots through the realm of informal politics. And yet beyond the Egyptian case, one could argue that this had proved to be relatively successful in Tunisia. Around the time of its 2014 constitutional referendum, Tunisia had gained, in spite of its economic crisis, an increasingly vibrant and empowered civil society. One could argue that, besides constitutional reforms, the post-revolutionary experience of Tunisian citizenship was rooted in a genuine interest in informal politics. Even though that process was also more likely to involve the young middle class, many civil society actors were proactively trying to involve the grassroots beyond the scope of formal politics. I shall briefly return to this point in following chapters, as one can certainly learn a lot from applying such a comparative approach.

However, before I proceed, let me dwell on the critique of web activism, which was formulated over the years that followed the uprisings. Many of the communication theories that came out around the time of the Arab Spring primarily focused on digital media and its more causal forms of political engagement. This critique often blamed the failures of civil movements on digital technologies. In doing so, it certainly brought to light concerning issues about the implications of surveillance capitalism and the political economy of social media. However, by reinforcing a general climate of disillusion, this critique also laid the groundwork for the dystopian form of technological determinism that prevails today. It has indirectly, and perhaps unconsciously, justified the argument of re-centralization and securitization. By hoping for some form of intellectual leadership, this critique is only reproducing the conditions for the elitist model of Habermas's public sphere. It reflects the perspective of a progressive intelligentsia, echoing the experience of the young leftist opposition engaged in the 2011 uprisings. Like the intelligentsia of the revolution, this academic critique relies on a top-down structural approach and tends to focus on the formal political sphere when trying to assess the outcome of a revolution.

Yet unlike the pro-revolutionary youth of the middle class, this academic critique of the new mass media often fails to engage in a constructive introspection. By feeding into our dystopian fears of mass communication, it reasserts the idea that mass audiences lack agency and critical thinking. In doing so, it ultimately widens the gap between the paternalistic discourse of a liberal elite and the actual realities of the grassroots. In fact, by limiting the argument to a structural critique of the media, it externalizes some aspects of the problem and often overlooks the sociology of civil movements. Most importantly, it implies that the only way to bring structural change is to reform policy, hoping to restore some form of intellectual leadership over the public sphere. The irony though, is that this critique has accentuated the feelings of fears and subjugation that are now associated with digital technologies. By the mid-2010s, these once-informal channels were viewed as the source of terrorist propaganda, populist sentiment and disinformation. This ultimately paved the way for an increased securitization of informal communication channels, reinforcing the implicit conviction that mass audiences were blindly receptive to hate speech, populism, extremist content and conspiracy theories.

Admittedly, the findings of my 2014 fieldwork partly corroborated this body of research. It certainly contributed to demystify the myth of a 'Twitter revolution', highlighting many limitations of online activism. Interviews in fact suggested that the rapidly expanding speed of online communication did not allow opposition voices to build genuinely organic grassroots networks at a natural pace. In that context, the language of the pro-revolutionary intelligentsia would remain disconnected from the political praxis of the street. Social media usage appeared to have accelerated the circulation of discursive power (cf. Figure 1). Under these conditions, it became harder to formulate a sustainable counter-discourse, one that could successfully support political change. We began to witness an obsolescence of narratives, and a clear disconnect between critical theory and political praxis. Beyond the circles of the leftist youth, the discursive tools of the revolution that initially came out of the mobilizations would no longer evoke the same sense of belonging. They were easily reframed and ascribed a different meaning by those who promoted a normative political message, one that would be marketable to the masses. In light of these findings, one could have concluded that digital media had introduced some kind of paradigmatic shift. Yet these developments were simply due to this unprecedented scale of mass communication.

Perhaps what has been weakened in recent years is the feeling of empowerment that one can experience on that level of the discursive cycle (east axis), when critical theory intersects with the language of the grassroots and the cultural practices of subversion. The circulation of discourse as we know it is undergoing a vertiginous – almost exponential – acceleration. New media frames and narratives are being shared every day, which generate influential slogans, political labels and trending hashtags. Yet whilst they gain instant reach and recognition, these newly established narratives are rapidly counteracted. On the one hand, activists and prominent figures of the political opposition are increasingly exposed to government-led smear campaigns. In many cases, their arguments are also reappropriated by those who casually engage in the rhetoric of progressive neoliberalism, which conveniently disregards the root causes of social exclusion and polarisation. Conversely, official narratives may be easily reframed or ridiculed thanks to cultural remix and the creative expressions of political satire. These media frames are then again reappropriated thanks to the responsiveness of proactive and ever emerging subcultures.

In order to examine the conditions for the consolidation of such counter-discourse, we have to zoom in on the transition that occurs between the first and the second quarters of the discursive cycle. This is where one can hope to see the consolidation of a critical theory informed by everyday practices of resistance. It is where we see new visions for socio-political change merging or diverging. From a communication perspective, this stage of the discursive cycle is also what determines the relevance and potential success of a counter-discourse.

In light of this, the findings of my research also revealed a problematic disconnect between critical theory and political praxis. In order to succeed, the critical theory of the revolution had to be empirically grounded, drawing on everyday life experiences of cultural and communicative resistance. The work of social theorists like Deleuze and Foucault (1977) amongst others posits that a relevant critical theory should report on real-life experiences of struggle for discursive power. In order to formulate a counter-discourse, the intelligentsia should cultivate an understanding of the grassroots, and engage with the perhaps more mundane expressions of political dissent, which can be also found in the private sphere as well in popular culture. Football supporters have, for example, played an important role in the mobilization of the 2011 Tunisian uprising, and were just as instrumental to the more recent civil movement of the 2019 Algerian Hirak. In Egypt, Cairo's public buses surprisingly became one of the last few environments for public expressions of political dissent, in the aftermath of the 2013 military coup. As for the young pro-revolutionary left, it would often find comfort in new forms of art and spirituality. Many started to attend the secluded social gathering of Sufi hadra, as a way to overcome depression and isolation. These environments are essential to the regeneration of informal communication networks. Like in the early days of the revolutionary protests, these settings shed light on political praxis. Accordingly, they have the potential to inspire a critical theory and contribute to the formulation of a counter-discourse. Unfortunately, they are often overlooked, because they are viewed as part of the popular and the masses.

Yet in the case of the 2011 uprisings, these forms of empowering communication practices were often limited to the early days of the protests, when the different voices of the revolution converged through the medium of the street. Beyond the scope of street mobilizations, this disconnect with political praxis revealed deeply rooted social divides, hindering any attempt to overcome the growing fragmentation of the public sphere. In that sense, it is fair to say that the polarisation of the post-revolutionary debate was not simply due to the systemic issue of media control. This disconnect between the theory and political praxis of the revolution points to a complex combination of social factors. To a large extent, one is sociologically conditioned to speak either one of these two political languages.

In that sense, it is fair to admit that there is only so much we can blame on digital technology. The challenge of reconciling these two practices of resistance is not limited to the media. However, digital media may be acting as a magnifying glass, in highlighting the social gap between the critical language of the intelligentsia and the realities of the streets.

Yet, once they came to demystify the narrative of 'Twitter revolution', many communication scholars continued to place the emphasis on social media as a power structure designed to control the masses. They went too far in the opposite direction, introducing a dystopian form of technological determinism. A number of theories started to consider why digital activism alone was not sufficient to support long-term political change. On the one hand, some communication experts argue that these dynamics are governed by a logic of consumerism. Any attempt at consolidating a counter-discourse is accordingly expected to take place outside of the social media market. This implies that counter-hegemonic voices should remain in the informal spaces of emergent media, running the risk of being always limited to a niche for fear of centralization. Others consider that counter-hegemonic communication practices are too short-lived and sporadic. In this case, the main concern is the fact that these informal practices of resistance do not rely on any organizational structure or clear political agenda. Such a dichotomy only exemplifies the fact that we are observing a disjuncture between critical theory and the everyday practices of resistance.

The irony is that although this structural critique of the media aims to deconstruct hegemonic discourse, it ultimately fails to shift focus away from the sphere of formal power. As a result, it is unable to envision an alternative to the discursive tools of power. Because it advocates for radical structural change at the macro-level, it expects the grassroots to rely on a similar approach to communication – one that is strategically designed and operates as a top-down process. Yet those who see themselves as belonging to this critique – myself included – also need to acknowledge that such a structural perspective comes from a place of privilege.

Therefore, as much as it borrows from constructionist epistemologies, this tradition occasionally contributes to (re)construct new narratives of structural powers. Such a critique (inadvertently) acts as a self-fulfilling prophecy, further alienating the grassroots from what represents the more formal tools of power. It assumes – and thereby reasserts – a distinction between political theory and the cultural resistance of the grassroots. It assesses the success of political action on the basis of normative expectations of systemic change and legal reforms. Critical thinkers, who have expressed reservations with regard to civil engagement in the digital age, tend to apply a predominantly structural perspective, which often overlooks the experiences of grassroots actors at the micro-level. Such a critique therefore tends to advocate for a political theory of resistance. In doing so, it demonstrates very little understanding of the more technical and operational considerations at stake in the realm of grassroots activism. Ironically, this structural critique of online activism thus indirectly contributed to produce cyber-dystopian narratives, which are now used to legitimize the securitization of the online space.

8

The agenda of global security and its implication for independent media

In this chapter, I will demonstrate that the argument of global security eventually came to condition the way we think about online political engagement in the MENA region. I will start by acknowledging how the framing of the Arab Spring evolved in the mid-2010s. This will bring me to explore the shifting priorities of international donors who supported the development of a local independent media sphere. I will examine the conditions in which civil society actors could expect to receive international support for grassroots communication. In doing so, I will also outline how the funding of these activities became contingent upon the agenda of global and national security. Simultaneously, I will highlight the fears that came to be associated with the unregulated space of social media, and consider why decentralized channels were eventually perceived as a threat. The chapter will present a new set of evidence, relying on interviews conducted between the first and the second wave of the Arab Spring.

My objective here is to illustrate the second half of the discursive cycle (cf. Figure 1), which relates to recentralization and securitization. In the years following the 2011 protests, international attention shifted away from civil society. The unfolding civil conflicts in Syria and Libya arguably reshaped the memory of the 'Arab Spring', delivering a general sense of cynicism. The events of 2011 were reframed as the source of political unrest in the region and remembered through an orientalist lens. In that context, the international audience became increasingly preoccupied with migration and the political stability of the region. This ultimately introduced a climate of public disillusionment, diverting public attention away from the continuous efforts of local civil society actors, who were still actively engaged in the realm of informal politics. Most importantly, it proved to have a significant impact on the region, by legitimizing the agenda of stability and national security upheld by the actors of the counterrevolution.

Social media was once again central to the debate, due to the online recruitment strategy of insurgency groups involved in the Syrian and Libyan civil wars. In Europe and the United States, the public coincidentally grew increasingly fearful of social media platforms, as they proved to be favourable environments for populist rhetoric. In addition, the media frenzy around the mid-2010s terrorist attacks only reinforced the security lens, drawing attention to the issue of jihadi propaganda circulating on both mainstream and encrypted platforms. Eventually, these public concerns over the circulation of 'extremist' content would lead to the development of a new market for strategic communication, intended to 'counter online extremism'.

In the aftermath of the 2015–16 terrorist attacks that targeted the European cities of Paris, Brussels, Munich and London, a number of policymakers appeared to have launched a crusade against the giants of the tech industry. They called for the enforcement of clear monitoring procedures to censor online incitements to hate and violence. Tech giants, for their part, publicly responded to the attack with a sort of indecisive ambivalence in an attempt to reassure users about the potential infringement of their privacy. A new market was about to emerge in the field of strategic communication. In order to divert attention away from public concerns over transparency and accountability, a number of tech companies supported the development of what became known as 'counter-narratives'. These new types of digital campaigns were strategically designed to counter online content deemed harmful and promoted on social media as part of the prevention of violent extremism (PVE). Stakeholders from the tech industry began to collaborate with the public sector on the promotion of impactful PVE messages. Their objective was to ensure that these 'counter-narratives' were perceived as credible and implicitly tackle the issue of violent extremism, without openly disclosing their counter-terrorism agenda. To this end, they called for the involvement of local civil society actors who had the potential to reach out to the grassroots. Civil society was accordingly invited to engage in this new market for strategic communication. By supporting the creation and promotion of these initiatives, tech companies would respond to public criticisms about hate speech and extremism without having to account for the lack of transparency around content moderation. Instead, they conveniently positioned themselves as the advocates of pluralism and freedom of expression who supported the inclusion of civil society actors.

In June 2017, Facebook announced the launch of the 'Online Civil Courage Initiative' (OCCI), a partnership with the 'Institute for Strategic Dialogue (ISD)' intended to offer 'financial and marketing support to UK NGOs working to counter online extremism' (Woollaston-Webber, 2017). The initiative provided funding dedicated to NGOs and civil society organizations engaged in a number of social issues related to inclusion, diversity and the representation of minority voices. Its goal was to facilitate online campaigns likely to tackle sensitive topics as a way to prevent exposure to 'violent extremism' and 'counter' online hate speech. In order to ensure the credibility of these campaigns, civil society actors were placed at the forefront of this project. Through the scope of the OCCI, they were invited to develop 'counter-narratives' with the potential to engage members from their local communities. Tech companies, for their part, would provide corporate technical tools to optimize the visibility of these messages and assess the degree of community engagement by relying on standardized online metrics. This new market for strategic communication was reproduced elsewhere, generating particular interest in countries, where governments were committed to demonstrate extra counterterrorism efforts. Multisector organizations involved in the prevention of 'violent extremism' (PVE) hosted international workshops across the MENA region. As part of these events, international donors, local NGOs and religious leaders were invited to share ideas about the alternative messaging that had the potential to engage the young, disillusioned audience. As much as these events and trainings were presented as an opportunity to include civil society actors, they often promoted the jargon of counterterrorism, reasserting some of the binary assumptions that prevailed in the security sector, such as law enforcement and the military.

It is in this context that local 'counter-narrative' campaigns were funded or collaboratively designed by governmental organizations. This extended to official religious authorities, such as the Rabita Mohammedia League of religious scholars in Morocco or the Al Azhar's Observatory for Combating Extremism in Egypt. Some of the organizations involved in the implementation of these initiatives had strong ties with MENA governments, as in the case of the non-profit Assakina organization supported by the Saudi Ministry of Foreign Affairs, the Sawab Centre supported by the US and UAE governments or the Global Center for Combating Extremist Ideology in Saudi Arabia (Etidal).

Within these multisector networks, the emphasis was placed on the role that civil society actors could play in engaging 'vulnerable' audiences, who were described as granting little credibility to official news sources. The intention behind the consolidation of these campaigns was, in essence, very similar to what drives governments' responses to disinformation and conspiracy theories. These projects stem from the realization that public trust is in decline and that official news channels – along with public institutions in general – are no longer considered as credible sources of information. Civil society actors were understandably seen as better placed to engage with the audiences at risk of exposure to violent or potentially harmful content.

On paper, this appeared to be a highly marketable idea. It spoke to the need to involve civil society on some of the public issues that had been initially restricted to the realm of formal politics. In Tunisia, the approach seemed to resonate, at first, with a broader range of public policies intended to empower civil society, stimulating genuine enthusiasm amongst civil society actors from the urban middle class. A number of communication projects were accordingly launched under the supervision of a governmental unit called the National Institution for Counter-Discourse ('Instance Nationale pour Le Discours Alternatif'). As much as they were expected to restore trust in national politics, these civil society actors saw this as an opportunity to redirect attention towards a shared sense of ownership over public institutions. Their objective was to promote an alternative culture of citizenship, by inspiring trust in the 2014 constitution and the recent reforms of the judiciary system. This was, in their view, a vision of public trust that contrasted entirely with the way national security had traditionally been addressed under the previous regime. In their view, the real challenge was to restore the legitimacy of the political project initiated by the revolution, without serving the credibility of the elected elites. From a reformist perspective, their involvement was strategically justifiable. Such hopeful endeavours nevertheless remained constrained by the framework of public bureaucracy. Ultimately, their ambitious vision was compromised by the security lens that conditioned the language and expectations of international donors.

In 2015, UN Secretary-General Ban Ki-moon presented a Plan of Action (PoA) for the prevention of violent extremism (PVE), which was to be used as a template for the implementation of national strategies. The UN PoA was structured around a number of core pillars and recommendations aligned with the new American counter-terrorism doctrine developed under the Obama administration. The idea was to shift policies away from a 'coercive' approach to apply a 'more holistic' framework that would involve a broader range of social actors, beyond the scope of the military, law enforcement and the traditional security sector. In this context, strategic communication was granted a particular significance. Communication activities were expected not only to counter terrorist propaganda, but also to contribute to the involvement of civil society actors and the independent media sphere in the growing PVE market. The PoA advocated strategic communication as part of a range of practices geared towards 'dialogue', 'reconciliation' and the engagement of 'vulnerable' communities with the help of civil society. It highlighted the importance of the independent media sphere amongst other social imperatives, such as gender equality and education. More specifically, the PoA presented strategic communication as an opportunity to provide a potentially safer environment for bloggers and independent journalists. Besides, this framework also referred to the issue of privacy and state surveillance, calling for a national strategy that would comply with human rights in the realm of strategic communication (Hussein, 2021: 75). Overall, this holistic take on the prevention of extremism was framed as an attempt to empower civil society actors. In theory, this could have allowed them to benefit from the international support required to work on those deeper social issues, which had been consistently neglected due to global security imperatives. In practice however, the field of strategic communication remained a one-way stream of influence, which was predominantly conditioned by the very same agenda of global and national security that had been historically invoked to repress civil society. In fact, the international pressure around the prevention of 'violent extremism' had pernicious effects on civil society, because its engagement was engineered as part of a top-down security response to the threat of terrorism.

In addition to corporate actors from the tech industry, international players like the EU reasserted the importance of strategic communication in the region. In 2016, the European parliament announced the establishment of a Task Force for Outreach and Communication in the Arab world. EU policymakers issued a briefing on EU Strategic Communication with the Arab World, in which they presented the rationale for strategic outreach and communication activities in the region. The briefing commented on the need to respond to the terrorist threat, while managing Europe's relationship with Arab neighbours in the midst of the humanitarian crisis that resulted from civil conflicts. The Arab Spring was explicitly viewed as a failure and implicitly described as the trigger of a 'security vacuum', which had paved the way for the resurgence of terrorism:

> [...] the 'Arab Spring' was not entirely a success story. [...] The ensuing humanitarian crisis and the flow of refugees have once again tested Europe's relationship with its Arab neighbours [...] At the same time, the threat posed by terrorist groups like ISIL/Da'esh and Al-Qaeda, [...] has brought the need to counter the jihadi narrative and violent extremism more broadly to the fore, including through more strategic outreach and communication with the Arab countries"
>
> (European Parliament, 2016: 2)

In this context, strategic communication was expected to bring together governmental and civil society actors to officially 'strengthen the overall media environment' and raise awareness about 'disinformation activities' (European Parliament, 2016). The objective was to re-centralize the debate and restore the credibility of the more official communication platforms, which were subjected to surveillance and regulation. Simultaneously, these strategic communication activities intended to promote the image of the EU in the region through the scope of initiatives implemented by civil society partners and foreign cultural offices. The emphasis was placed on media capacity, alternative media content exploring new genres and formats, and initiatives designed to support the sphere of independent journalism. Through the scope of art, culture and journalism, the EU would benefit from the framework of soft power and cultural diplomacy to improve its image. According to the official EU narrative, the core objective was to 'strengthen the capacity of the media and civil society', whilst 'winning the heart and minds of Arab societies' (European Parliament, 2016: 6).

From the perspective of local independent media, the imperative of global and national security presented different challenges. Across the region, these concerns have significantly influenced the priorities and expectations of international donors likely to support the engagement of civil society in the alternative media sphere. Many of the campaigns and workshops involving 'counter-narratives' or 'alternative narratives' intended to reach an audience which was assumed to be inherently vulnerable to 'extremism' because of socioeconomic or political marginalization. Though this idea may seem to acknowledge the sociological parameters that are too often eclipsed by the fear of terrorism, it only reinforced the stigma of marginalization. In its early phase of development, this new communication market also relied on another form of technological determinism: the belief that social media would provide measurable indicators of impact to assess the potential success of these campaigns. Following a logic of cost-effectiveness, civil society partners were encouraged to allocate their resources to online campaigning when implementing projects around public trust, media capacity or youth engagement. Corporate practices of online marketing were initially used to assess the visibility and credibility of these actors amongst the targeted audience. Yet the reliability and the relevance of these online metrics of engagement remained highly questionable. Most importantly, international donors and stakeholders from the tech industry placed the incentive of these projects on short-term quantifiable reach. In doing so, they overlooked the importance of organic social interactions and community relationships, which is arguably essential to public trust. Had they applied a bottom-up perspective genuinely informed by civil society, they would have perhaps realized that social capital relies on interpersonal and organic communication. Instead, they transposed the 'one-to-many' communication stream of the old media into the supposedly more inclusive and interactive sphere of social media.

Ultimately, this would generate new challenges for the local civil society organizations eager to secure funding for youth engagement, media capacity or independent journalism.

Those who were more likely to interact with grassroots communities on the ground were now expected to communicate *strategically* online. Insidiously, this would affect their ability to remain involved in the more organic experiences of bottom-up communication that continued to consolidate counter-publics in the peripheries of the public sphere. On the one hand, civil society partners involved in these initiatives would have the opportunity to receive funding or technical skills, while demonstrating capacity to a broader range of potential benefactors. On the other hand, embracing the language of international donors would often bring them to compromise on the framing of their activities. Due to the security-sensitive nature of these campaigns, civil society partners were not always able to operate in full transparency. Under the holistic framework introduced by the UN and the United States' new counterterrorism doctrine, international players occasionally attempted to downplay the security tone, poorly concealing it through other realms of activities. Locally, the emphasis was placed on education, entrepreneurship, community resilience or media capacity. Yet the design and implementation of these communication projects would nevertheless centre around the jargon and priorities of international donors, implicitly revealing the incentive of global security.

Civil society would then have to navigate these pressures without compromising on its pro-revolutionary ethos. In Tunisia, local CSOs experienced the same tensions I described earlier with regard to the activist blogosphere. On the one hand, the sector had been proactively engaged in constitutional reforms. It continued to advocate for freedom of speech and social justice, while denouncing corruption and nurturing informal politics. To a large extent, civil society proved to have gained more agency in post-revolutionary Tunisia than in many of the countries typically considered well-established democracies. On the other hand, those civil society actors, who appeared to be more successful at securing resources, were often viewed as part of a privileged urban elite. They benefitted from a high level of education, an international network, as well as the linguistic skills and political literacy required to frame their activity in response to donors' priorities.

In this context, international concerns over security and migration only added to the ethical challenges faced by civil society. Stuck between a rock and a hard place, some civil society partners came to apply a reformist approach within the field of strategic communication. They welcomed the development of technical skills and resources likely to benefit the sphere of emergent media, whilst hoping to challenge the security lens. They would thereby find themselves in an ambivalent posture, risking their credibility as legitimate intermediaries and potential representatives of the grassroots.

This aura of compromised credibility was, to a large extent, detrimental to local civil society organizations. It was continuously weaponized by populist leaders to suggest that local NGOs leaning towards the civil pro-revolutionary opposition intended to serve foreign interests. In reality, the ways in which these organizations negotiate ethical considerations in relation to technical constraints are, of course, far more complex. The sector includes a broad spectrum of institutions, ranging from social enterprises to small non-profit associations, with various degrees of proximity to the grassroots, political elites and international donors. Across the scope of non-governmental organizations, there is unequal access to skills and resources to navigate bureaucratic constraints and limited funding opportunities.

a. The Tunisian case

In Tunisia however, some of the more established civil society actors would occasionally find their credibility compromised. The independent media sphere in particular was not always seen as fully 'independent' in the eyes of the general population. Whilst they were considered as more reliable, some of the alternative news platforms that gained recognition in the aftermath of the revolution were often perceived as being part of a politicized community of activists, or inclined towards a particular ideological perspective. A range of independent media platforms including Nawaat, Inkyfada and I Watch gained recognition by delivering in-depth investigative reporting and denouncing cases of corruption in the political and mainstream media sphere. However, this market was generally viewed as limited to a niche audience and almost entirely dependent on foreign donors, which affected its sustainability and occasionally undermine its claim to impartiality. Those who gained recognition by regulatory bodies like the National Union of Tunisian Journalists were becoming more established, thus likely to be associated with the national media outlets. This institutional recognition was likely to inspire a greater sense of distrust, given that the national media market was known to be biased and corrupted. In 2019, non-profit organizations like Youth Can and Youth Decides offered events, workshops and talk shows, which were proactively promoted on their official Facebook pages. Yet these initiatives appeared to have a relatively small level of engagement on social media, and had been condemned in Facebook posts for serving the interests of a privileged elite of civil society actors.

With the exception of local community radio stations, the mainstream media outlets were said to cultivate outdated genres and forms of storytelling that no longer resonated with the younger public. Mainstream media outlets were generally not considered as reliable, due to a lack of rigorous investigation and relationships of clientelism with political elites. Institutions in charge of the professionalization of journalists like IPSI (the Institute of the Press and Information Sciences) along with official bodies of media regulation were described as unable to promote and implement clear mechanisms of accountability:

> Certain people have a real control over the official media environment in Tunisia, and when the media coverage does not comply with their views, it is automatically blocked. I personally think that it is due to an outdated structure that has kept applying an archaic system over the years and it is the same in many other official institutions in Tunisia, beyond the media environment, like in the sectors of health, transports, education. But that inability to innovate and evolve is particularly visible in the media because the media needs to adapt and reflect society day to day.
>
> (Member of a local NGO, Tunis; January 2020)

Besides the political economy of the mainstream media, its framing of social issues had increased feelings of exclusion amongst the youth. Younger demographics felt at odds with the stereotypical representations of the youth that would prevail in the national media discourse. The national media had produced both negative and positive stereotypes of the Tunisian youth that misrepresented its voices in the public debate. The former related to the depiction of the urban, affluent and highly educated youth, often idealized and presented as successful entrepreneurs likely to conform with social norms. In contrast, the latter was typically associated with the more disfranchised youth from inland Tunisia, portrayed as a threat to the social order.

Mirroring the priorities that international donors imposed upon civil society, the national media also remained centred on the issue of terrorism. This only added to the stigmatization of disfranchised youths, diverting attention away from the question of social inequality. Coverage of terrorism dominated the agenda of the mass media, only to serve a trend towards sensationalism and without being appropriately addressed in the public debate. Many civil society actors engaged in the field of art, culture and independent journalism were thus hoping to provide more relevant content to address social issues from a new angle that would contrast with the national media and political discourse:

> As you know there was an attack here in Tunis in 2015 on Mohammed Khamis Avenue, and I will always remember the coverage by traditional Tunisian media, which was highly problematic. The national media could only describe the attacker as an alien, and they never really wanted to address the real issues and sociological causes, what the real reason was. Whereas us all, the youth, we know perfectly well what the real problem is. There is a minimum of responsibility, coming from the media to contemplate on the real social causes of terrorism; cause in reality this is all due to precarity. During that period, none of main media outlets decided to conduct a real investigation; trying to really understand what brings a young individual to do this.
>
> (Co-founder of an art initiative for the youth, Tunis; January 2020)

The disconnect between mainstream media and the perspective of the disfranchised youths essentially widened the gap between formal and informal politics. Young audiences manifested interest in soft news topics and innovative formats. They would share videos of local and regional YouTube influencers focusing on sport, entertainment, political satire or popular culture. Within the professionalized sector of traditional media, this was often interpreted as a lack of public engagement. The conventional wisdom was that younger demographics were somehow not interested in politics because of their apparent detachment from mainstream news channels with a focus on the national political debate. In reality, the popularity of emerging media demonstrated an acute political awareness and a desire to tackle public issues from a refreshing angle, employing media content crafted by the audience. Some actors from the independent media scene proactively advocated in favour of emerging media. In 2019, the Tunisian media watchdog 'I Watch' launched an 'alternative media' portfolio of activities bringing young talents and YouTube influencers to collaborate on a range of projects around alternative journalistic practices, media genres and storytelling. The programme included public events, workshops and artistic collaborations between cartoonists and creators, promoting comic book satire, YouTube chronicles, rap or slam. This reminds us that civil society remains, in many cases, instrumental to the development of emerging media, invalidating populist attacks to its reputation. Simultaneously, it shows why its ethos and credibility should never be compromised by the agenda of global security.

A critical approach to media development however reminds us that donors continue to make sense of the local media market through a Eurocentric lens. The intention is to 'educate' the audience, commonly viewed as misguided and vulnerable. It is this insidiously paternalistic attitude that continues to condition international support to media development. The 'strings attached' of international funding generate particular challenges in cases where civil society intends to focus on communication and public trust. They may affect the sense of community ownership that creates added value in emergent media. Simultaneously, they involve more risks for civil society actors working towards media freedom and independent journalism. This became very clear in light of the new security-driven approach to strategic communication that pretended to support the inclusion of civil society.

In Tunisia, the state of emergency was implemented in 2015 under the administration of former President Beji Caid Essebsi. The country had suffered a series of terrorist attacks and was under international pressure to demonstrate counterterrorism efforts due to the high estimated numbers of Tunisian recruits who had joined jihadi insurgencies in Syria. The government was expected to develop a national counterterrorism strategy in line with the 2015 UN 'Plan of Action to Prevent Violent Extremism'. Along with Lebanon and Morocco, Tunisia was among the first countries in the region to elaborate its national strategy on the basis of these UN recommendations (Hussein, 2021). However, this process was primarily motivated by national concerns over the expectations of the foreign governments involved in the international cooperation on counterterrorism. As a matter of fact, the Tunisian committee in charge of drafting the national strategy for the prevention of violent extremism was placed under the supervision of the Tunisian Ministry of Foreign Affairs. The main partner advising the committee on the development of the strategy was none other than the Executive Director of the United Nations Counter-Terrorism Centre (UNCCT).[1] Foreign actors, including the European Union, the UN and the UK Home office played an important role in the implementation of the first social initiatives designed to bring the plan of action into effect. Some of the early projects geared towards a social approach to the prevention of 'violent extremism' were conditioned by the incentives and preliminary assumptions of international donors. They were also supervised by foreign executives, who did not always understand the complexities and particularities of the Tunisian context.

This was especially the case with regard to initiatives related to strategic communication. The Research Information and Communication Unit (RIKU) of the UK Home Office also collaborated with the Tunisian government, promoting the infamous 'Prevent' framework originally used in the UK. The strategy was in other words advised by the very same policy which had already been heavily contested in the British press and criticized by grassroots organizations tackling discriminatory policies and Islamophobia in the UK (e.g. CAGE).[2] Indeed, the UK PVE framework was criticized for stigmatizing minorities associated with the threat of terrorism. Within the broader security sector and the emerging market of strategic communication, the trend was to direct international aid to the areas perceived as the most vulnerable to extremism. As a result, most of the projects funded by international donors were therefore implemented in the 'Tunisie de l'intérieur' and the regions bordering Libya and Algeria. Consequently, the neighbourhoods of Tunis and the other coastal regions beyond Tunis were dramatically neglected. Sousse, Monastir and the broader Sahel region, for example, did not benefit from the same resources. And yet these areas presented an alarmingly high degree of social inequalities, in spite of the existence of a more privileged middle class.

The international imperative around the prevention of violent extremism quickly transpired through the funding available to civil society. Indeed, the UN PoA along with the priorities of the EU called for a proactive involvement of civil society in the field of strategic communication. At the time, it had been argued that these policies intended to engage a broader range of social actors, by broadening perspectives beyond the security sphere. However, many of the civil society actors interviewed for my research stated that this process ultimately resulted in a pernicious professionalization of civil society. Tunis-based organizations that benefitted from a well-connected international network were more likely to understand the expectations set by international donors and secure the available grants. Alternatively, local community associations that would have been better placed to engage with a relevant audience of beneficiaries were far less likely to receive funding. Over time, this may have contributed to shaping the image of a privileged community of metropolitan civil society actors, who had grown to become disconnected from the grassroots.

And it is precisely this general sentiment that eventually resonated with the anti-establishment rhetoric of Kais Said during the presidential election of 2019. The demand for strategic communication skills in the prevention of 'violent extremism' occasionally triggered opportunistic responses from some of the most resourceful civil society organizations. The issue was recurrently invoked to fund a broad range of initiatives related to youth representation, gender equality, education as well as the development of the independent media sphere. As a result, many civil society actors became well-versed in the political jargon underpinning the prevention of violent extremism. This raises an important question around the shift that this supposedly 'holistic' PVE approach was expected to introduce. Instead of supporting the media capacity of civil society actors, it limited the scope of communication activities to global security imperatives. Most importantly, it took advantage of their credibility and grassroots reach to serve a PVE agenda that was more often than not irrelevant to the particularities of local contexts. At the same time, the national media repeatedly covered terrorism from a sensationalist angle, which only reaffirmed the stigma of socioeconomic and political marginalization. The Tunisian public longed for an inclusive and constructive take on the matter, which could account for the real social and existential causes of the problem. However, although the independent media sphere was expected to meet this need, it was not always perceived as fully independent.

This context created a window of opportunity for political actors like Saied, who relied on informal communication practices to campaign during the 2019 presidential election. I mentioned earlier the fact that an informal approach to political campaigning is often more successful in motivating voters' engagement. This is exemplified by the case of conservative parties like Ennahda or the Egyptian Muslim Brotherhood, which both initially relied on a long history of grassroots associative work to gain representation after the 2011 uprisings. Another example can be found in the events that led to the election of Tunisian president Kais Saied.

During the second round of the 2019 presidential race, Saied was competing against the businessman and media mogul Nabil Karoui. The two candidates capitalized on very different resources and campaigning strategies. Karoui eventually stood out as a representative of the political establishment. The candidate had been arrested on charges of tax evasion and money laundering. He was also under investigation by the Independent High Authority for Elections (ISIE) for having allegedly benefitted from the exposure he gained from his own media outlet Nessma TV. This introduced a debate on issues of corruption within the national media sphere. The controversy revealed that traditional media outlets had lost credibility amongst the youths and other disfranchised segments of the Tunisian society who felt excluded and misrepresented in the national public sphere. Media watchdogs and civil society actors voiced their concerns about the partiality of national news channels calling for clear mechanisms of transparency and accountability to prevent relationships of clientelism between the media and political elites. The High Authority for Independent Audiovisual Communication (HAICA) in charge of monitoring media coverage of the campaign reported that other official media outlets (including TV channels El Hiwar Ettounsi, AttessiaTV, Zitouna TV, Hannibal TV and the radio Al Quran Al-Karim) had transgressed the rules and regulations set to ensure media independence (Kapitalis, 2019). Opposite Karoui, Kais Saied, on the other hand, had gained popularity amongst the youths by engaging in grassroots communication practices, which contrasted with traditional approaches to political campaigning. A local civil society actor interviewed at the time stated:

'Having coffee at the local café is part of the Tunisian culture. It is the only leisure available to young people in Tunisian society. [...] As you know, usually, an election campaign requires a lot of money, but in the case of president Kais Saied ... well, he almost did not spend anything. Because he invested time and kept meeting people in local cafés across the country. He spent four years visiting different cities and meeting with members of the youths'.

(Interviewee, SOAS CGMC dataset, Tunis, January 2020)

In the days following the announcement of Saied's election, supporters inspired by the unexpected outcome of the campaign reclaimed ownership of the public space, working collaboratively to refurbish the streets, which had been poorly maintained by local municipalities. The initiative was charged with a powerful symbolic message, reaffirming the agency of the youths over the streets. In October 2019, the regional news platform Al-Monitor reported that 'since the run-off presidential election held Oct. 13 elevated the outsider Kais Saied to Tunisia's presidency, cleaning campaigns and painting initiatives have been popping up around the country, organized via Facebook' (Foroudi, 2019).

During this period, Saied's campaign unexpectedly stimulated the enthusiasm of the Tunisian youths: an electorate which was preferably engaged in informal politics, because it had felt underrepresented and marginalized from the formal political sphere. It was thanks to the informality of the streets and local cafes that the candidate won the election, ultimately demonstrating the political consciousness of the youths to the political establishment:

> During the last presidential election, everyone was surprised cause they did not expect such an important election turnout within the youths. They kept saying 'youths don't vote', 'youths don't follow politics', and in the end we have a president that is supported by the youths, who have been very influential on social media. A candidate, who came from nowhere, who was not really involved in the traditional political sphere. He was elected thanks to youths' support and they informal power and influence on society.
>
> (Interviewee, SOAS CGMC dataset, Tunis, January 2020)

Amongst international observers, however, Saied was predominantly described as a populist. Many did not expect him to have such an important reach amongst the Tunisian youths, because of his conservative views on the topics of death penalty, inheritance law and homosexuality. Most international commentators therefore disregarded the question of his popularity amongst young voters, arguing that his anti-establishment rhetoric was nothing but the sign of the declining trust in partisan politics:

> During the 2019 his political rhetoric amongst the youths has been described as 'populist'. Personally I am not a fan of this term, I believe it is quite a vague term to describe the complexity of what is going on. This is how it was particularly described by political elite. I think the political elites found it convenient to labelled his approach as 'populist' precisely because he has these vague accusations of the entire political class. By doing this, he was tapping into a widespread disapproval of the political class, which typically gets labelled as populism. How we want to label it is one thing, but when

it comes to the more complex mechanisms of his campaign, I think this deserves a real investigation.

Fadil Alirizia, Founder of Meshkal.org,
Tunis, September 2021

To some extent, this argument implied that his support base lacked judgement or political awareness, hence reasserting prevailing assumptions about the ostensible passiveness of the youths in the public debate. It presupposed that Saied's electorate remained ill-equipped or misinformed, thus refuting their agency as well as their call for mobilization in the particular case of the campaign. This prevailing perspective resonated with Western concerns about the erosion of the political centres and the rise of populism. The use of decentralized campaigning practices was analysed through a European lens, with little consideration for the particularities of the Tunisian context. Within this discourse, grassroots campaigning was associated with a potential threat to Tunisia's burgeoning democracy. As a result, the reasons behind its success were altogether disregarded.

This partly explains why the subsequent events took many international observers by surprise. Indeed, many analysts did not initially grasp the significance of the mobilizations that led to the coup of 25 July 2021. It was on that day that Tunisians marched the streets to protest inefficient lockdown restrictions, which had severally accentuated the economic crisis. This led President Kais Saied to reaffirm his anti-establishment position, taking action against the leading coalitions and political parties sitting in parliament. On that day, Saied dismissed Prime Minister Hicham Mechichi and invoked article 80 of the Tunisian constitution to dissolve the parliament for a period of thirty days.

Many international commentators took a strong stand against Saied's decision, labelling it as an attack against Tunisian democracy. Yet in the early days of the political crisis, local independent media platforms reported that many Tunisian protesters initially considered this to be a legitimate attempt at holding political elites accountable. Once again, like in the case of the 2019 campaign, the international media had failed to address the context behind protesters' grievances. In the midst of the global epidemic, foreign observers could only witness the events from up far and were thus unable to relay the voices of the mobilized youths. This occasionally led them to project their own fear of populism on the Tunisian case, in ways that ultimately benefitted Saied's anti-establishment rhetoric. Two months after the coup, local civil society actors involved in the independent media sphere raised the fact that the international discourse around Saied may have ironically contributed to his popularity:

> [The perspective of international commentators] may even have an effect when it comes to strengthening Saied's base. Many of us have noticed that he was getting even more popular recently given the international discourse around him. [His support base] would think 'oh look at these foreigners trying to intervene in domestic politics'. Political figures opposing Saied had to clearly stake out that they are either not meeting with foreign delegations or putting out statements suggesting they might criticise the president but 'actually stand out against any form of international intervention'. The international discourse attacking the president has generated a clear discomfort. Overall this international discourse may very well be feeding into the recent polarisation inside Tunisia. The interaction between these political narratives has been under-studied but deserves more attention.
>
> (Independent journalist and civil society actors, *Fadil Alirizia, Founder of Meshkal.org, Tunis, September 2021*)

In some regards, the reading of international commentators discounted the political awareness of Tunisian civil society. It implied that the civil mobilizations had paved the way to the coup and discounted a long history of controversies involving formal institutions, coalitions and parties as well as other political actors – besides Saied. It also dismissed the role that protesters played, shifting our attention away from the streets to focus once again on the political sphere and the drama involving leading parties and the presidential palace.

In contrast to international commentators, local independent news platforms highlighted the fact that those taking part in the demonstrations remained cautious and critically engaged in the public mobilizations (Ben Mbarek, 2021). Since the 2019 election, they had manifested the desire to rethink, question and disrupt the normative framework of political institutions. However, this did not necessarily translate into a blind faith in populist rhetoric. To a certain extent, the series of civil mobilizations that were initiated around the time of the election reaffirmed some aspects of the 2011 revolution, calling for a substantial transformation of the political culture, a 'fundamental chang[e] in the political system' (Ben Mbarek, 2021). Tunisian analysts proposed a different interpretation, re-exploring the context of 2019 campaign and examining the reasons why elected officials had lost their legitimacy. In contrast to international observers, many local analysts interpreted the coup as the result and continuation of a long political crisis that predated the election. They challenged the idea according to which the coup marked the end of Tunisian democracy, diffusing blame among political actors to deliver a sense of shared responsibility over the events. In doing so, they also reaffirmed the feeling of agency that young voters, protesters and civil society actors had asserted over the months leading to the election.

That is not to say that Saied's repressive politics was not damaging to freedom of speech and the independent media sphere. On the contrary, it is very clear that local activists and independent journalists are now facing more personal threats, attacks, arrests and prosecution. At the time of writing, Tunisian blogger and activist Amina Mansoor had just been sentenced to six months of jail for posting a Facebook comments, which criticized the president. In light of this, it is clear that the fears related to the rise of populism are certainly legitimate. However, these fears are often counter-productive when it comes to envisioning an alternative to populist rhetoric. In reality, these apprehensions alone do not help address the genuine feelings of exclusion and misrepresentation that drive anti-establishment sentiment amongst the grassroots.

b. The Egyptian case

Egypt was perhaps amongst the countries where the agenda of counterterrorism was the most outwardly detrimental to civil society. In July 2013, General Abdel-Fattah al-Sisi gave a speech in which he demanded a 'mandate to combat terrorism' (The Tahrir Institute for Middle East Policy, 2013). The military leader called everyone to join the opposition against the Friday marches held by Morsi's supporters. Over the following weeks, the tension between the Muslim Brotherhood and its opponents resulted in multiple clashes in the cities of Cairo, Mansoura, Damietta and Tanta. The violence culminated on 14 August 2013, when the Egyptian security forces killed over 800 supporters of the Muslim Brotherhood, who were participating in a large sit-in on Rabaa al-Adawiya and al-Nahda squares.

The military rhetoric on terrorism and national security would subsequently always be linked to the traumatic memory of these events. Over the first few years following the military coup, the legacy of the 'Rabaa al-Adawiya' massacre helped manufacture the legitimacy of the military regime, conjuring up a sense of victory over the Muslim Brotherhood (Amnesty International, 2019). The clearing of the squares served the counterrevolutionary narrative of the 'June 30' so-called revolution. In November 2013, an anti-protest law was issued by interim President Adly Mansour, which intended to regulate the right to public meetings, processions and peaceful demonstrations (Hamzawy, 2016). The securitization and recentralization of the public sphere ultimately fed into the polarisation that was already perceptible during the presidential and constitutional debates of 2012. It allowed the new military regime to portray the opposition as a threat and blame it for the worsening of the economic crisis during 2011–13 the post-revolutionary transition. In 2014, the country repeatedly experienced long periods of power cuts, which the military regime officially blamed on Morsi's administration and its Muslim Brotherhood affiliates, who had previously served as the Minister of Electricity. These electricity shortages presumably resulted from poor quality fuel but were strategically described as 'terrorist acts' and intentional 'sabotage' (Mada Masr, 2014).

The crackdown on the Muslim Brotherhood, which was carried out under the banner of counterterrorism, was not limited to public services. It affected a broad range of social institutions, including nongovernmental organizations, the judiciary, the higher education sector and the media (Zollner, 2019). The agenda of counterterrorism was repeatedly used to legitimize these forms of coercion and repression, both domestically and in the eyes of the international community. The new military regime appeared to be clearly aligned with the shifting priorities of the EU and its emphasis on political stability and migration. Its security discourse also resonated with US foreign policy under the Trump administration. Amongst former activists and civil society actors, the general impression was that international players were quick to disengage, in spite of the hopes that had been expressed about the civil opposition in the early stages of the 2011 uprisings. Any political references to the 'Arab

Spring' would become limited to the case of Libya and Syria, suggesting that civil mobilizations would inevitably result in conflict. Amongst Western governments, this trope spoke to real concerns about the rise of new political forces, which could have jeopardized foreign interests by adding to the geopolitical complexity of the region. In essence, the subtext of this discourse was that such a totalitarian regime was a lesser evil than the potential chaos of emerging militias.

Simultaneously, the arguments of stability and national security were conveniently used to repress opposition voices domestically. In a 2017 interview, a lawyer and local political analyst stated:

> All that Egypt has done is decide to take the banner of counterterrorism and make everything the purview of national security, so every single act can be criminalised and defined as harming the state. And if you are harming the state, it is an issue of national security, which carries terrorism charges and carries death penalty as a maximum charge, if you are arrested. It is everything from insulting the judiciary, the president or the police to insulting the state or trying to bring down the state. (...) They are now expanded these charges to being terrorism charges.
>
> (Lamia, 2017)[3]

As reported by Human Rights Watch (2017: 1), local independent human rights groups documented cases of arbitrary arrests and enforced disappearances. Between 2013 and 2016, it was estimated that forty-four individuals had died from torture whilst detained by the police (Human Rights Watch, 2017). Along with Muslim Brotherhood supporters, pro-revolutionary activists and human rights defenders were prosecuted on a number of charges. These included participation in terrorist activities, engaging in human rights activities without a license, spreading false information or inciting rebellion with the intention to harm national security (Human Rights Watch, 2017). When they were not directly facing prosecution, activists were regularly exposed to government-led smear campaigns. Back in 2011, Egyptian human rights groups appealed to the UN, denouncing the SCAF's targeted efforts to discredit local civil society groups by using online pro-government channels (Hassan and Shenker, 2011). Online rumours were circulated to suggest that these local actors were funded by foreign entities with a secret agenda. These human rights organizations, which were already operating within a restrictive legal framework, would eventually be exposed to further regulations and state interference in their operational activities.

In May 2017, President al-Sisi signed a new law granting extraordinary state powers over local NGOs. The new bill would drastically affect the funding opportunities and freedom of expression of all civil society actors, including those associated with foreign entities (Transparency International, 2017). Under penalty of law involving prison terms and fines, any publications issued by civil society organizations would have to be formally approved by the government. Along with the argument of 'public order' and 'public morality', 'national security' was once again invoked in the framing of these tighter regulations. Through the security lens, the right to freedom of association was easily dismissed on the grounds that it represented a political threat to the status quo. Simultaneous to the promulgation of the law, twenty-one websites – including those hosting independent media platforms – were blocked for allegedly spreading disinformation, terrorist content or violent extremism. The very same month, a smear campaign was circulated on national media attacking activists who had taken part in international conferences reporting on human rights abuses (Transparency International, 2017).

In 2018, President Sisi passed a new 'cybercrime' legislation allowing a court to block any website deemed a threat to the state. The new law exposed content providers to 'jail terms of up to five years and fines ranging between 10,000 and 20 million Egyptian pounds' (Al Jazeera News, 2018). The law even extended the scope of these penalties to users, who may have unintentionally accessed websites banned for threatening the country's economic interests and national security. The same year, the Egyptian parliament passed another law, subjecting social media accounts with more than 5,000 followers to prosecution if they were to publish false news (Reuters, 2018). In line with the rhetoric of the Trump administration, the Egyptian government intended to tackle the issue of disinformation as part of its broader project of Internet securitization. Without providing any clear definition of 'fake news', the bill reserved all powers to implement the law to the Supreme Council for the Administration of the Media. 'Fake news' was weaponized to repress civil activists like the women's rights advocate Amal Fathy, who was arrested in May 2018 for posting a Facebook video holding the government accountable for the issue of sexual harassment (Amnesty International, 2018). In this case the charges included 'spreading false news', 'harming national interest' and incitement to terrorism (Michaelson, 2018c). This only intensified in the recent context of the global pandemic, which further legitimized the implementation of tighter mechanisms of control and surveillance over local information channels. In 2020, EuroMed Rights released a report stating that opportunities for social media activism were continuously shrinking:

> The narrative behind eliminating coronavirus fake news became a new Trojan horse to further curtail the space for independent voices. Arrests for social media posts are frequent, and while repression was already the norm, the current circumstances have rendered it more concerning as 'the government is simply using this COVID-19 situation to do whatever they please'.
>
> (EuroMed Rights, 2020: 2–3)

The country experienced a peak of Covid-19 cases between March and June 2020, during which activists and journalists were arrested and accused of spreading misinformation detrimental to the management of the health crisis. They were charged on the basis of the laws on Anti-Cybercrimes (2018) and Anti-terrorism (Ifex, 2021).

Within this highly restrictive legal framework, surveillance and censorship considerably affected access to alternative media. Mada Masr, the last independent news website operating in Egypt could no longer be accessed by a local audience from 2017. At the time of writing, VPNs and mirror sites remained the only way to bypass surveillance and censorship. However, their servers and websites were blocked in the country and would often need to be downloaded from abroad. Open-source privacy networks designed to browse the web anonymously, such as Tor, would be blocked and their legality remained unclear. On the part of users, these tools would also involve a certain degree of digital literacy as well as a compromise on the cost or speed of internet connection.

On the eve of the 2018 presidential election, the legitimacy that President Sisi had gained in the aftermath of the coup had faded away. However, the argument of national stability was so deeply rooted in the political discourse that it excluded any alternative to the military leadership in the eyes of the general population. Behind the muted contestation of Sisi's authority was the hope that another military figure could eventually rise to power. One month before the 2018 election, al-Sisi gave a revealing speech at the inauguration of the Zohr natural gas field in the governorate of Port Said. The President referred to the 2013 mandate he had requested to 'combat terrorism', stating that he 'could do it again' and 'will never let anyone manipulate Egypt's security as long as [he was] alive' (Sayed, 2018). Five years after the coup, the narrative of national security and the legacy of the 'Rabaa al-Adawiya' massacre remained existentially central to his regime.

The 2018 presidential race was scheduled for the month of March. Applications for candidacies were open for a period of two weeks in January 2018. However, most of the potential candidates, who had expressed interest in running for the elections, were either treated as ineligible, jailed or coerced into withdrawing their candidacy. By the start of the campaign, President al-Sisi was only competing with candidate Mousa Mostafa Mousa, who had officially endorsed the President before entering the race.

In December 2017, an Egyptian army officer named Colonel Ahmed Konsowa had been prosecuted by a military court and was found guilty of expressing political opinions while he was technically still serving as a military officer (Reuters, 2017). He was sentenced to jail for six years on the grounds that he had publicly expressed interest in running for the elections via his YouTube channel, before submitting an official resignation from the military.

Former candidate and Ministry of Foreign Affairs Ahmad Shafiq was deported from the United Arab Emirates after announcing his intention to compete in the presidential election (Michaelson, 2018a). A rumour circulated, suggesting that the former leadership of the Armed Forces – allegedly Chief Commander Tantawi – had convinced Shafiq that he should withdraw his candidacy with the pretext of genuine concerns for his safety. Shafiq subsequently withdrew from the race in January stating that he was not 'the ideal person to lead the state's affairs' (Michaelson, 2018a).

The strongest challenger was Sami Anan, a member of the SCAF and former Chief of Staff, who had been dismissed by former President Morsi in August 2012. He was soon arrested and interrogated on charges of running for election without prior approval from the military and was formally accused of inciting popular mobilization against the armed forces (Michaelson, 2018a). Eventually, Anan was banned from the presidential race on the grounds that any internal tensions within the military would threaten Egypt's political stability and harm national security. And yet President al-Sisi himself had previously announced his intention to run in the presidential election of March 2013 without having formally resigned from the military services.

One of the last would-be candidates was the leftist human rights lawyer Khaled Ali (Michaelson, 2018b), who eventually announced his decision to withdraw from the race on the day following the arrest of Sami Anan. At this stage, Ali had already collected 20,000 constituents' signatures, only slightly short of the 25,000-target required to validate his candidacy (Kestler-D'Amours, 2018).

On 2 April 2018, it was announced that President Sisi had won the elections with 97 per cent of votes, with a voter turnout of 41.5 per cent. But the most revealing fact about the elections was that, according to the figures released by the electoral commission, 1.76 million Egyptians appeared to have voted for the popular footballer Mo Salah, who was obviously not included as a candidate on the electoral list. This proportion of invalid ballots (7.27 per cent) was higher than the 2.9 per cent of votes in favour of Moussa Mostafa Moussa. A year later, in April 2019, the Egyptian parliament approved constitutional amendments allowing President Sisi to remain in power until 2030.

Overall, these recent developments illustrate the extent to which the argument of countering disinformation and violent extremism became instrumental to the implementation of tighter media regulations and state surveillance policies in countries like Egypt. In such environments, the only avenues left for the expression of political dissent are within the realm of the popular, as was the case during the 2018 elections. In one of his latest pieces, Egyptian media analyst Hossam Fazulla (2020) further illustrates this point by referring to a broader range of interesting examples. He mentions the 2016 grassroots campaign organized in support of the street performance group 'Atfal Shaware' (Street Children), which informally contested the decision to ban the use of cameras in the streets of Egypt. Another meaningful instance of these peripheral expressions of dissent was creative enough that it involved young children playing in the streets:

> In 2017, the streets of Egypt were occupied by children playing with a simple plastic pendulum toy which they called Bedan El-Sisi, or El-Sisi's testicles. The toy gained its sarcastic name and popularity after a short video was

shared online of an anonymous individual asking a young boy: 'What is the name of that toy?' 'Bedan El-Sisi' the kid replies. In Egyptian slang, the term 'testicle' signifies something unpleasant and distasteful. (…) Not only was this intervention playful and sarcastic, but it also made a significant intervention in both reclaiming public spaces whilst side-stepping perceptions of threatening, conventional political action.

(Fazulla, 2020)

This ultimately brings us to rethink the way we view the mass audience and the realm of popular culture, as well as the implications of the security discourse on disinformation.

9

Lebanon: Before, during and after the 2019 revolution

In order to introduce a discussion on the second wave of the 'Arab Spring', I will now explore the particular context in which the 2019 Lebanese revolution occurred and consider how the global security lens legitimized the authority of the leading political forces in the years preceding the mobilizations. In this chapter, I will apply a chronological perspective and will start by outlining some aspects of the prevailing political discourse prior to the 2019 uprisings. This will bring me to reflect on the security-driven market of strategic communication, which I already discussed in relation to the Tunisian and Egyptian cases. I will then comment on the main achievements of the revolution from a communication perspective and identify some of the challenges that young activists have been facing in the post-revolutionary phase.

By the time of Lebanon's 2022 general elections, it became very clear that the experiences of the Egyptian and Lebanese pro-revolutionary youths were, in many regards, very similar. This may come as a surprise to those who indulged in the narrative of Lebanese exceptionalism by perpetuating the myth of an endemic sectarianism. The Lebanese revolution demonstrated that sectarianism was a social construct with real-life consequences, which had been enforced by the leading political actors who remained in power after the 1975–90 civil war.

In contrast to many other countries in the region, Lebanon was not governed by a single ruling elite. Its political landscape was historically divided and the construct of *taifa* (sect) has been traditionally used by the political establishment to create an illusion of unified sectarian identities. In some regards, the notion of *taifa* served as a substitute for the imagined community of the nation-state (Anderson, 1983). That system allowed a handful of sectarian leaders to *divide and conquer*, essentially disempowering civil society by means of fragmentation. It was thanks to sectarian rhetoric that the figures of the leading parties and militias maintained legitimacy, after the 1989 National Reconciliation Accord known as the Taif Agreement. The significance given to the concept of *taifa* laid the groundwork for a long history of divisive identity politics exacerbated by regional geopolitical tensions, foreign military occupation and a series of conflicts opposing various armed groups and militias.

In the years preceding the 17 October protests, international concerns over the political stability of the region gave prominence to a climate of sectarian tensions, which had long been engineered by religious and political leaders. The labels of 'terrorism' and 'extremism' would eventually feed into a strategy of political othering, increasing the polarisation between the two main coalitions dividing the political sphere: on the one hand was the Pro-Bashar '8 March Alliance' mainly composed of Hezbollah, the Shia Amal Movement and the Free Patriotic Movement. On the other was the Hariri-led '14 March Alliance', which included the Sunni Future Movement along with the Kataeb Party and the Christian right-wing Lebanese Forces.

Between 2013 and 2015, tensions relating to the war in neighbouring Syria resulted in a spike in terrorist attacks targeting Hezbollah's bastions. These included Shia majority districts like Beirut's southern suburbs of Dahieh, or the town of Hermel located 80 km east of Tripoli (BBC News, 2015; France 24, 2015). A number of attacks also appeared to be targeting the Lebanese army, which Sunni factions considered to be collaborating with Hezbollah. In this context, the issue of security and stabilization arguably played an important role in the rhetoric of the two camps dominating the political sphere. Ironically, Hezbollah began to frame its involvement in the Syrian conflict as another form of the *war on terror*. The normalization of the movement in the political landscape was in part justified by the need to defeat jihadi groups (McGregor, 2016). This narrative tapped into the fears related to the spike of terrorist attacks. As for the rhetoric of the 14 March Alliance, it suggested that the recruitment of local Sunni fighters by jihadi groups was due to a feeling of socio-political exclusion, emphasized by the interference of Hezbollah in national politics.

During that time, the very same political actors who claimed to be fighting a certain kind of extremism would continue to use a polarizing rhetoric charged with religious symbolism. For example, this was the case in many of the annual speeches that Hezbollah's Secretary-General Hassan Nasrallah gave as part of the Shia commemoration of Ashura. Every year, Shia Muslims gathered in the southern suburb of Beirut (Dahieh) to honour the memory of Imam Hussein, who was killed during the historical battle of Karbala. Since 2008, the symbolism around the seventh century battle of Karbala has been used to support 'Hezbollah's self-proclaimed ideology of resistance' (Yazbeck, 2017: 470). In fact, it has been argued (Yazbeck, 2017) that, in the case of Hezbollah, the imagery of Karbala has significantly contributed to reasserting the construct of the *taifa*, which became the locus of identity politics in the absence of a consolidated nation state. This was particularly obvious in 2013, when Nasrallah and Hezbollah's deputy general Naim Qassem recurrently evoked the battle of Karbala to credit the engagement of their affiliates fighting in Syria. In his 2013 Ashura speech, Nasrallah drew an explicit analogy between his supporters and the martyrs of Karbala, 'who died with Hussein on the tenth of Muharram' (Yazbeck, 2017: 475). That same year, Sheikh Ahmad al-Assir, a Sunni cleric from Sidon, conversely publicly preached vividly against Hezbollah. Under his charismatic influence, some of his followers clashed with Hezbollah supporters in the city of Sidon (Middle East Eye, 2017). His men also engaged in violence against the Lebanese army, eventually opening fire at a military checkpoint, which resulted in a number of causalities in June 2013 (Shaheen, 2015). The following year – during the Ashura commemoration of November 2014 – Nasrallah once again drew from the imagery of warfare to legitimize the 'martyrdom' of Hezbollah fighters, praising the 'party's victories over the "extremists" in Syria' (Gebeily, 2014). He was referring to the events of late October 2014, when Hezbollah clashed with al-Qaeda-linked groups at the Syrian-Lebanese border, while the Lebanese army fought al-Qaeda affiliates in Tripoli. These events show that, throughout the early 2010s, the rhetoric of religious and political leaders was carefully designed to perpetuate sectarian divide.

That climate of sectarian tensions soon turned out to have a devastating impact on the economy, by causing a decrease of foreign currency inflows and reducing the support of Sunni-majority Gulf States, due to negative sentiment about the growing influence of Hezbollah (Blair, 2022). Most importantly, it reinforced a feeling of marginalization in cities like Tripoli, which became stigmatized and labelled as breeding grounds for jihadi recruits.

In 2016, a deal was made between the Sunni-dominated Future Movement, Hezbollah officials and the Free Patriotic Movement (FPM). The leader of the Future Movement Saad Hariri was appointed as prime minister, while the founder of the FPM Michel Aoun was elected president. The political compromise of 2016 was expected to restore the belief in the national security apparatus and facilitate the joint activities of the army, the intelligence services and the Ministry of Interior. To quote a participant interviewed for this research, the narrative around the 2016 political deal suggested that 'chaos should no longer prevail in Lebanon'. A year later, the army mobilized to fight ISIS on the Lebanese front, while Hezbollah led a successful offensive, defeating Jabat al-Nusra fighters on the Syrian side. Hezbollah would then capitalize on its victory against terrorist groups, while FPM leaders Aoun and Gebran Basil occasionally invoked the need to fight terrorism. It was argued that these collaborations allowed a successful crackdown on terrorist cells and led to a fall of terrorist attacks.

The Lebanese army, which had also collaborated with the intelligence services of the ISF in Syria would continue to receive the support of the United States and was perceived as an efficient player in counter-terrorism work. Yet as much as the international community was primarily invested in the issue of global security, this no longer reflected the main concerns of the Lebanese population. On the eve of the 2018 parliamentary election, the most concerning public issue in fact pertained to the country's economic challenges and the stability of the currency. International players would however only consider this a priority insofar as it was defined as a root cause of extremism. To some extent, global concerns over terrorism gave more significance to sectarian conflict, thus supporting the narrative of Lebanese exceptionalism. They reinforced the belief that sectarianism was endemic and that the country was plagued by identity politics.

In 2017, Prime Minister Saad Hariri mandated an inter-ministerial working group to draft the Lebanese 'National Strategy for Preventing Violent Extremism'. At that time, the global imperative of counterterrorism was perfectly aligned with the security narrative upon which the 2016 Lebanese government had built its legitimacy. Accordingly, the strategy was drafted so as to demonstrate compliance with the 2015 UN Plan of Action to Prevent

Violent Extremism. However, research later demonstrated that the Lebanese strategy had failed to rethink 'violent extremism' in relation to the country's history of fragmented politics (Hussein, 2021: 72). Any genuine attempt at defining political violence in the Lebanese context should have pointed to the role and accountability of the warlords who had always benefitted from sectarian divide. Yet the national strategy, which was approved in 2018, conveniently avoided the question. Instead, 'violent extremism' was subsumed to three categories of attitudes and behaviours: '(1) the spread of individual and collective hatred that may lead to structural violence; (2) the rejection of diversity and nonacceptance of others, and the use of violence as a means of expression and influence; and (3) a behaviour that threatens values that ensure social stability' (Hussein, 2021: 78). In spite of the fact that the draft strategy involved a consultation with other social actors beyond the ministries, it did not facilitate the inclusion of civil society actors. It also failed to challenge the terminology of 'violent extremism' in relation to the history of Lebanese politics.

In the end, the security incentives driving the new market of strategic communication did not support the development of a local independent media sphere, prior to the October 2019 revolution. This was not surprising, considering that the national media market was very fragmented and dominated by partisan outlets, with limited opportunities for independent journalism. Amongst the main national TV channels were the partisan Future TV owned by the Hariri camp, Hezbollah-backed Al Manar TV, the National Broadcasting Network (NBN TV) owned by the Amal movement and the Christian pro-government Lebanese Broadcasting Company (LBC) (Cochrane, 2007, 2008). The national media landscape was also characterized by a range of print media with political affiliations (e.g. newspapers like the pro-Hezbollah al-Akhbar, anti-Hezbollah Nidaa al-Watan, liberal and central-left An-Nahar and the right-wing Christian newspaper Al-Joumhouria). The public television network TL Liban, in spite of being non-partisan, was not appealing to the youth and was often criticized for providing irrelevant media coverage. A month before the revolution, a local campaigning expert suggested to me that the best places to debate and engage constructively about politics would be funerals, since they were amongst the few places gathering a random and fairly representative sample of the population. In contrast, the national media market, was, in his view, rather detrimental to public deliberation:

> You don't really find any proper debate that is voiced on TV. In politics, no one wants a debate, everyone caters just to a very limited target audience, they are not trying to convince someone else's [electorate]. (...)
> (Political activist and campaigner, Beirut, Lebanon; September 2019)

The national media had also failed to relay the perspectives of the younger audience, reproducing outdated journalistic practices and stereotypical representations of the youths, who would be perceived as passive and disengaged. But the revolution eventually demonstrated that the public was eager for alternative media content and formats that could relay the peripheral voices of the progressive youth:

> You watch media for knowledge and information but also because you need to relate to something. (...) In the last couple of years there was a very strong disconnection between young people and the national media stations in Lebanon. (...) Cause the national TV shows are either politicised or irrelevant. Now people have started to watch TV again, just to catch up with recent events and the revolution. Before the revolution a lot of people had lost interest. Because it is not representative of the population, especially the youths. Youths, females, activists ... you don't see them.
> (Young female civil society actor, Beirut, January 2020)

Only a very limited number of independent and non-partisan media platforms had started to deliver alternative content relevant to the interests of the younger demographic. These included Daraj and the activist media platform Megaphone, which the independent journalist Timour Azhari described as the 'voice of Lebanon's uprising' (Azhari, 2019). Although Megaphone was already active before the 2019 protests, the revolution significantly expanded its reach amongst the diaspora and pro-revolutionary youth.

If anything, it was indeed the revolution that stimulated the development of the independent media sphere in recent years. On the eve of the October protests, there certainly was a window in the market for alternative information channels such as Megaphone. Young audiences were eager for original media content reflecting a progressive editorial line that would be delivered through social media platforms like Instagram. Some of the independent journalists viewed themselves as activists and would initially volunteer or work as freelancers to launch these new channels. During interviews, they described the practice of independent journalism as 'an indispensable tool' that would enable them to 'break the monopoly of image and language, while contributing to a broader movement for change' (Independent journalist and activist, Beirut, April 2022). They saw independent media as part of a broader infrastructure that would be conducive to structural change that might extend to other voices from the young opposition, such as newly formed parties or student unions.

Prior to the revolution, these initiatives would have been fairly limited due to the financial challenges already faced by most of the traditional media competing on the national market. After 2016, a number of well-established news outlets such as the daily newspaper As-Safir had to close. This was still the case around the time of the revolution, when Hariri's Future TV (2019) and the English-language newspaper Daily Star (2021) also had to shut down. The advertising model was no longer sufficient to fund the broad range of channels owned by politicians, now that the sponsorship of Gulf countries like Qatar and Saudi Arabia was shrinking. In contrast, the few independent outlets that covered the 2019 uprisings from within the revolution had gained traction and were now more likely to secure grants to develop the sphere of independent journalism. This new generation of activist-journalists had in fact gained experience covering elections back in 2017–18. They initially operated anonymously to avoid being associated with any specific political agenda and experimented freely with a new approach, which became particularly relevant to the revolutionary protests.

Beyond the emergence of an independent media sphere, the greatest achievement of the Lebanese revolution was the fact that it challenged the legacy of the civil war. It defeated the feeling of sectarian segregation that divided the country into different geographical zones. The revolution contributed to challenge the stereotypical image of the cities and neighbourhoods that had been stigmatized due to sectarian politics. This was the case for Tripoli, which had been repeatedly framed as a dangerous hot zone conducive to the recruitment of jihadi fighters. During the revolution, the city became an allegory of the entire country, evoking a long history of sectarian conflicts caused by years of government neglect and political clientelism. Poverty combined with the proximity of the Syrian civil war had paved the way for a series of armed conflicts opposing the pro-Bashar Alawite community of Jabal Mohsen[1] to the Sunni-majority neighbourhood of Bab el-Tebbaneh (Facon, 2020). But it was the stigma associated with sectarian conflict that had left Tripoli isolated from the rest of the country. Before the revolution, many Lebanese people had never even visited Tripoli. This was said to have affected opportunities for social cohesion, adding to the economic and geographic isolation of the city. The revolution gave a voice to Tripolitans. It acknowledged their feelings of marginalization and validated their struggle as valuable to the revolutionary project. That was the reason why Tripoli became known as the 'bride of the revolution'.

The same could be said about the Shia-majority city of Nabatieh, historically dominated by Hezbollah and the Amal movement. The revolutionary protests demystified the stereotype, according to which Nabatieh was nothing but a stronghold of Hezbollah. They revealed that the two political groups were not unanimously acclaimed. Like in the rest of the country, the pro-revolutionary youth demanded an alternative to the system of sectarian quotas. As in the case of Tripoli, the revolution gained a particular significance in the city of Nabatieh. This was the place where Hezbollah's narrative of resistance was, until then, assumed to resonate with the city's history of occupation by the Israeli Defense Forces in the early 1980s (Houssari, 2019).

From a communication perspective, the Lebanese revolution deconstructed the symbolism around sectarianism. It relied on a set of new symbols to overrule the old arsenal of discursive tools used in sectarian rhetoric. In doing so, it intended to create a sense of unifying national identity. Protests took place in strategically central public spaces like Martyrs' Square in both Beirut and Tripoli. Demonstrations and road blocks were also organized at the intersection of divided areas like Ring Bridge, which connects East and West Beirut (Frakes, 2019). The Lebanese flag became a sign of civilian empowerment and an emblem of the fight against sectarian politics. As part of the revolutionary efforts made to overcome the fragmentation of the public space, protesters created disruption by blocking roads across the country. They burned tires and gathered on strategic junctions, reclaiming ownership of physical networks of circulation and communication. They demonstrated that militias no longer had a monopoly over geographical areas and represented the revolution as a movement that was, for a little while, widespread across the country:

> When we were in the streets, even with the most brutal form of police violence, we were euphoric, we were happy. It was an insane feeling. Nobody was on pills anymore, nobody needed to see their therapist. Even if we were not winning, even if it did not translate into any political win, but, this act of convening and being fearless for a split of second, and owning the space ... And this familiarity that you have with people that you never met was insane, it was moving. [...]
>
> (Activist, Beirut, April 2022)

Protesters chanted slogan designed to oppose all the figures of the political establishment, attacking the district-based offices of the dominant parties. Groups were created on WhatsApp to organize the logistics of the road blocks, and protesters travelled, sometimes for the first time, to other cities building real-life social networks during protests, which turned out to be a bonding experience. Tents were erected on Martyrs' Square, in the area surrounding parliament in downtown Beirut, where different groups would gather to share ideas about revolutionary demands and tactics. The different actors of the revolution could meet and share perspectives on the objectives and priorities of the opposition. Over the first ten days of the protests, this certainly contributed to a cross-fertilization of ideas, bringing together critical theory and political praxis:

> Those townhouse meeting happened daily, on Martyrs square, on a daily basis, a lot of debates going on, some of them high level politics, some of them much more tactics, it opened a lab of ideas and dreams and demands, the feminists played a huge role in pushing their discourse through the revolution ... At some point it was also a catalyst to express the hopes for the kind of country we aspire to.
>
> (Activist and independent journalist, Beirut, April 2022)

The revolution was extensively documented on social media platforms and WhatsApp groups. In fact, alongside the development of the independent media sphere, revolutionary activists organically supported media literacy by relying on personal networks of reliable sources to fact-check information. Many revolutionaries were developing new media skills and learning how to identify and verify potentially relevant user-generated content on the spot. This proved to be increasingly useful as counterrevolutionary forces would often spread misinformation, in an attempt to create confusion and regain control over the public discourse. Meanwhile, the Western debate on disinformation was still reliant on the assumption that mass audiences were most likely deprived of media literacy and vulnerable to 'fake news'. Yet the informal communication practices of the Lebanese revolution in fact demonstrated that audiences often had the skills required to engage critically with the media and challenge disinformation, which in this case reflected the agenda of the political elites. The perspective of pro-revolutionary youths was accordingly very much aligned with the critique of 'post-truth whiteness', in suggesting that the issue of disinformation was nothing new. In their view – and in contrast to what a Eurocentric lens would lead us to believe – this climate of 'post-truth' politics predominantly originated from the political status quo:

> Quite often 'fake news' is associated with social media and I think it's bullshit because I think it has always existed. It's actually the main thing that traditional media does, in our part of the world – both traditional media and security services work hand in hand, so they are the fake news machine. The only issue is that social media makes this much more available and accessible to everyone and makes the virality immediate. In a few seconds a video can circulate and be treated as a true information, and there is also no traceability, for example on Whatsapp [...] I think it gets amplified because it is associated with new media and I also think that it is a very Western debate. It was forced into our faces but we have been dealing with fake news, since forever.
>
> (Independent journalist, Beirut, April 2022)

During the first phase of the uprisings – the thirteen days leading up to the announcement of Saad Hariri's resignation – the revolution was pure euphoria. Yet sadly, as in the Egyptian case, counterrevolutionary forces eventually succeeded in regaining control of both the offline and virtual public space. Many young activists suggested to me that the analogy with Egypt was in fact very relevant, even though the counterrevolution was not constituted of a monolithic bloc.

Following the early days of the uprisings, Hezbollah's intimidation tactics on WhatsApp groups became increasingly visible. In late October and late

November, supporters of Hezbollah and the Amal Movement would clash with protesters on the Ring Bridge and destroy the tents erected by revolutionaries on the squares. The number of protesters mobilizing on the street began to decrease. In mid-November, President Michel Aoun gave a speech in which he dismissed revolutionary demands for a technocratic government, calling for the end of the protests. Nasrallah started demonizing protesters and tried to antagonize them by drawing analogies between the road blocks and some of the tactics used during the civil war. The OTV channel released a report claiming that the revolutionary protests were funded by Saudi Arabia, and that amoral sexual practices were taking place on the square. Others, like the Kataeb Party, saw the revolution as an opportunity to rebrand themselves and tried to appear as the most likely ally of the revolution within the political sphere. As in post-revolutionary Tunisia and Egypt, the revolution was eventually reappropriated. The assassination of the activist Lokman Slim, who was accused of being an agent of Israel by Hezbollah, generated a peak of anxiety. Independent journalists like Raiq Baissy would continue to receive personal threats and others like Samir Khaled would be bullied in targeted smear campaigns. In late March 2022, the independent media platform Daraj reported that pro-Hezbollah bot accounts were proactively targeting opposition voices and independent journalists. These attacks resulted in a number of complaints submitted to the Internal Security Forces' Cybercrime and Intellectual Property Rights Bureau, which would then prosecute journalists on the grounds of 'defamation, slander, and inciting harm' (Seifeddin, 2022). Over time, counterrevolutionary forces made sure to re-fragment the public debate, which left young revolutionary voices increasingly more isolated. And as I will show, this process was accentuated by the pandemic and the economic crisis. By means of fragmentation, the public debate was in fact being re-centralized and securitized around the political status quo of sectarianism.

Almost three years after the 17 October revolution, the political sphere was still dominated by the same players. Following the second wave of the Arab Spring, the first parliamentary elections were about to take place. These were originally scheduled for 27 March 2022, but were postponed to 15 May of that year. Public outrage reached its peak by the time of the parliamentary campaign. The endless financial crisis was exacerbated by the tragedy of Beirut explosion of 2020, for which no accountability was provided.

Prior to the events of Beirut blast, public discontent was already fuelled by the deterioration of the economic situation and the instability of the currency. The political elites had mismanaged the public debt, which was piling up after the 1975–90 civil war. The Lebanese economy was primarily reliant on the Gulf States' contribution to the financial industry along with tourism (7 per cent of the GDP) and the support of a resourceful diaspora. The budget deficit was already alarming in 2011, following the first wave of the Arab Spring. In 2016, however, the banks started to offer attractive interest rates, which incentivized deposits in both Lebanese pounds and US dollars. The governor of the central bank introduced financial engineering, which led to a short-term influx of foreign currency. However, due to the fact that these policies were not accompanied by the economic reforms required for success, the central bank accumulated liabilities. Lebanon's debt rapidly increased, while political leaders indulged in a public sector pay rise before the general election of 2018. In that context, the October 2019 decision to impose a tax on WhatsApp calls was received as an invitation to take to the streets. This was the last straw, the tipping point of a long history of economic measures driven by personal greed, which had always benefitted the warlords of the civil war and allowed them to perpetuate a climate of sectarian divide. The liquidity crisis became perceptible in August 2019 when Lebanon suffered from a fall in remittances combined with a rapid outflow of US dollars. This limited opportunities for foreign exchange, which translated into a noticeable difference between the official exchange rate and that available in the black market.

Following the mass protests of 17 October, Lebanese commercial banks closed for two weeks (Azhari, 2019b). They later imposed high fees as well as weekly limits of foreign currency withdrawal. During the pandemic, another limit on withdrawals was eventually imposed on the local currency (Geldi, 2021). As a result of the monetary policies implemented by the central bank, people would no longer be able to withdraw money, including from local currency accounts.

By February 2021, the currency had collapsed. While the official exchange rate to the dollar set by the central bank was at 1,500 Lebanese pounds, it was determined at 3,900 by regular banks and had reached 9,300 on the black market (Geldi, 2021). Around the same time, the International Consortium of Investigative Journalists released a report exposing leaked documents presenting evidence that members of the political class had set offshore firms and shell companies abroad, while they encouraged people to deposit their savings in local banks (Independent, 2021). Meanwhile, it was estimated that 74 per cent of the population was now living in poverty. In late 2021, the government once again failed to subsidize the most essential goods, generating unprecedented sanitary issues, such as period poverty (France 24, 2021). The energy ministry lifted initial subsidies on fuel, which inevitably increased the cost of all services involving transportation (Middle East Eye, 2021). Further, electricity plants were unable to deliver twenty-four-hour power supplies due to fuel shortages and Lebanese households would thus encounter extra fuel costs. The energy market would soon collapse due to energy shortages and the country suffered a twenty-four-hour national blackout in October 2021. In 2022, these conditions were aggravated by inflation and the global increase of fuel and energy prices caused by the conflict in Ukraine (The World Bank, 2022). People would become ever more reliant on the local black market for energy supplies, which reinforced the geographic segregation that the revolution initially intended to break through. People could no longer travel easily from region to region, as had been the case during the early phase of the revolution.

The economic crisis was only made worse by the tragic events of the 2020 Beirut explosion. In the midst of the Covid-19 pandemic, a warehouse containing a large storage of ammonium nitrate (2,750 tonnes) exploded in the Port of Beirut on 4 August 2020. The chemical had been unsafely stored for a period of over six years, in spite of the fact that senior officials knew about the risks of explosion (BBC News, 2021). The magnitude of the blast was felt beyond a perimeter of 240 km, causing an estimated 219 deaths, as well as thousands of injuries and more than 10 billion dollars in property damages. It was estimated that, as a result of the explosion, the public debt reached approximately '495 per cent of gross domestic product in 2021' (Blair, 2022).

More than a year later, no one had yet been held accountable and the public's conviction was that the political leadership was deliberately hindering the investigation. In fact, the well-established parties once again tried to channel public frustrations through sectarian rhetoric, blaming each other for the shortcomings of the judicial enquiry. This was precisely what had caused the

Tayouneh clashes opposing supporters of Hezbollah and the Amal Movement to an unidentified group, which allegedly belonged to the Christian Lebanese Forces.[2] The army was also involved and confusion remains as to who initiated the hostilities. The clashes sadly re-enacted the imagery of the civil war, as they took place on the previous front line dividing Christian and Muslim areas, in the neighbourhood of Tayouneh on 14 October 2021. They were described as the worst armed confrontation since the Lebanese conflict of 2008. Prior to these events, the leaders of Hezbollah and the Amal Movement – Nasrallah and Nabih Berri – had questioned the impartiality of Tarek Bitar, the judge in charge of the legal investigation into the 2020 blast. On the morning of the Tayouneh incident, armed supporters of Hezbollah and the Amal Movement gathered in front of the Justice Palace in Eastern Beirut to protest against Bitar's appointment. They soon clashed with militia fighters, whose affiliation remained unclear. Many suggested that these were members of the Christian right-wing Lebanese Forces, a party and paramilitary group fiercely opposed to Hezbollah. Rocket propelled grenades were fired and snipers shot into the crowd, causing seven deaths and dozens of injuries.

The incident introduced a climate of contentious politics similar to the polarisation which led to the Egyptian military regime opposing the Muslim Brotherhood after the 2011 uprisings. The circumstances around the Tayouneh incident were extensively debated online and footage of the clashes would circulate on social media platforms. Audiences reacted to the events calling for further investigations and speculating as to what had triggered the shootings. A heated debate unfolded on Twitter under the hashtag '#May7' and '#MiniMay7'. In fact, in the months preceding the 2022 parliamentary election, the 2021 clashes had undeniably contributed to shift the trajectory of public discourse.

Both Hezbollah and the right-wing Lebanese Forces capitalized on public fear and confusion to restore their legitimacy within their support base. Beyond the pro-revolutionary youths, those who heard about the clashes within close-knit and secluded communities would most likely become more receptive to the political framing of the event, which was reminiscent of the civil war (Baydoun, 2022). In fact, young revolutionaries were increasingly concerned about the effect that such a polarizing incident would have on the upcoming election. The economic crisis combined with the pandemic and the tragedy of the explosion had created a perfect storm, maintaining a sense of fear in the population, along with constant uncertainty and isolation.

Some of the more pessimistic activists I interviewed suspected that these conditions would reopen the wounds of the postcolonial crisis, which historically stimulated the need to reaffirm one's sectarian identity. They believed that audiences would thus once again become receptive to the symbolism of the old parties' populist rhetoric. In their view, the only way for the revolutionary opposition to survive was to apply the exact same communication strategy as the one used by the most established players in the political sphere. One activist in fact stated that the revolution would now have to rely on the same type of symbolism, which had forged sectarian identities. He argued that the only way forward was to create the same sense of belonging, which could be found in partisan slogans, uniforms or military songs. He added that the opposition would also need to rely on charismatic leaders, due to what he described as the 'father issue' resulting from the postcolonial identity crisis.

Like many of the leftist pro-revolutionary activists I had interviewed in Egypt, he was now convinced that the only way to succeed in consolidating the opposition was to rely on mainstream campaigning practices, involving retail politics. He believed that the revolution would have to be led by its own political elite and that its message should be carefully crafted to appeal to the masses. He was certainly not alone in thinking that the revolutionary movement should move towards institutionalization and compromise. On the eve of the 2011 parliamentary election, many activists feared that the independent candidates would fail to consolidate a viable coalition. As in the Egyptian case, they would engage in an introspective critique in the hope of understanding how the revolution could have succeeded. In retrospect, some came to the conclusion that the opposition should have perhaps been more open to political compromise. They suggested to me that it may have been more strategic to join the rally around the Kataeb Party, which had rebranded itself as the voice of the anti-establishment opposition, in spite of its history of involvement in the civil war. They deplored the fact that the revolutionary movement was now divided into a reformist versus a radical wing. Others shared their frustration about the fact that the planning of the revolution was in their view often envisioned as a form of casual 'event management':

> I remember the first weeks of the revolution. That was the most beautiful way to demand decency, dignity and human rights; and then it ended. But a revolution is not simply an event we can plan. It's not about event management. A revolution is a feeling. If you don't feel it, you are not there. And they continue to think about it as an event 'let's do it on Sunday'. But it should not be like that. If you organise a marathon in Jounieh to raise awareness about corruption, it won't change anything. The leading political forces still master the art of political rhetoric, and that is also a skill we need to gain; being 'good' in politics is not enough.
>
> (Civil society actor and activist, Byblos, March 2022)

Due to the brain drain caused by the socio-economic and political crisis, they wondered whether one could institute a new leadership formed by a young political intelligentsia. Most importantly, they doubted that these opposition voices would be able to reach out to a significantly large audience in light of the increasing polarisation opposing Hezbollah to the Lebanese Forces.

By the time of the 2022 parliamentary election, the counterrevolution had regained control over physical networks of communication. A participant interviewed described how, the pandemic had even deprived people of the ability to connect through physical touch and maintain the interpersonal interactions, which had proved to be essential to the revolution. Posters supporting the right-wing Lebanese Forces were displayed everywhere along the coastal road connecting Beirut to Tripoli in the North. Voters would be assigned to the voting stations located in their district of origin, which would be administered by the party assumed to be the most established in a specific region. The young members of the opposition assigned to the voting station of Nabatieh dreaded the idea of being exposed to Hezbollah's flag and intimidating display of symbolic power on the day of the election. They also had a legitimate fear that voters' anonymity might be compromised in case individuals were suspected of being opposed to Hezbollah. In spite of revolutionary demands, no centralized polling station had been set up in Beirut, which would have allowed people to cast their vote without being reminded of any sectarian delineation.

Since the assassination of the activist Lokman Slim, Hezbollah had demonstrated it could easily spread conspiracy theories to demonize opponents and influence trending hashtags by using social media bots. As was the case in post-revolutionary Egypt, the social media sphere quickly became weaponized by counterrevolutionary forces to regain control over the public space by means of fragmentation. This was emphasized by a number of independent journalists who became particularly exposed to the false claims and intimidation tactics used by Hezbollah:

> Fake accounts are like an unofficial arm of campaigns (…). These are accounts that omit a name or clear identity, but work in a way that seems coordinated in terms of a unified message and the target (…) They allow electronic armies, such as those affiliated with Hezbollah, to wage battles and carry out campaigns. This has made it an arena of daily confrontation, which will likely intensify with an eye on the parliamentary elections on May 15. It cannot be denied that the Lebanese parties, through their own campaigns and those of the security services, have succeeded in reducing the space for virtual dialogue having already eliminated the space for dialogue on the ground.
>
> (Seifeddin, 2022)

Some proactive members of the pro-revolutionary opposition suspected that those who had the courage to oppose all the dominant parties might be labelled as traitors and ostracized within their own community. In their view, the imperative was to formulate a very clear message, outlining the evidence incriminating all the well-established parties, in a political language that truly had the potential to rally the majority.

How would the young intelligentsia of the opposition create a new kind of sustainably unifying narrative that had the potential to be embraced by a majority? This question would once again prove to be crucial to the revolutionary strategy. Some activists remained somewhat confident that the worsening of the socioeconomic conditions would only give more credit to the independent candidates, aligned with the revolutionary youth. In their view, this gave more grounds to the idea of a civil opposition united against the entire establishment behind the system of sectarian politics. These few participants appeared to be optimistic, convinced that the revolution already had demonstrated it could channel the language of the majority. In the end, the results of 2022 general elections certainly demonstrated that the revolution was relatively successful in challenging the political status quo by limiting the influence of Hezbollah and its allies. However – although the Free Patriotic Movement[3] had lost support – Hezbollah and the Amal retained their seats in parliament and the right-wing Lebanese Forces gained the majority thanks to the climate of polarisation resulting from the Tayouneh incident. The election turnout was significantly low due to the general feeling of cynicism surrounding the elections and the cost of fuel required to travel to the voting stations. In spite of these drawbacks, a number of independent candidates and representatives of non-aligned opposition parties were successfully elected, as was the case for Marc Daou (from the Taqaddom opposition group and 'United for Change' list) and Elias Jradi (from Together Towards Change).

However, the challenges faced by the pro-revolutionary opposition also led to internal tensions.

During the course of the parliamentary campaign, the influential opposition candidate Jad Ghosn was occasionally discredited online by other figures of the opposition aligned with the Kataeb Party. This occurred after he expressed reservations about their political programme and decided to join the MMFD (Citizens in the State) party, which represented the more radical wing of the pro-revolutionary opposition. In spite of his popularity across the country, Ghosn eventually lost a tight race against the candidate of the Lebanese Forces Razi al-Hajj by a mere eighty-eight votes, in a district of Mount Liban. These results were contested, due to a dispute over a torn bag of diaspora votes at a polling station of Baskinta village. But some of Ghosn's supporters stated that the real challenges faced by the candidate came down to the social media posts of some of his opponents within the opposition. Social media influencers like Gino Raidy or Ramzi Abou Ismail were said to have discredited the candidate online, and the Kataeb Party had circulated a piece entitled '6 reasons not to vote for Jaad' via its online channel. This illustrated the fact that polarisation had also increased within the revolutionary camp.

Conclusion: The media as a bridge between the political theory and political praxis of the revolution

The communication practices of a revolution are not disconnected from that of the hegemony. Instead, they simply evolve and re-emerge as part of a cycle of discursive power. Whilst they entail a creative process of disruption in their early phase of development, they are also subject to reappropriation, re-centralization and securitization. In order to succeed, the different social actors engaged in a revolution should thus carefully analyse the role they are each likely to play in this cycle.

At first, the counter-discourse of the revolution incorporates some of the communication tools applied in the sphere of power. This process of disruption already involves a form of reappropriation, which serves the interests of peripheral voices. At this stage, the creativity with which one is able to transpose the tools of discursive power delivers a sense of agency and emancipation. These are the kind of practices, which I situate at the upper pole (north axis) of the discursive cycle. They partly rely on one's ability to transpose some of the tools of discursive power into the sphere of counter-power. A number of findings outlined in this research happen to illustrate this phenomenon.

In Egypt, it was, for example, suggested that the development of a new generation of tech-savvy entrepreneurs supported by the 'Gil Mustaqbal' project was, to a certain extent, conducive to the emergence of web activism. In Tunisia, the pro-revolutionary youth from the highly educated middle also made good use of their skills and resources to stimulate the development of a thriving civil society. This demographic was able to speak the language of formal politics, which contributed to secure international funding for the development of an informal political sphere after the 2011 revolution. The civil society actors, who benefitted from this particular form of political literacy, were also well-placed to advise policy, remaining well-represented in the post-revolutionary public sphere. Like in Egypt, this transfer of discursive power was also visible in the realm of online activism. In both countries, the early generation of bloggers and online activists would share ideas and influences from different cultures of political resistance within the opposition. Some were close to the Islamist opposition, while others had views rooted in Marxist ideologies. Yet as long as the practice of web activism was still limited to a niche, they were able to cross-fertilize each other's ideas. Each of these formal political literacies would be challenged in a constructive way, thanks to the initially decentralized setting of the blogosphere. By the time of the 2011 uprisings, these networks of political dissent were able to draw the attention of international media as they reported on the uprisings by producing online content sometimes available in foreign languages. These multiple examples show how the tools of discursive power were transposed and reapplied in creative ways to serve the opposition.

However, as soon as the revolution gained momentum, many of these young activists realized that their ability to leverage the discursive tools of power was no longer beneficial to the revolution. At this stage, the main challenge was to apply a communication strategy that would speak to the majority and remain relatable to the grassroots. In Tunisia and Egypt, evidence from the post-revolutionary blogosphere revealed that many young activists from the urban middle class were in fact attached to the idea of intellectual leadership. Some suggested that 'revolutions [would have to be led] by a minority', stating that they did not '[expect the support of the majority]' (The Big Pharaoh, 8 May 2012).[1] The progressive youth from the middle class was conflicted. In spite of its leftist-libertarian ethos, its intention was to act as an enlightened intelligentsia and lead the way towards the political theory of the revolution. In the Egyptian case, this partly explains why it was unable to reach out to the electorate of the Muslim Brotherhood. On another level, this aspect of the civil opposition formed by the young middle class also accounts for the framing of the 2011 uprisings by international media. In the early phase of the uprisings, this highly educated tech-savvy middle class became the faces of the Arab Spring in the coverage of foreign news outlets. This particular representation of the revolution was perhaps reassuring to the Western audience, because it resonated with an idealized memory of the Enlightenment. As per the traditional model of Habermas's public sphere, the assumption was that the revolution would be led by a liberal intellectual elite that would enlighten the masses. Accordingly, digital technologies had supposedly played an important role, allowing this young tech-savvy intelligentsia to liberalize the debate. One could argue that such narrative was in fact ultimately detrimental to the civil opposition because it emphasized its singularity, highlighting the sociological gap between this demographic and the more conservative working class.

Meanwhile, the counterrevolution was happy to restore its legitimacy by playing the card of populism. Well-established political groups regained control over the virtual and physical spaces of the revolution, when the young civil opposition was no longer able to interact with the grassroots. In Egypt, the Muslim Brotherhood and military establishment reappropriated the strictly populist dimension of revolutionary slogans and narratives. Simultaneously, the actors of the counterrevolution started to campaign in rural regions. They proactively engaged in retail politics, while maintaining their visibility over traditional mass media. Simultaneously, the actors of the counterrevolution reappropriated the sphere of social media to reproduce a (one-to-many) mass media logic of political campaigning. In other words, while the pro-revolutionary youth appeared to be speaking the language of an intellectual elite, the political leadership proved to have a monopoly over populist channels and rhetoric.

A similar process occurred in Tunisia over the years leading up to the 2019 presidential race. Following, the 2011 uprisings, Facebook – amongst other social media platforms – was as influential as any other mainstream news outlets. During the 2019 campaign that led to the election of Kais Saied, the platform was in fact considered as one of the most popular information sources, and was accordingly used as a strategic tool for political campaigning (Aliriza, 2019). A number of well-established parties and political actors had invested considerable resources into social media campaigns, which were conveniently not subject to the same regulations as the national media outlets covering the presidential race (Aliriza, 2019). These online campaigns started to inspire the same scepticism as the traditional media, which was viewed as biased and affected by political clientelism. In this particular context, Kais

Saied stood out from the race by applying a decentralized communication strategy that contrasted with that of his opponents. Instead of relying on media visibility and online campaigns, he simply capitalized on his own version of retail politics, interacting face-to-face with his electorate in local cafes across the country. For a little while, his communication strategy did appear to be decentralized and inclusive of the grassroots.

In Lebanon, interviews suggested that counterrevolutionary forces had also attempted to regain control of the public space by means of fragmentation. Members of the pro-revolutionary youths described how WhatsApp groups were rapidly infiltrated to spread disinformation intended to discredit activists and intimidate protesters. Hezbollah had long capitalized on its narrative of self-proclaimed resistance and would continue to frame its opponents as the agents of a Western conspiracy aligned with Isreali interests. As always, the concern was that this populist rhetoric would further ostracize the young opposition, in suggesting that it would not be fairly representative of the grassroots. Following the Tayouneh clashes, the polarisation opposing Hezbollah and the Amal movement to the right-wing parties dominated the debate, creating more grounds for fragmentation.

These developments ultimately reveal two common denominators in each of the three countries considered. The first one relates to the process of re-centralization, which I described as part of the discursive cycle. Whether they emerge online or offline, these peripheral networks are easily hijacked to reinforce the hegemony of the political status quo. Online research and ethnographic evidence indicate that both the online and offline settings used by revolutionary activists were reappropriated by the political establishment. This simply refers to the second shift of discursive power that I situate at the lower pole (south axis) of the cycle. It also illustrates the interplay between revolution and counterrevolution, which has been conceptualized in the work of Hannah Arendt (2016).

The second common denominator is perhaps less obvious but, in my view, far more interesting. Across these different contexts, it appears that the progressive youth from the highly educated middle class is not always viewed as a legitimate representation of the grassroots. In fact, the real opportunities for large-scale grassroots activism are often limited to the early days of a revolutionary uprising. These short-lived experiences appear to be the most efficient settings when it comes to creating an alternative sense of belonging. During these very brief periods of time, street mobilizations facilitate organic interpersonal communication. These relationships seem to be far more powerful than the populist construct of national or sectarian identity. Unfortunately, in most cases, these civil opposition movements can hardly sustain access to these social settings long enough to consolidate the strategy and political theory of the revolution.

In fact, beyond the scope of street mobilizations, the reach of the progressive youth is often limited to the diaspora and international audience. During the course of a post-revolutionary transition, this community often struggles to speak a political language that is relatable to the grassroots. Evidence collected from interviews and the activist blogosphere in fact suggests that the progressive youths often find themselves secluded within their own echo chamber. Following the first wave of the Arab Spring, communication scholars attributed this phenomenon to the practice of digital activism. The main argument then was that this new form of public engagement was built on a pervasive attention economy and a logic of political consumerism, which would remain detrimental to any civil opposition. Many aspects of my research certainly corroborate this argument, which is instrumental when it comes to demystifying the cyber-utopianism of the early 2000s.

However, the flipside of this argument is that it supports another form of technological determinism. In contrast to the utopia of the early 2000s, today's political discourse on digital technology is essentially dystopian. This climate of fears and scepticism has created more grounds for re-centralization and securitization. Public concerns over hate speech and disinformation are invoked to justify tighter media regulations as well as increased surveillance and censorship. In the mid-2010s, this political discourse thrived thanks to the argument of national and global security.

In Egypt, this narrative was repeatedly used to repress civil society and limit opportunities for freedom of expression. In other countries like Tunisia, the imperative of global security had more insidious effects on civil society. Global concerns of violent extremism led to the development of a new market for strategic communication, which was supposed to rely on the credibility of civil society actors. However, the international donors and tech companies, who supported the development of this new communication market, often promoted the adoption of large-scale marketing practices combined with a logic of cost-effectiveness. This was more likely to be detrimental to the credibility of civil society actors, who had the potential to build community trust by experimenting with an authentically organic approach to grassroots communication. In Lebanon, these security concerns only reinforced the stigma associated with the history of sectarian conflict, without supporting the media and communication skills of local civil society actors.

In recent years, the perception of threat associated with decentralized networks of communication has proved to be a disservice to civil society. Yet it is still this perception of threat that dominates today's political discourse on disinformation. It is the same logic of recentralization that led to the censorship of activists documenting the unlawful eviction of Palestinian families from the neighbourhood of Sheikh Jarrah in May 2021. In that case, most of the material censored through biased content moderation was labelled as 'hate speech' or 'incitement to violence'. Our disillusion about digital technologies is recurrently used to justify increased securitization, because it remains essentially rooted in the assumption of technological determinism. As long as technology is viewed as the main source of the problem, one will be expected to find a quick fix through technological solutions.

Yet my research indicates that the main communication challenges faced by the pro-revolutionary youth are primarily sociological. The role that this young progressive middle class plays in the revolution presents them with an interesting conundrum. On the one hand, they are often well-placed to transpose the discursive tools of power into the sphere of counter-power. On the other, their privilege often prevents them from interacting organically with the grassroots. Here I am specifically referring to this disjuncture that I situate on the east axis of the discursive cycle. This young intelligentsia often struggles to formulate a political message that can successfully reach the grassroots. Its first impulse is to capitalize on the literacy of the elite, before mastering the everyday culture of informal politics.

At this point of my conclusion, I have to admit that there is a meta-level to this discussion. The case of the young pro-revolutionary middle class inevitably brings me to reflect on the ways in which liberal progressive elites have attempted to defeat populism in recent years. This underlying debate raises the same questions as the one addressed by Nancy Fraser in her recent work. While we engage in a critique of reactionary populism, we should also question our assumptions about these audiences, which appear to be receptive to populist rhetoric. It is ultimately counter-productive to dismiss the sensitivities of the grassroots, when they sentiment does not align with the views of the progressive elites. Those of us who advocate for structural change in the language of the intelligentsia should also undertake a critical introspection. As suggested by Fraser in her critique of progressive neoliberalism, populism is too often met with a form of liberal paternalism. In that case, the main objective is to protect and educate grassroots audiences, which are viewed as inherently passive and vulnerable. Such a representation of the grassroots only creates more grounds for polarisation. Most importantly, it often underestimates the agency of the audience as well as its ability to support social change through informal communication practices in the peripheries of the public sphere.

The Arab Spring is too often judged according to normative expectations of 'democratic success', which are commonly derived from the case of the European Enlightenment. Political analysts consistently revert to the model of Western democracies as a reference point to assess the success of progressive-revolutionary movements elsewhere in the world. One rarely dares to consider what these experiences of resistance may teach us about the recent political crises that occurred across Europe and the United States. Yet in countries like Tunisia, Egypt or Lebanon, the progressive wing of the opposition has a particularly informative understanding of what it takes to defeat reactionary populism. Its struggle for freedom of expression reveals that a culture of informal politics expressed through peripheral communication channels is in fact crucial to citizenship. It also shows that it would be counter-productive to substitute reactionary populism for the liberal paternalism of an elite. Indeed, the case studies presented in this book demonstrate that the progressive youth may compromise its reach and credibility, when trying to restore some form of intellectual leadership. However, mobilizing on the streets and in the realm of emergent media is instrumental when it comes to relaying and amplifying the voices of the grassroots. In other words, it is the practice of informal communication, which is the most likely to support pluralism and freedom of speech. These experiences certainly relate to recent debates around the decline of public trust, which has been described in Western countries traditionally viewed as 'established' democracies. Those concerned with the rise of populism in the West may for once learn from other contexts to improve the conditions for public trust through informal communications.

This idea is not entirely new. As argued in my earlier chapters, other theories have acknowledged the importance of informality in the field of Cultural Studies. I have also mentioned the contribution of feminists like Nancy Fraser (1990), who highlighted the significance of peripheral communication. What makes this argument particularly relevant today is the fact that it has been recently neglected in favour of a structural critique of new media. This critique is primarily concerned with the political economy of digital media as well as its implications as a system of control. Such a perspective tends to dismiss the creative power of the audience and its ability to occasionally disrupt the medium and its message. Simultaneously, growing concerns over disinformation tend to accentuate this climate of dystopian cynicism. Today, this question remains central to the field of political communication. Researchers are dedicating their attention to understanding how one should 'counter' propaganda, 'fake news' and conspiracy theories, while decrying the rise of 'post-truth politics' (Ball, 2017; Pomerantsev, 2016). Some commentators went so far as to blame postmodernism for the spread of disinformation (D'Ancona, 2017). They claim that we are now living in an era, which overrides the scientific value of truth. This perspective seems to advocate for the restoration of modernity, to validate a positivist notion of truth. It suggests that one may authenticate media content by relying solely on rationalism and the development of ever-more advanced technological tools. In spite of our cynicism, we continue to view rationalism, expert knowledge and scientific progress as the pillars of a democratic society. As a result, we tend to disregard the importance of social capital and creativity. These are typically some of the skills that drive the circulation of discourse from the sphere of power to the realm of counter-power. I argue that these parameters are too often overlooked in the context of today's debate on disinformation, because of the argument of 'post-truth' whiteness (Masood and Muhammad, 2020; Mejia et al., 2018). This debate is infused with assumptions about the psychology of the audience, which are reminiscent of early crowd psychology. Mass audiences are increasingly viewed as gullible and vulnerable to disinformation. Accordingly, it is also generally admitted that they should be educated and carefully introduced to the art of public deliberation. Yet, evidence clearly shows that – even in a highly repressive environment – audiences spontaneously come to exercise their creative power.

Appendices

Blogger	Blog	Hyperlink
Wael Abbas	Al Wa'I al Masry	http://misrdigital.blogspirit.com/
Zeinobia	Egyptian chronicles	http://egyptianchronicles.blogspot.co.uk/
Yassin Ayari	Malhit	http://mel7it3.blogspot.co.uk/
Behayya	Behayya	http://baheyya.blogspot.co.uk/
Fares Mabrouk	Fares Mabrouk Blog	http://www.faresmabrouk.com/
Lina Ben Mhenni	A Tunisian Girl	http://atunisiangirl.blogspot.co.uk/
UnderAshes	UnderAshes	http://underash.blogspot.co.uk/
_Z_	Débat Tunisie	http://www.debatunisie.com/
The Big Pharaoh	The Big Pharaoh	http://www.bigpharaoh.org/
Fustat	Fustat	http://fustat.blogspot.co.uk/
Slim Amamou	NoMemorySpace	https://nomemoryspace.wordpress.com/

Figure 8 Overview of the Blogosphere Dataset: 2011–13, Tunisia and Egypt.

Tweets mentioning the five leading candidates between 10.04.2012 and 24.05.2012					
	Hamdeen Sabahy	Ahmad Shafiq	Mohammed Morsi	Amru Mussa	Abdel Moneim Abu Al Futuh
Total Tweets	6023	15492	8480	4181	6369
#tags	18220	49048	32450	19348	17328
[@tags]	3759	9057	5677	2668	2926
ReTweets	2629	7302	4707	2280	2247
Source: R-Shief research tool, http://r-shief.org/					

Figure 9 Summary of the Data Sampled from the R-Shief Database.

Online comments posted prior to the 2012 constitutional referendum	
Article	Number of comments posted (Sept–Dec 2012)
1	243
2	15763
3	100
4	117
5	83
6	91
7	65
8	95
9	68
10	130
11	48
12	145
14	113
15	48
16	52
17	38
18	77
19	44
20	46
21	31
22	51
23	29
24	38
25	31
26	36
27	76
28	28
29	234
30	125

Figure 10 Overview of the Comments Sampled from the 'Dostour Sharek' Archive.

Egyptian News Sources Selected from the Nexis Lexis News Database
Al Ahram Al Arabiya
Al Ahram Al Duwali
Al Gomhurriah (Arabic)
Al Messa (Arabic)
Al Ahram
Al Ahram Gate
Al Ahram Gate (Arabic)
Al Ahram Hebdo
Al Ahram Messai
Al Ahram Weekly
Al Masry Al Youm (Arabic)
Alborsanews.com
Amcham Egypt project News
Arab Finance
Arab Finance (Arabic)

Figure 11 Sources Selected to Identify the Visibility of the 5 Leading Candidates across the LexisNexis Database.

Sentiment Analysis conducted on a sample of Arabic Hashtags covering the campaign (May 2012) (Laila Shereen Sakr, 2012)						
Arabic hashtags for names of candidates	*Shafiq* [Ahmad Shafiq]	*Hamdeen* [Hamdeen Sabahy]	*AbouFotouh* [Abdel Moneim Abu al Futuh]	*Moussa* [Amru Mussa]	*Morsi* [Mohammed Morsi]	KhaledAli [Khaled Ali]
Percentage of positive sentiment	77.66%	84.84%	72.6%	69.05%	99.83%	93.49%
Percentage of the sample	41.51%	11.4%	13.53%	8.53%	11.74%	7.34%
Daily Tweet Volume	7460	3912	2457	2978	3128	1171
Votes – election round 1	23.66%	20.72%	17.47%	11.13%	24.78%	0.58%
Source: http://www.jadaliyya.com/pages/index/5716/egypt-presidential-elections-and-twitter-talk						

Figure 12 Findings of the Sentiment Analysis Computed by Sakr (2012): First Round of the 2012 Presidential Campaign, Egypt.

Notes

Chapter 3

1   *'Generation of the Future'*.
2   Note to the editor: the only evidence of this comes from anonymized interview transcripts from my research.
3   From the Arabic 'فلول' (remnants from the old regime).
4   https://www.opendemocracy.net/en/north-africa-west-asia/impact-of-coalition-on-ennahda-and-nidaa-tounes/.

Chapter 4

1   http://baheyya.blogspot.co.uk/2012/05/striver.html.
2   http://baheyya.blogspot.co.uk/2014/01/a-military-constitution.html.
3   [Translated] http://www.debatunisie.com/archives/2011/02/19/20430474.html.
4   Pseudonyms are used to maintain participants' anonymity.
5   [Translated] http://underash.blogspot.co.uk/2012/12/blog-post.html.
6   السـماء أعـلى   الى بعيـدا تُحلق الثــورة
الأرض فــوق تمشى ــ السياسـة و
7   [Translated] http://atunisiangirl.blogspot.co.uk/2012/01/droit-de-reponse.html.
8   Union Générale des travailleurs Tunisiens.
9   Union des Travailleurs de Tunisie.
10   [Translated] http://mel7it3.blogspot.co.uk/2011/08/le-15-aout-la-mascarade.html.
11   http://www.faresmabrouk.com/2013/05/27/lhorizon-du-possible-1/.
12   http://baheyya.blogspot.com/2012/12/on-morsis-opponents.html.
13   http://www.bigpharaoh.org/2012/10/20/we-are-yearning-for-a-viable-alternative/.
14   Ibid.
15   Ibid.
16   [Translated] http://nomemoryspace.wordpress.com/2012/05/31/romain-gavras/.
17   [Translated] http://www.faresmabrouk.com/2013/05/27/lhorizon-du-possible-1/.

18 Error message appearing onscreen when the government prevented access to the Internet.

19 Reference to famous blogger and Twitter activist Slim Amammou.

20 Reference to blogger Lina Ben Mhenni.

21 [Translated] http://www.debatunisie.com/archives/2011/09/11/22005894.html.

22 http://mel7it3.blogspot.co.uk/2011/12/meritons-nous-tunezine-non-mais-onpeut.html.

23 http://www.bigpharaoh.org/2012/05/08/what-did-egypts-revolutionaries-do-wrong/.

Chapter 5

1 Study conducted as part of the 2012–2014 ESRC Google Data Analytics Programme (Voter Ecology Project).

2 R-Shief is an open-source project, which provides free access to a database of tweets posted in English and Arabic between 2008 and 2013. The website is also developing a set of data visualization tools designed to conduct social media analysis in Arabic.

3 I am specifically referring to Amru Mussa's moussacampaign and Abu al Futuh's MaadiCampaign.

Chapter 7

1 Pseudonyms are used to maintain participants' anonymity.

2 Famous Egyptian blogger active on the activist blogosphere prior to 2011.

3 *Electronic agents* or electronic army.

4 Pseudonyms are used to maintain participants' anonymity.

5 Pseudonyms are used to maintain participants' anonymity.

6 Bread, freedom, social justice.

7 The al-Karama Party (Dignity party).

8 Pseudonyms are used to maintain participants' anonymity.

9 Pseudonyms are used to maintain participants' anonymity.

10 Pseudonyms are used to maintain participants' anonymity.

11 Egyptian bloggers, famous among the activist community.

12 Pseudonyms are used to maintain participants' anonymity.

13 Pseudonyms are used to maintain participants' anonymity.
14 Pseudonyms are used to maintain participants' anonymity.
15 Pseudonyms are used to maintain participants' anonymity.
16 Pseudonyms are used to maintain participants' anonymity.
17 Pseudonyms are used to maintain participants' anonymity.
18 Pseudonyms are used to maintain participants' anonymity.
19 Pseudonyms are used to maintain participants' anonymity.
20 Pseudonyms are used to maintain participants' anonymity.
21 Pseudonyms are used to maintain participants' anonymity.
22 Reference to the clashes that took place in November 2011 between young revolutionaries and the police in the Mohammed Mahmoud street, which leads to Tahrir Square.
23 Amir, leftist pro-revolutionary activist, Cairo, spring 2014.

Chapter 8

1 Notes to the reviewers and editors: these information come for anonymized interviews.
2 https://www.cage.ngo/prevent.
3 Pseudonym.

Chapter 9

1 District of Tripoli.
2 After the civil war, the Lebanese Forces became a party but continued to operate as a paramilitary organization. Since 2005, it was part of the 14 March Alliance led by Saad Hariri.
3 The party lost twenty seats.

Chapter 10

1 http://www.bigpharaoh.org/2012/05/08/what-did-egypts-revolutionaries-do-wrong/.

Bibliography

Abaza, M., 2013. Walls, Segregating Downtown Cairo and the Mohammed Mahmud Street Graffiti. *Theory, Culture & Society*, 30(1), pp. 122–39.

Adorno, T. W. and Horkheimer, M., 1947. *Dialectic of Enlightenment, Philosophical Fragments*. Translated by E. Jephcott., 2002. California: Stanford University Press.

Ahram Online, 2013. Full English Translation of Egypt's New Protest Law. 25 November. Available at: https://english.ahram.org.eg/News/87375.aspx [Accessed: 22 May 2022].

Akkerman, T., 2011. Friend or Foe? Right-Wing Populism and the Popular Press in Britain and the Netherlands. *Journalism*, 12(8), pp. 931–45.

Al Jazeera News, 2018. Egypt's Sisi Signs New Law Tightening Government Control Online. 18 August. Available at: https://www.aljazeera.com/news/2018/8/18/egypts-sisi-signs-new-law-tightening-government-control-online [Accessed: 22 May 2022].

Al Maghlouth, N., Arvanitis, R., Cointet, J.-P. and Hanafi, S., 2015. Who Frames the Debate on the Arab Uprisings? Analysis of Arabic, English, and French Academic Scholarship. *International Sociology*, 3(4), pp. 1–24.

Aliriza, F., 2019. Fears over Facebook's Role in Election Campaign. *Meshkal*. 5 September. Available at: https://meshkal.org/fears-over-facebooks-role-in-election-campaign/ [Accessed: 22 May 2022].

Allagui, I. and Kuebler, J., 2011. The Arab Spring and the Role of ICTs. *International Journal of Communication*, 5, pp. 1435–42.

Alterman, J. B., 2011. The Revolution Will Not Be Tweeted. *The Washington Quarterly*, 34(4), pp. 103–16.

Alvares, C. and Dahlgren, P., 2016. Populism, Extremism and Media: Mapping an Uncertain Terrain. *European Journal of Communication*, 31(1), pp. 46–57.

Amnesty International, 2014. Egypt's Plan for Mass Surveillance of Social Media an Attack on Internet Privacy and Freedom of Expression. 4 June. Available at: https://www.amnesty.org/en/latest/news/2014/06/egypt-s-attack-internet-privacy-tightens-noose-freedom-expression/ [Accessed: 22 May 2022].

Amnesty International, 2018. My Wife Was Imprisoned for Speaking out against Sexual Harassment in Egypt. 21 August. Available at: https://www.amnesty.org/en/latest/campaigns/2018/08/my-wife-was-imprisoned-for-speaking-out-against-sexual-harassment-in-egypt/ [Accessed: 22 May 2022].

Amnesty International, 2019. Egypt: Bitter Legacy of Rabaa Massacre Continues to Haunt Egyptians. 14 August. Available at: https://www.amnesty.org/en/latest/news/2019/08/egypt-bitter-legacy-of-rabaa-massacre-continues-to-haunt-egyptians/ [Accessed: 22 May 2022].

Anderson, B., 1983. *Imagined Communities: Reflections on the Origins and Spread of Nationalism*. London: Verso.

Anderson, L., 2011. Demystifying the Arab Spring. *Foreign Affair*, 90(3), pp. 2–7.

Angeli, C., Bonk, C. J. and Hara, N., 2000. Content Analysis of Online Discussion in an Applied Educational Psychology Course. *Instructional Science*, 28, pp. 115–52.

Anderson, J., Dean, J. and Lovink, G., 2006. *Reformatting Politics: Information Technology and Global Civil Society*. New York: Routledge.

Anderson, L., 2011. Demystifying the Arab Spring. *Foreign Affair*, 90(3), pp. 2–7.

Aouragh, M. and Alexander, A., 2011. The Egyptian Experience: Sense and Nonsense of the Internet Revolution. *International Journal of Communication*, 5, pp. 1333–58.

Appadurai, A., 1996. *Modernity at Large: Cultural Dimensions of Globalization*. Minneapolis, MN: University of Minnesota Press., H., 1963. On the Revolution. London: Penguin Books.

Arendt, H., 2016. (First published 1963). On Revolution. London: Faber & Faber. Main - Faber Modern Classics edition.

Azhari, T., 2019. Lebanon's Banks Reopen after Two-Week Closure. *Al Jazeera*. 1 November. Available at: https://www.aljazeera.com/economy/2019/11/1/lebanons-banks-reopen-after-two-week-closure [Accessed: 22 May 2022].

Azhari, T., 2019. Megaphone: The Voice of Lebanon's Uprising. *Al Jazeera*. 8 December. Available at: https://www.aljazeera.com/features/2019/12/8/megaphone-the-voice-of-lebanons-uprising [Accessed: 22 May 2022].

Bakhtin, M., 1981. *The Dialogic Imagination*. London: University of Texas Press.

Ball, J., 2017. *Post-Truth: How Bullshit Conquered the World*. London: Biteback.

Bayat, A., 2010. *Life as Politics: How Ordinary People Change the Middle East*. Sanford: Stanford University Press.

Baydoun, R., 2022. How Media Controls Your Opinion. Sarde Podcast. April 2022. Available at: https://www.youtube.com/watch?v=KdSkMxf9ZwM [Accessed: 22 May 2022].

BBC News, 2015. Beirut Attacks: Suicide Bombers Kill Dozens in Shia Suburb. 12 November. Available at: https://www.bbc.co.uk/news/world-middle-east-34795797 [Accessed: 22 May 2022].

BBC News, 2021. Beirut Port Blast: The Tensions around the Investigation. 14 October. Available at: https://www.bbc.co.uk/news/world-middle-east-58913864 [Accessed: 22 May 2022].

Beinin, J., 2012. *The Rise of Egypt's Workers*. Washington: The Carnegie Papers.

Beinin, J. and Vairel, F., 2013. *Social Movements, Mobilization and Contestation in the Middle East and North Africa*. Second Edition. Stanford: Stanford University Press.

Benhabib, S., 2011. The Arab Spring: Religion, Revolution and the Public Sphere. Transformation of the Public Sphere. Available at: http://publicsphere.ssrc.org/benhabib-the-arab-spring-religion-revolution-and-the-public-square/ [Accessed: 4 August 2015].

Ben Mbarek, G., 2021. Tunisia. The Protesters Who May Have Helped Bring Down Mechichi Government. *Nawaat*. 27 July. Available at: https://nawaat.org/2021/07/27/tunisia-the-protesters-who-may-have-helped-bring-down-mechichi-government/ [Accessed: 22 May 2022].

Ben Mhenni, L., 2012. *Tunisian Girl: Blogueuse Pour Un Printemps Arabe*. Montpellier: Editions Indigene.

Benjamin, W., 1936. *The Work of Art in the Age of Mechanical Reproduction*. Translated by J. A. Underwood., 2008. London: Penguin Books.

Bennett, W. L. and Livingston, S., 2018. The Disinformation Order: Disruptive Communication and the Decline of Democratic Institutions. *European Journal of Communication*, 33(2), pp. 122–39.

Bennett, W. L. and Segerberg, A., 2011. Social Media and the Organization of Collective Action: Using Twitter to Explore the Ecologies of Two Climate Change Protests. *The Communication Review*, 14(3), pp. 197–215.

Bennett, W. L. and Segerberg, A., 2012. The Logic of Connective Action. *Information, Communication & Society*, 15(5), pp. 739–68.

Bennett, W. L. and Segerberg, A., 2013. *The Logic of Connective Action Digital Media and the Personalization of Contentious Politics*. Cambridge: Cambridge University Press.

Bergmann, E., 2018. *Conspiracy & Populism: The Politics of Misinformation*. London: Palgrave Macmillan.

Berry, D. M., 2011. The Computational Turn: Thinking about the Digital Humanities. *Culture Machine*, 12, pp. 1–22.

Bessi, A., et al., 2014. The Economy of Attention in the Age of (Mis)information. *Journal of Trust Management*, 1, p. 12.

Biekart, K. and Fowler, A., 2013. Transforming Activism 2010+: Exploring Ways and Waves. *Development and Change*, 44(3), pp. 527–46.

Bindra, J., 2018. How Blockchain can Transform India. *TEDX Chennai*. 18 May.

Blair, E., 2022. Explainer: Lebanon's Financial Crisis and How It Happened. *Reuters*. 23 January. Available at: https://www.reuters.com/markets/rates-bonds/lebanons-financial-crisis-how-it-happened-2022-01-23/ [Accessed: 22 May 2022].

Boler, M. and Davis, E., 2018. The Affective Politics of the 'Post-Truth' Era: Feeling Rules and Networked Subjectivity. *Emotion, Space and Society*, 27, pp. 75–85.

Bontcheva, K. and Posetti, J., 2020. Balancing Act: Countering Digital Disinformation While Respecting Freedom of Expression Broadband Commission Research Report on 'Freedom of Expression and Addressing Disinformation on the Internet'. Unesco, Broadband Commission for Sustainable Development.

Borsch, C., 2006. The Exclusion of the Crowd The Destiny of a Sociological Figure of the Irrational. *European Journal of Social Theory*, 9(1), pp. 83–102.

Boubekeur, A., 2017. Islamists, Secularists and Old Regime Elites in Tunisia: Bargained Competition. In M. Assebrug and H. Wimmen, eds. *Dynamics of Transformation, Elite Change and New Social Mobilization*. London: Routledge.

Bourdieu, P., 1991. *Language and Symbolic Power*. Cambridge, UK: Polity.

Breuer, A., 2012. *The Role of Social Media in Mobilizing Political Protests, Evidence from the Tunisian Revolution*. Bonn: German Development Institute.

Briggs, C. L. and Bauman, R., 1992. Genre, Intertextuality, and Social Power. *Journal of Linguistic Anthropology*, 2(2), pp. 131–72.

Cacciatore, M. A., Scheufele, D. A. and Iyengar, S., 2016. The End of Framing as We Know It; and the Future of Media Effects. *Mass Communication and Society*, 19(1), pp. 7–23.

Calhoun, G. ed., 1992. *Habermas and the Public Sphere*. Cambridge, MA: The MIT Press.

Cardon, D., 2010. *La Démocratie Internet, Promesse Et Limites*. Paris: Seuil.

Castells, M., 2004. *The Network Society: A Cross-Cultural Perspective*. Northampton: Edward Elgar Publishing.

Castells, M., 2007. Communication, Power and Counter-Power in the Network Society. *International Journal of Communication*, 1, pp. 238–66.

Castells, M., 2009. *The Rise of the Network Society: Information Age: Economy, Society and Culture Volume 1*. Malden: Blackwell Publishing.

Castells, M., 2012. *Networks of Outrage and Hope*. Cambridge: Polity Press.

Cavatorta, F., 2015. Salafism, Liberalism, and Democratic Learning in Tunisia. *The Journal of North African Studies*, 20(5), pp. 770–83.

Cavatorta, F. and Mekki, N., 2021. How Can We Agree on Anything in This Environment? Tunisian Media, Transition and Elite Compromises: A View from Parliament. *The International Journal of Press/Politics* 2021, 26(4), pp. 822–41.

Cavatorta, F. and Merone, F., 2013. Moderation through Exclusion? The Journey of the Tunisian Ennahda from Fundamentalist to Conservative Party. *Democratization*, 20(5), pp. 857–75.

Chadwick, A., 2013. *The Hybrid Media System: Politics and Power*. Oxford: Oxford University Press.

Chatfield, A. T. and Alhurjran, O., 2009. A Cross-Country Comparative Analysis of E-Government Service Delivery among Arab Countries. *Information Technology for Development*, 15(3), pp. 151–70.

Chomsky, N. and Herman, E. S., 1988. *Manufacturing Consent: The Political Economy of the Mass Media*. London: The Bodley Head.

Christensen, M. and Christensen, C., 2011. The Arab Spring as Meta-Event and Communicative Spaces. *Television & New Media*, 14(4), pp. 351–64.

Clennon, O. D., 2018. *Resisting Post-truth Whiteness: The Grassroots as Sites of Black Radical Activism in: Black Scholarly Activism between the Academy and Grassroots*. Manchester: Palgrave Pivot, pp. 131–49.

Cochrane, P., 2007. Lebanon's Media Sectarianism. *Arab Media & Society, Feature Article* (May), pp. 1–13.

Cochrane, P., 2008. Lebanon's Media Battle. Arab Media & Society. *Feature Article* (September), pp. 1–6.

Coleman, G., 2011. Hacker Politics and Publics. *Public Culture*, 23(3), pp. 511–16.

ConstituteProject.org (The Comparative Constitution Project), 2022. Egypt's Constitution of 2012. *Historical*. 27 April. Available at: https://www.constituteproject.org/constitution/Egypt_2012.pdf?lang=en [Accessed: 22 May 2022].

Cottle, S., 2006a. *Mediatized Conflict: Developments in Media and Conflict Studies*. Maidenhead: Open University Press.

Cottle, S., 2006b. *Mediatized Conflict: Understanding Media and Conflicts in the Contemporary World*. New York: Open University Press.

Cottle, S., 2011. Media and the Arab Uprisings of 2011: Research Notes. *Journalism*, 12(5), pp. 647–59.

Curran, G. and Gibson, M., 2012. WikiLeaks, Anarchism and Technologies of Dissent. *Antipode*, 45(2), pp. 294–314.

Curtis, M., 1991. Walter Lippmann Reconsidered. *January*, 28(2), pp. 23–31.

D'Ancona, M., 2017. *Post Truth: The New War on Truth and How to Fight Back*. London: Ebury.

Dartnell, M., 2006. Web Activism as an Element of Global Security. In A. Karatzogianni, ed. *Cyber Conflict and Global Politics*. New York: Routledge, pp. 61–78.

Dayan, D., 2000. Television. Le Presque-Public. *Réseaux*, 18(100), pp. 427–56.

Dayan, D. and Katz, E., 1994. *Media Events: Live Broadcasting of History*. Cambridge, MA: Harvard University Press.

Dean, J., 2003. Why the Net Is Not a Public Sphere. *Constellations*, 10(1), pp. 95–112.

Dean, J., 2005. Communicative Capitalism: Circulation and the Foreclosure of Politics. *Cultural Politics*, 1(1), pp. 51–73.

Dorfman, A. and Mattelart, A., 2019. (First published 1971) *How to Read Donald Duck: Imperialist Ideology in the Disney Comic.* London: Pluto Press.

Dunn, A., 2011. Unplugging a Nation: State Media Strategy during Egypt's January 25 Uprising. *The Fletcher Forum of World Affairs*, 35(2), pp. 15–24.

Elseewi, T. A., 2011. A Revolution of the Imagination. *International Journal of Communication*, 5, pp. 1197–206.

Erhaim, Z and Mahlouly, D. 2023. 'Pro-Palestinian Activism: Resisting Digital Occupation'. In Miladi, N. (ed.) '"https://www.bloomsbury.com/uk/global-media-coverage-of-the-palestinianisraeli-conflict-9780755649907/"' 'Global Media Coverage of the Palestinian-Israeli Conflict: Reporting The Sheikh Jarrah Evictions', London: I.B. Tauris Bloomsbury. August 2023.

Erll, A., 2011. Traumatic Pasts, Literary Afterlives, and Transcultural Memory: New Directions of Literary and Media Memory Studies. *Journal of Aesthetics & Culture*, 3, pp. 1–5.

Erll, A. and Rigney, A., 2009. *Mediation, Remediation, and the Dynamics of Cultural Memory.* Berlin: Walter de Gruyter.

EuroMed Rights, 2020. Dangerous Liaisons: Social Media as a (Flawed) Tool of Resistance in Egypt. September. Available at: https://euromedrights.org/wp-content/uploads/2020/09/Study_on_social_media_in_Egypt.pdf [Accessed: 22 May 2022].

European Commission, 2018. Action Plan against Disinformation. *Joint Communication to the European Parliament, the European Council, the Council, the European Economic and Social Committee and Committee of the Regions.*

European Parliament, 2016. Briefing: EU strategic Communication with the Arab World. May. Available at: https://www.europarl.europa.eu/RegData/etudes/BRIE/2016/581997/EPRS_BRI_2016_581997_EN.pdf [Accessed: 22 May 2022].

Facon, C., 2020. Tripoli: The Bride of The Revolution. *Orientxxi.* 8 January. Available at: https://orientxxi.info/magazine/tripoli-the-bride-of-the-revolution,3543 [Accessed: 22 May 2022].

Fahmi, G., 2019a. Are We Seeing a Second Wave of the Arab Spring? *Chatham House.* 22 March. Available at: https://www.chathamhouse.org/2019/03/are-we-seeing-second-wave-arab-spring [Accessed: 5 May 2022].

Fahmi, G., 2019b. Five Lessons from the New Arab Uprisings. *Chatham House.* 12 November. Available at: https://www.chathamhouse.org/2019/11/five-lessons-new-arab-uprisings [Accessed: 5 May 2022].

Farah, R., 2012. The Arab Spring: A Revolution or Just an Outburst? *Al-Monitor.* 25 January. Available at: http://www.al-monitor.com/pulse/culture/2012/01/arab-societies-and-bedouin-cultu.html# [Accessed: 2 September 2015].

Fazulla, H., 2020. Mickey Mouse and Activism in Egypt. *The Middle East Research Hub.* 21 October.

Flaxman, S. et al., 2016. Filter Bubbles, Echo Chambers, and Online News Consumption. *Public Opinion Quarterly*, 80(S1), pp. 298–320.

Flichy, P., 2010. *Le Sacre de l'amateur, Sociologie des Passions ordinaires à l'ère numérique*. Paris: Seuil.

Flichy, P., 2011. *The Internet Imaginary*. Cambridge, MA: The MIT Press.

Foroudi, L., 2019. Painting the Town: How Kais Saied Inspires Change on Tunisian Streets. *Al-Monitor*. 22 October. Available at: https://www.al-monitor.com/originals/2019/10/the-people-want-clean-roads-kais-saied-effect-takes-over.html#ixzz7VKteStVJ.

Foucault, M., 1971. *L'ordre du discours: Leçon inaugurale au Collège de France prononcée le 2 décembre 1970*. Paris: Gallimard.

Foucault, M. and Deleuze, G., 1977. Intellectuals and Power. In D. F. Bouchard, ed. *Language, Counter-Memory, Practice: Selected Essays and Interviews*. Ithaca: Cornell University Press, pp. 205–17.

Frakes, N., 2019. Lebanon's Protesters Occupy Central Beirut Road in Display of Unity. 17 December. Available at: https://www.al-monitor.com/originals/2019/12/lebanon-protests-block-roads-beirut-ring.html#ixzz7U0TjYNdJ [Accessed: 22 May 2022].

France 24, 2015. Deadly Explosions Rock Hezbollah Stronghold in Beirut. 12 November. Available at: https://www.france24.com/en/20151112-severalwounded-two-blasts-dahieh-southern-beirut-lebanon-hezbollah [Accessed: 22 May 2022].

France 24, News Series, 2021. Women Face Period Poverty as Lebanon's Economic Crisis Deepens. 1 July. Available at: https://www.france24.com/en/middle-east/20210701-women-face-period-poverty-as-lebanon-s-economic-crisis-deepens [Accessed: 22 May 2022].

Fraser, N., 1985. What's Critical about Critical Theory? The Case of Habermas and Gender. *New German Critique*, 35, pp. 97–131.

Fraser, N., 1990. Rethinking the Public Sphere: A Contribution to the Critique of Actually Existing Democracy. *Social Text*, 25(26), pp. 56–80.

Fraser, N., 2007. Transnationalizing the Public Sphere. *EIPCP*. Available at: http://eipcp.net/transversal/0605/fraser/en [Accessed: 1 May 2012].

Fraser, N., 2016. Progressive Neoliberalism versus Reactionary Populism: A Choice that Feminists Should Refuse. *NORA – Nordic Journal of Feminist and Gender Research*, 24(4), pp. 281–4.

Fraser, N., 2017. Progressive Neoliberalism versus Reactionary Populism: A Hobson's Choice. In Heinrich Geiselberger, ed. *The Great Regression*. Cambridge: Polity, pp. 40–8.

Fuchs, C., 2010. Labor in Informational Capitalism and on the Internet. *The Information Society*, 26, pp. 179–96.

Fuchs, C., 2012a. Behind the News. *Social Media, Riots, and Revolutions. Capital & Class*, 36(3), pp. 383–91.

Fuchs, C., 2012b. Some Reflections on Manuel Castells' Book Networks of Outrage and Hope. *Social Movements In the Internet Age*. Triple C, 10(2), pp. 775–97.

Fuchs, C., 2017. From Digital Positivism and Administrative Big Data Analytics towards Critical Digital and Social Media Research! *European Journal of Communication*, 32(1), pp. 37–49.

Gebeily, M., 2014. Ashura: Lebanon's Shia Defiant in Face of ISIL Threat. *Al Jazeera.* 5 November. Available at: https://www.aljazeera.com/news/2014/11/5/ashura-lebanons-shia-defiant-in-face-of-isil-threat [Accessed: 22 May].

Gehad, R., 2014. Egypt Amends Penal Code to Stipulate Harsher Punishments on Foreign Funding. 23 September. Available at: https://english.ahram.org.eg/News/111488.aspx [Accessed: 22 May 2022].

Geldi, M., 2021. Lebanese Cannot Access Money in Banks since Late 2019. Anadolu Agency. 27 February. Available at: https://www.aa.com.tr/en/economy/lebanese-cannot-access-money-in-banks-since-late-2019/2158782 [Accessed: 22 May 2022].

Gerbaudo, P., 2012. *Tweets and the Streets, Social Media and Contemporary Activism.* London: Pluto Press.

Gerbaudo, P., 2018. Social Media and Populism: An Elective Affinity? *Media, Culture & Society* 2018, 40(5), pp. 745–53.

Glassey, O. and Leresche, J. P., 2012. La participation politique (re)visitée par les TIC: la réinvention des échelles du débat public. *Argumentum, Journal of the Seminar of Discursive Logic, Argumentation Theory and Rhetoric*, 10(1), pp. 109–27.

Gleverec, H., Masse, E. and Magret, E., 2008. *Cultural Studies, Anthologie*. Paris: Armand Colin.

Greenberg, N., 2019. *How Information Warfare Shaped the Arab Spring: The Politics of Narrative in Tunisia and Egypt*. Edinburgh: Edinburgh University Press.

Grenfell, M. J., 2010. *Bourdieu, Language and Linguistics*. London: Continuum–3PL.

Grimmer, G. and Stewart, B. M., 2013. Text as Data: The Promise and Pitfalls of Automatic Content Analysis Methods for Political Texts. *Political Analysis*, pp. 1–31.

Groshek, J. and Koc-Michalska, K., 2017. Helping Populism Win? Social Media use, Filter Bubbles, and Support for Populist Presidential Candidates in the 2016 US Election Campaign. *Information, Communication & Society*, 20, p. 9.

Guidère, M., 2012. *Le Choc des révolutions arabes: De l'Algérie au Yémen, 22 pays sous tension*. Paris: Autrement Frontières.

Habermas, J., 1962. *The Structural Transformation of the Public Sphere: An Inquiry into a Category of Bourgeois Society*. Translated by T. Burger., 1989. Cambridge: MIT Press, 1991.

Habermas, J., 1984. *The Theory of Communicative Action Vol. 1, Reason and the Rationalization of Society*. Boston: Beacon Press.

Habermas, J., 2006. Political Communication in Media Society: Does Democracy Still Enjoy an Epistemic Dimension? The Impact of Normative Theory on Empirical Research. *Communication Theory*, 16, pp. 411–26.

Halbwachs, M., 1997. *La Mémoire Collective*. Paris: Albin Michel.

Hall, S., 1993. Encoding and Decoding in the Television Discourse. In S. During, ed. *The Cultural Studies Reader*. London: Routledge, pp. 90–103.

Hall, S., 1997. Representation and the Media. In S. Talreja, S. Jhally and M. Patierno, eds. *Transcripts of Stuart Hall's lecture at The Open University*. Northampton, MA: Media Education Foundation, pp. 5–22.

Hall, S., 2000. Reconstruction Work: Images of Post-War Black Settlement. In J. Procter, ed. *Writing Black Britain 1948 to 1998: An Interdisciplinary Anthology*. New York: Manchester University Press, pp. 82–94.

Hameleers, M., Bos, L. and de Vreese, C. H., 2017. The Appeal of Media Populism: The Media Preferences of Citizens with Populist Attitudes. *Mass Communication and Society*, 20(4), pp. 481–504.

Hamzawy, A., 2016. Egypt's Anti Protest Law: Legalising Authoritarianism. Carnegie Middle East. 24 November. Available at: https://carnegieendowment. org/2016/11/24/egypt-s-anti-protest-law-legalising-authoritarianism-pub-66274 [Accessed: 22 May 2022].

Hart, V., 2003. Democratic Constitution Making. *United States Institute for Peace, Special Report* (107). July Issue, pp. 1–12.

Hassan, A. and Shenker, J., 2011. Egyptian Human Rights Groups Accuse Junta of Smear Campaign. *The Guardian*. 24 August. Available at: https://www. theguardian.com/world/2011/aug/24/egypt-human-rights-military [Accessed: 22 May 2022].

Houssari, N., 2019. Nabatieh Rises against Hezbollah and Amal. *Arab News*. Available at: https://www.arabnews.com/node/1574416/middle-east [Accessed: 22 May 2022].

Howard, P. N., Woolley, S. and Calo, R., 2018. Algorithms, Bots, and Political Communication in the US 2016 Election: The Challenge of Automated Political Communication for Election Law and Administration. *Journal of Information Technology & Politics*, 15(2), pp. 81–93.

Hiltz, S. R. and Turoff, M., 1978. *The Network Nation: Human Communication via Computer*. Reading, MA: Addison-Wesley.

Hinds, M., 2003. *The Triumph of the Flexible Society: The Connectivity Revolution and Resistance to Change*. Westport: Praeger.

Hine, C., 2000. *Virtual Ethnography*. London: Sage.

Hirst, M., 2012. One Tweet Does Not a Revolution Make: Technological Determinism. *Media and Social Change, Global Media Journal Australian Edition*, 6(2), pp. 1–11.

Hogan, B., 2008. Analyzing Social Network via the Internet. In N. G. Feilding and R. M. Lee and G. Blank, eds. *The Sage Handbook of Online Research Methods*. London: Sage, pp. 141–60.

Houston, J. B., 2018. Community Resilience and Communication: Dynamic Interconnections between and among Individuals, Families, and Organizations. *Journal of Applied Communication Research*, 46, pp. 19–22.

Houston, J. B., Spialek, M. L., Cox, J., Greenwood, M. M. and First, J., 2015. The Centrality of Communication and Media in Fostering Community Resilience: A Framework for Assessment and Intervention. *American Behavioral Scientist*, 59, pp. 270–83.

Howard, P. N., 2010. *The Digital Origins of Dictatorship and Democracy: Information Technology and Political Islam*. New York: Oxford University Press.

Howard, P. N. and Hussein, M.H., 2013. *Democracy's Fourth Wave? Digital Media and the Arab Spring*. New York: Oxford University Press.

Human Rights Watch, 2017. We Do Unreasonable Things Here. *Torture and National Security in al-Sisi's Egypt*. September.

Hussein, S., 2021. Preventing Violent Extremism the Lebanese Way: A Critical Analysis of the Lebanese PVE Strategy. *Perspective on Terrorism,* 15(5), pp. 71–84.

Ibrahim, A., 2015. Egypt's Power Outages Continue to Intensify. *Middle East Eye*. 12 February. Available at: https://www.middleeasteye.net/news/egypts-power-outages-continue-intensify [Accessed: 22 May 2011].

Ifex, 2021. Egypt: Fake News and Coronavirus Trials. 31 March. Available at: https://ifex.org/egypt-fake-news-and-coronavirus-trials/ [Accessed: 22 May 2022].

Independent, 2021. As Lebanese Got Poorer, Politicians Stowed Wealth Abroad. 6 October. Available at: https://www.independent.co.uk/news/world/europe/beirut-hassan-diab-british-virgin-islands-britain-world-bank-b1933118.html [Accessed: 22 May 2022].

Iskander, E., 2011. Connecting the National and the Virtual: Can Facebook Activism Remain Relevant after Egypt's January 25 Uprising? *International Journal of Communication*, 5, pp. 1225–37.

Jamaoui, A., 2015. The Impact of the Coalition on Ennahda and Nidaa Tounes. *Open Democracy*. 11 March.

Jenkins, H., 1992. *Textual Poachers: Television, Fans and Participatory Culture*. NewYork: Routledge.

Jenkins, H., 2006a. *Fans, Bloggers and Gamers, Exploring Participatory Culture*. New York: New York University Press.

Jenkins, H., 2006b. *Convergence Culture: Where Old and New Media Collide*. New York: New York University Press.

Jumet, K. D., 2014. The Egyptian Uprisings from 2011 to 2013: Who Says They Were About Democracy? 2014 APSA Annual Meeting & Exhibition Washington, DC. 28–31 August. Available at: http://papers.ssrn.com/sol3/papers.cfm?abstract_id=2454846 [Accessed: 2 August 2015].

Kanna, A., 2012. Urban Praxis and the Arab Spring. *City: Analysis of Urban Trends, Culture, Theory, Policy, Action*, 16(3), pp. 360–8.

Kant, I., 2011. *The Critique of Pure Reason*. Washington: Pacific Publishing Studio.

Kapitalis, 2019. Presidentielle: Hichem Snoussi (Haica) approuve la decision de l'Isie de ne pas avoir elimine Nabil Karoui. 18 September.

Karatzogianni, A. ed., 2009. *Cyber Conflict and Global Politics*. New York: Routledge.

Katz, E. and Lazarsfeld, P., 1955. *Personal Influence: The Part Played by People in the Flow of Mass Communications*. Glencoe, IL: Free Press.

Kestler-D'Amours, J., 2018. How Egypt Presidential Election Is Rendered Irrelevant. *Al Jazeera*. 24 January. Available at: https://www.aljazeera.com/news/2018/1/24/how-egypt-presidential-election-is-rendered-irrelevant [Accessed: 22 May 2022].

Khatib, L., 2012. *Image Politics in the Middle East*. London: I.B. Tauris.

Khondker, H. H., 2011. Role of the New Media in the Arab Spring. *Globalizations*, 8(5), pp. 675–9.

Kramer, B., 2018. Populism, Media and the Form of Society. *Communication Theory*. Communication Theory, 28, pp. 444–65.

Latour, B., 1993. *We Have Never Been Modern*. Cambridge, MA: Harvard University Press.

Lawson, G., 2012. The Arab Uprisings: Revolution or Protests? In N. Kitchen, ed. *IDEAS Reports–Special Reports*. London: SR011. LSE IDEAS, pp. 12–16.

Lazarsfeld, P. F., Berelson, B. and Gaudet, H., 1948. *The People's Choice: How the Voter Makes up His Mind in a Presidential Campaign*. New York: Columbia University Press.

Le Bon, G., 1982. *The Psychology of Socialism*. New York: Rootledge. Le Bon, G., 2009. (First published 1895). *Psychology of Crowds*. Southampton: Sparkling Books Limited.

Levinson, M., 2017. *Fake News in Real Context*. New York: Connected Editions.

Lim, M., 2012. Clicks, Cabs, and Coffee Houses: Social Media and Oppositional Movements in Egypt, 2004–2011. *Journal of Communication*, 62(2), pp. 231–48.

Lippmann, W. (1998). First published 1922. Public Opinion. London: Transaction Publishers.

Liu, B., 2010. Sentiment Analysis: A Multi-Faceted Problem. *IEEE Intelligent Systems*, 25(3) 2010, pp. 76–80.

Logan, M. R., 1981. L'intertextualité au carrefour de la philologie et de la poésie. *Littérature*, 41, pp. 47–9.

Lopes de Souza, M. and Lipietz, B., 2011. The 'Arab Spring' and the City: Hopes, Contradictions and Spatiality. *City: Analysis of Urban Trends, Culture, Theory, Policy, Action*, 15(6), pp. 618–24.

Lopes de Souza, M. and Lipietz, B., 2012. Introduction: Where Do We Stand? New Hopes. *Frustration and Open Wounds in Arab Cities. City: Analysis of Urban Trends, Culture, Theory, Policy, Action*, 16(3), pp. 355–9.

Lotan, G., Graeff, E., Ananny, M., Gaffney, D., Pearce, I. and Boyd, D., 2011. The Revolution Were Tweeted: Information Flows during the 2011 Tunisian and Egyptian Revolutions. *International Journal of Communication*, 5, pp. 1375–405.

Lynch, M., 2011. After Egypt: The Limits and Promise of Online Challenges to the Authoritarian Arab State. *Perspective on Politics*, 9(2), pp. 301–10.

Lynch, M., Freelon, D. and Aday, S., 2017. Online Clustering, Fear and Uncertainty in Egypt's Transition, Democratization. *Democratization*, 24(6), pp. 1159–77.

Maboudi, T. and Nadi, G. P., 2014. Bringing the Constitution Online: The Struggle over Egypt's New Constitution. 2014 APSA Annual Meeting & Exhibition Washington, DC. 28–31 August. Available at: https://www.american.edu/spa/gov/upload/democracry2013-nadi-maboudi.pdf [Accessed: 2 August 2015].

Masr, Mada, 2014. Electricity Minister to Replace Alleged MB Members. 24 August. Available at: https://www.madamasr.com/en/2014/08/24/news/u/electricity-minister-to-replace-alleged-mb-members/ [Accessed: 22 May 2022].

Malik, A. and Awadallah, B., 2011.The Economics of the Arab Spring. Centre for the Study of African Economies. Available at: http://www.csae.ox.ac.uk/workingpapers/pdfs/csae-wps-2011-23.pdf [Accessed: 2 August 2015].

Mason, P., 2011. *Why It's Kicking Off Everywhere, The New Global Revolutions*. London: Verso.

Masood, A. and Nisar, M., 2020. Speaking out: A Postcolonial Critique of the Academic Discourse on Far-Right Populism. *020*, 27(1), pp. 162–73.

Mazzoleni, G. and Bracciali, R., 2018. Socially Mediated Populism: The Communicative Strategies of Political Leaders on Facebook. *Palgrave Communication*, 4(50), pp. 1–10.

McCarthy, R., 2018. When Islamists Lose: The Politicization of Tunisia's Ennahda Movement. *Middle East Journal*, 72(3), pp. 365–84.

McCombs, M., 2004. *Setting the Agenda*. USA: Blackwell Publishing Malden.

McCombs, M. and Shaw, D.L., 1972. The Agenda-Setting Function of Mass Media. *Public Opinion Quarterly*, 36, pp. 176–87.

McGregor, A., 2016. Unwanted Ally: Hezbollah's War against the Islamic State, Jamestown Foundation, 22 January 2016. *Terrorism Monitor Volume*, 14(2), pp. 9–12. Available at: https://www.refworld.org/docid/56a7924c4.html [Accessed: 22 May 2022].

McLuhan, M., 1967. *War and Peace in the Global Village*. New York: Bantam Books.

McLuhan, M., 1994. (first published 1964). *Understanding Media: The Extensions of Man*. Cambridge: The MIT Press.

Mejia, R., Beckermann, K. and Sullivan, C., 2018. White Lies: A Racial History of the (Post)Truth. *Communication and Critical/Cultural Studies*, 15(2), pp. 109–26.

Mellor, N., Ayish, M., Dajani, N. and Ayish, M. I., 2011. *Arab Media, Globalization and Merging Media Industries*. Cambridge: Polity.

Meraz, S., 2009. Is There an Elite Hold? Traditional Media to Social Media Agenda Setting Influence in Blog Networks. *Journal of Computer-Mediated Communication*, 14, pp. 682–707.

Meraz, S. and Papacharissi, Z., 2013. Networked Gatekeeping and Networked Framing on#Egypt. *The International Journal of Press/Politics*, 20(10), pp. 1–26.

Merrin, W., 2014. *Media Studies 2.0*. New York: Routledge.

Merrin, W., 2019. President Troll: Trump, 4Chan and Memetic Warfare. In Catherine Happer, Andrew Hoskins and William Merrin eds., *Trump's Media War*. London: PalgraveMacmillan, pp. 201–26.

Michaelson, R., 2018a. Egypt Arrests Ex-General Who Stood for Election against Sisi. *The Guardian*. 23 January. Available at: https://www.theguardian.com/world/2018/jan/23/former-egyptian-general-arrested-by-military-after-announcing-presidential-bid-sami-anan [Accessed: 22 May 2022].

Michaelson, R., 2018b. Khaled Ali Withdraws from Egyptian Presidential Race. *The Guardian*. 24 January. Available at: https://www.theguardian.com/world/2018/jan/24/khaled-ali-withdraws-egyptian-presidential-race-abdel-fatah-al-sissi [Accessed: 22 May 2022].

Michaelson, R., 2018c. 'Fake News' Becomes Tool of Repression After Egypt Passes New Law. *The Guardian*. 27 July. Available at: https://www.theguardian.com/global-development/2018/jul/27/fake-news-becomes-tool-of-repression-after-egypt-passes-new-law [Accessed: 22 May 2022].

Middle East Eye and Agencies, 2017. Lebanese Cleric Ahmad Al-Assir Sentenced to Death over Sidon Clashes. 29 September. Available at: https://www.middleeasteye.net/news/lebanese-cleric-ahmad-al-assir-sentenced-death-over-sidon-clashes [Accessed: 22 May 2022].

Middle East Eye and Agencies, 2021. Lebanon Removes All Subsidies on Fuel Causing Further Spike in Prices. 20 October. Available at: https://www.middleeasteye.net/news/lebanon-fuel-prices-rise-subsidies-end [Accessed: 22 May 2022].

Mourtada, R. and Salem, F., 2011a. Facebook Usage: Factors and Analysis. *Arab Social Media Report*, 1(1), pp. 1–20.

Mourtada, R. and Salem, F., 2011b. Civil Movement: The Impact of Facebook and Twitter. *Social Media Report*, 1(2), pp. 1–29.

Moussa, M. and Scapp, R., 1996. The Practical Theorizing of Michel Foucault; Politics and Counter-Discourse. *Cultural Critique*, 33, pp. 87–112.

Morley, D., 1986. *Family Television: Cultural Power and Domestic Leisure*. London: Routledge.

Morley, D., 1992. *Television, Audiences and Cultural Studies*. London: Routledge.

Murphy, E., 2009. Globalization and Network Civility in the Arab Region. In S. Stetter, ed. *Middle East and Globalization: Encounters and Horizons*. London: Palgrave McMillan, pp. 41–58.

Myles, J. F., 2010. *Bourdieu, Language and the Media*. New York: Palgrave McMillan.

Myles, J. F., 2013. Instrumentalizing Voice: Applying Bakhtin and Bourdieu to Analyze Interactive Voice Response Services. *Journal of Communication Inquiry*, 20(10), pp. 1–16.

Noble, S., 2018. *Algorithms of Oppression: How Search Engines Reinforce Racism*. New York: NYU Press.

Ong, W. J., 2002. *Orality and Literacy: The Technologizing of the World*. London: Routledge.

Papacharissi, Z., 2014. *Affective Publics*. Oxford: Oxford University Press.

Papacharissi, Z., 2015. Affective Publics and Structures of Storytelling: Sentiment, Events and Mediality. *Information, Communication & Society*, pp. 3–18.

Phillips, J., 2012. The Arab Spring Descends into Islamist Winter: Implications for U.S. Policy. The Heritage Foundation. 20 December.

Pomerantsev, P., 2016. Why We're Post-Fact. *Granta*. Online Edition. 20 July.

Pomerantsev, P., 2019. *This Is Not Propaganda*. London: Faber and Faber.

Pool, I. D. S., 1983. *On Free Speech in an Electronic Age, Technologies of Freedom*. Cambridge, MA: Harvard University Press.

Postill, J. and Pink, S., 2012. Social Media Ethnography: The Digital Researcher in a Messy Web. *Media International Australia*, 145, pp. 123–34.

Puchot, P., 2012. *La Révolution Confisquée, Enquête sur la transition démocratique en Tunisie*. Paris: Sindbad.

Rajewsky, I. O., 2005. Intermediality, Intertextuality, and Remediation: A Literary Perspective on Intermediality. *Intermédialité*, 6, pp. 43–64.

Ramsey, G., 2012. Activists, Individualists and Comics: The Counter-Publicness of Lebanese Blogs. *Television & New Media*, 20(10), pp. 1–18.

Reuters, 2017. Egyptian Army Officer Jailed after Announcing Presidential Candidacy: Lawyer, Family. 19 December. Available at: https://www.reuters.com/article/us-egypt-politics-idUSKBN1ED2EL [Accessed: 22 May 2022].

Reuters, 2018. Egypt Targets Social Media with New Law. 17 July. Available at: https://www.reuters.com/article/us-egypt-politics-idUSKBN1K722C [Accessed: 22 May 2022].

Richardson, T., 1996. Foucauldian Discourse: Power and Truth in Urban and Regional Policy Making. *European Planning Studies*, 4(3), pp. 279–92.

Riegert, K. and Rushkoff, D., 2003. *Open Source Democracy, How Online Communication Is Changing Offline Politics*. London: Demos.

Saebo, O., Rose, J. and Molka-Danielsen, J., 2010. eParticipation: Designing and Managing Political Discussion Forums. *Social Science Computer Review*, 28(4), pp. 403–26.

Saltanat, J., 2010. E-government in Kazakhstan: Challenges for Transitional Country. Available at: http://www.nispa.org/files/conferences/2010/papers/201004220915450.janenovasaltanat.pdf [Accessed: 22 May 2012].

Sayed, N., 2018. Op-Ed Review: Sisi's Messages Interpreted as Stern Warning to Destabilizers. 2 February. Available at: https://www.egypttoday.com/Article/1/41753/Op-ed-review-Sisi%E2%80%99s-messages-interpreted-as-stern-warning-to [Accessed: 22 May 2022].

Sefeddin, M., 2022. Lebanon: (Fake) Twitter Accounts Continue to Incite. *Daraj*. 22 March.

Seifeddine, M. (2022) Lebanon: (Fake) Twitter Accounts Continue to Incite. Daraj. 24 March. Available at: https://daraj.media/en/88931/

Semetko, H. A. and Krasnoboka, N., 2003. The Political Role of the Internet in Societies in Transition: Russia and Ukraine Compared. *Party politics*, 9(1), pp. 77–104.

Shaheen, K., 2015. Fugitive Lebanese Cleric Ahmad al-Assir Fails to Avoid Arrest with '70s Makeover' 17 August. Available at: https://www.theguardian.com/world/2015/aug/17/fugitive-lebanese-cleric-ahmad-al-assir-arrest-70s-makeover-beirut [Accessed: 22 May 2022].

Shereen Sakr, L., 2012. Egypt's Presidential Elections and Twitter Talk. *Jadaliyya*. 26 May. Available at: http://www.jadaliyya.com/pages/index/5716/egypts-presidential-elections-and-twitter-talk [Accessed: 3 August 2015].

Shereen Sakr, L., 2013. A Digital Humanities Approach: Text, the Internet, and the Egyptian Uprising. *Middle East Critique,* 22(3), pp. 247–63.

Shukrallah, H., 2011. *Egypt, the Arabs, and the World, Reflections at the Turn of the Twenty-First Century*. Cairo: The American University in Cairo Press.

Snider, E. A. and Faris, D. M., 2011. The Arab Spring: U.S. Democracy Promotion in Egypt. *Middle East Policy*, 18(3), pp. 49–62.

Sobelman, D., 2001. Gamal Mubarak President of Egypt? *Middle East Quarterly*, 8(2), pp. 31–40.

Soffer, O., 2010. 'Silent Orality': Toward a Conceptualization of the Digital Oral Features in CMC and SMS Texts. *Communication Theory*, 20, pp. 387–404.

Southwell, B. G. and Thorson, E. A., 2015. The Prevalence, Consequence, and Remedy of Misinformation in Mass Media Systems. *Journal of Communication*, 65, pp. 589–95.

Sreberny, A., 2008. The Analytic Challenges of Studying the Middle East and Its Evolving Media Environment. *Middle East Journal of Culture and Communication*, 1, pp. 8–23.

Stäheli, U., 2011. Seducing the Crowd: The Leader in Crowd Psychology New German. *Critique,* 114, 38 (3), pp. 63–77.

Stein, E., 2012a. After the Arab Spring: Power Shift in the Middle East?: Revolutionary Egypt: Promises and Perils. In N. Kitchen, ed. IDEAS Reports–special reports, SR011, pp. 23–7.

Stein, E., 2012b. Revolution or Coup? Egypt's Fraught Transition. *Survival: Global Politics and Strategy*, 54(4), pp. 45–66.

Stepanova, E., 2011. The Role of Information Communication Technologies in the 'ArabSpring'. *Implications beyond the Region. PONARS Eurasia Policy Memo*, 159, pp. 1–6.

Sterne, J., 2003. Bourdieu, Technique and Technology. *Cultural Studies*, 17(13/14), pp. 367–89.

Steuer, C. and Doron, A., 2020. What Counter-Revolution in Tunisia and Egypt? The Legacies of the RCD and the NDP in Party Systems and the Informal Economy. *Confluences Méditerranée*, 4(115), pp. 129–44.

Stort, C., 2017. The Social Psychology of Crowds – Ideas, Identity and Impact. Keele University Inaugural Lecture, Published on 3 November.

The Tahrir Institute for Middle East Policy, 2013. El Sisi Asks for Mandate to Combat Terrorism. 24 July. Available at: https://timep.org/timeline/jul24-13/ [Accessed: 22 May 2022].

Tarde, G., 1962. *The Laws of Imitation.* Translated by E.C. Parsons, from 2nd French edition. Gloucester, MA: Peter Smith.

Tarde, G., 1969. *On Communication and Social Influence*. Selected papers. Chicago: University of Chicago Press.

Tarde, G., 1989. *L'opinion et la foule*. Paris: Presses Universitaires de France.

Tatarchevskiy, T., 2011. The Popular Culture of Internet Activism. *New Media and Society*, 13(2), pp. 297–313.

Thakor, 2019. The Real Problem with Deep Fakes. TEDxWesleyanU. 21 September.

Thorson, E., 2016. Belief Echoes: The Persistent Effects of Corrected Misinformation. *Political Communication*, 33(3), pp. 460–80.

Tomlinson, J., 1991. *Cultural Imperialism: A Critical Introduction*. New York: Continuum.

Transparency International, 2017. Egypt: Stop the Onslaught Against Civil Society. 7 June. Available at: https://www.transparency.org/en/press/egypt-stop-the-onslaught-against-civil-society [Accessed: 22 May 2022].

Tschirgi, D., Kazziha, W. and McMahon, F., 2013. *Egypt's Tahrir Revolution*. London: Lynne Rienner.

Tufekci, Z., 2013. 'Not This One': Social Movements, the Attention Economy, and Microcelebrity Networked Activism. *American Behavioral Scientist*, 57(7), pp. 848–70.

Tufekci, Z., 2014. After the Protest. *The New York Times*. 19 March. Available at: http://www.nytimes.com/2014/03/20/opinion/after-the-protests.html? [Accessed: 2 August 2015].

Tufekci, Z., 2017. *Twitter and Tear Gas: The Power and Fragility of Networked Protest*. London: Yale University Press.

Turkle, S., 2012. *Alone Together, Why We Expect More from Technology and Less from Each Other*. New York: Basic Books.

Turner, F., 2008. *From Counterculture to Cyberculture: Stewart Brand, the Whole Earth Network and the Rise of Digital Utopianism*. Chicago: The University of Chicago Press.

United Nations, 2013. UN Data country profile, United Nations Statistics Division. Available at: http://data.un.org/CountryProfile.aspx? [Accessed: 1 May 2013].

Van Aelst, P. and Walgrave, S., 2002. New Media, New Movements? The Role of the Internet in Shaping the 'Anti-Globalization'. *Movement, Information, Communication & Society*, 5(4), pp. 465–93.

Wahby, N., 2017. Institutions and Populism in the Global South – Lessons for the Brexit–Trump Era Noura Wahby University of Cambridge. *City & Community*, 16(2), pp. 139–44.

Warkotsh, J., 2012. Bread, Freedom, Human Dignity: Tales of an Unfinished Revolution in Egypt, COSMOS Working paper. Available at: http://cadmus.eui.eu/bitstream/handle/1814/26187/2012WP14COSMOS.pdf?sequence=1 [Accessed: 10 August 2015].

Warner, M., 2002. Public and Counterpublics. *Public Culture*, 14(1), pp. 49–90.

Wallsten, K., 2007. Agenda Setting and the Blogosphere: An Analysis of the Relationship between Mainstream Media and Political Blogs. *Review of Policy Research*, 24(6), pp. 567–87.

Webster, J. and Kiazesk, T., 2017. The Dynamics of Audience Fragmentation: Public Attention in an Age of Digital Media, *Journal of Communication*. 62, pp. 39–56.

Wolf, A., 2017. *Political Islam in Tunisia: The History of Al-Nahda*. Oxford: Oxford University Press.

Woollaston-Webber, V., 2017. Facebook Launches Online Civil Courage Initiative to Tackle Rising Extremism in the UK. *Wired*. 23 June. Available at: https://www.wired.co.uk/article/facebook-online-civil-courage-iniative [Accessed: 22 May 2022].

The World Bank, 2022. Food and Energy Price Shocks from Ukraine War Could Last for Years. 26 April. Available at: https://www.worldbank.org/en/news/pressrelease/2022/04/26/food-and-energy-price-shocks-from-ukraine-war [Accessed: 22 May 2022].

Yazbeck, N., 2017. The Karbalization of Lebnon: Karbala as ieu de mémoire in Hezbollah's Ashura Narrative. *Memory Studies*, 11(4), pp. 469–82.

Young, M. ed., 2019. Are We Seeing a New Wave of Arab Spring Uprisings in 2019? Carnegie Middle East Center. 7 November. Available at: https://carnegie-mec.org/diwan/80260 [Accessed: 5 May 2022].

Youngs, G. ed., 2013. *Digital World: Connectivity, Creativity and Rights*. New York: Routledge.

Zollner, B., 2019. How Egypt's Muslim Brotherhood Has Carried on. Carnegie Middle East Center. 11 March. Available at: https://carnegie-mec.org/2019/03/11/surviving-repression-how-egypt-s-muslim-brotherhood-has-carried-on-pub-78552 [Accessed: 22 May 2022].

Zulli, D., 2018. Capitalizing on the Look: Insights into the Glance. *Attention Economy, and Instagram, Critical Studies in Media Communication*, 35(2), pp. 137–50.

Zuboff, S., 2020. *The Age of Surveillance Capitalism: The Fight for a Human Future at the New Frontier of Power*. London: Profile Books.

Index

www.ingramcontent.com/pod-product-compliance
Lightning Source LLC
Chambersburg PA
CBHW062027270326
41929CB00014B/2350